TEACHING ISLAMIC STUDIES IN THE AGE OF ISIS, ISLAMOPHOBIA, AND THE INTERNET

TEACHING ISLAMIC STUDIES IN THE AGE OF ISIS, ISLAMOPHOBIA, AND THE INTERNET

EDITED BY COURTNEY M. DORROLL

INDIANA UNIVERSITY PRESS

This book is a publication of

Indiana University Press
Office of Scholarly Publishing
Herman B Wells Library 350
1320 East 10th Street
Bloomington, Indiana 47405 USA

iupress.indiana.edu

Manufactured in the United States of America

Cataloging information is available from the Library of Congress.

ISBN 978-0-253-03979-8 (hardback)
ISBN 978-0-253-03980-4 (paperback)
ISBN 978-0-253-03983-5 (ebook)

1 2 3 4 5 24 23 22 21 20 19

To Liv, you are my life

CONTENTS

FOREWORD

From Khomeini to Trump: A Reflection on
Islamic Studies in America

Richard C. Martin

MY PERSPECTIVE ON TEACHING UNIVERSITY undergraduate cours-
es on Islam in times of crisis in the Middle East originated with the Iranian
Revolution in 1979, four years after earning a PhD and landing a tenure-
track teaching appointment in a religious studies program. In my newly
stocked toolbox of teachable knowledge, I had syllabi on Islamic surveys,
Sufism, Islamic religious thought, and early and medieval Islam. I could
teach modern Islam if pressed. The taking of American diplomatic hos-
tages by youthful Iranian supporters of Ayatollah Khomeini challenged
my ability to explain and interpret Islam and Muslim societies on the basis
of what I had learned in graduate school and a half year spent in Egypt.

In a 1982 essay in *Daedalus* titled "The Effects of Modernization on
Religious Change," the anthropologist Mary Douglas wrote a candid essay
on this problem, which began by saying, "Events have taken religious studies by surprise. This set of university institutions devoted to understanding religion without the constraints of the divinity school has generally
included religious change in its subject matter. No one, however, foresaw
the recent revivals of traditional religious forms. . . . No one credited the
traditional religions with enough vitality to inspire large-scale political re-
volt."[1] The dominant media of the day—television—brought the events
of the Iranian Revolution and images of angry Muslims into American
homes during the 444-day Iran hostage crisis in Tehran. Teaching about
Islam was on a new and unsure footing.

The events of that era also introduced into religious studies and social sciences a discourse on fundamentalism epitomized by the Fundamentalism Project led by Martin E. Marty and R. Scott Appleby, which
was to contribute to curriculums on Islam and the Middle East in 1980s
and 1990s.[2] Other crises have occurred since, such as airplane hijackings

and two wars in Iraq, where Islam was implicated in ways that were beginning to be publicly debated. September 11, 2001, made by far the greatest demands on the old standby curriculum. However, today's university undergraduates were toddlers when Osama bin Laden signed off on the first major attack on American soil. Now, a new generation of students has come of age when a candidate for president of the United States can run on a message of associating Muslims, even American citizens who are Muslims, with terrorism and exclusion.

Should scholars well trained in Islamic studies adjust the curriculum they teach to speak to contemporary events? Are courses on the Qur'an, Islamic history, Islamic religious thought, and other traditional curriculum topics less relevant today? How do we make the curriculum relevant to today's undergraduates who learn and communicate largely through the internet and social media? These are some of the questions that are creatively raised in the essays that follow.

I have come to conclude from my own experience that universities can be effective discursive spaces for learning about Islam in and beyond the classroom. Classes on Islam, as the essays in the volume demonstrate, can be excellent pedagogical sources of knowledge about Islamic history, culture, literature, and societies. Beyond the curriculum as such, classes on Islam that have both Muslim and non-Muslim students enrolled are also structured spaces where questions and conversations can take place and students can learn from each other. The give and take between Muslim and non-Muslim students, if encouraged, can be lively and instructive. Sunni, Shia, and secular Muslim students may feel freer to have conversations they are not likely to have in strictly religious settings. Such conversations also take place in Muslim Student Association organizations, where Muslim students of all stripes work together to present "Islam" to non-Muslims at dinners featuring ethnic dishes and Muslim speakers. Residence halls are social spaces where Muslims and non-Muslims interact, in good ways and occasionally bad. The internet and social media are well-known contemporary sources of communication among students where faculty have little control over what is said and learned. However, the classroom, student organizations, and campus social spaces can render social media more effective insofar as they are face to face and dialogical. Curriculum that requires critical evaluation of internet sites and blogs on Islamic topics can provide valuable ways of learning to use social media in courses on Islam.

When I was an undergraduate student in the late 1950s, on the other hand, only one Muslim student, an exchange student from Jordan, was enrolled in the university where I attended. Muslim immigrants had arrived and settled in America at mid-twentieth century, but in small numbers. Atiyyeh and I became good friends during our four years of undergraduate studies. However, there was little opportunity or effort to learn about his faith, Sunni Islam. Presumably, he prayed and practiced his religion in private, necessarily without the benefit of a *masjid*, a common place of prayer, an Imam to lead the prayer and provide guidance and counsel, or family and friends with whom to celebrate the *'uyud*, the ritual festivals.

In retrospect, it was a missed opportunity for me, and perhaps for him also, to enlighten his new friends who were innocent of much, if any, knowledge about Islam. Not surprisingly in midcentury America, most colleges and universities did not yet offer courses that dealt with Islamic religion, history, or societies directly. By the time Atiyyeh and I graduated in 1960, I knew little more about Islam and Muslim societies than I did as an incoming freshman. Years later, after he became Minister of Education in Amman and I a professor of Islamic and religious studies, we found each other through a friend of a friend. Happily, we are now in touch by email from time to time. Sadly, after several years of sharing news and photos of family and selves growing older, the tone of our most recent correspondence has taken a sober turn, edged with uncertainty about growing anti-Muslim sentiment and violence, in Europe and America, but also in much of the Middle East.

The demographic profile of Muslims in America has changed dramatically since Atiyyeh and I were undergraduates. During the past half century, Muslims have become a significant minority in American social, political, and cultural life. Few universities these days do not have at least a few, foreign, second-generation Muslim American and/or Muslim convert students, some in large numbers; as mentioned above, Muslim Student Association chapters are active on many campuses. By one recent estimate over one thousand colleges and universities (still a small number) offer some courses in Islamic studies in various departments in the humanities and social sciences, including majors and minors with concentrations in Islamic studies. PhD programs conducting research on Islam and Muslims, such as Near Eastern Languages and Cultures (NELC), have grown from producing less than 1 percent of all PhDs earned up to the 1970s, to 3 percent in the 1980s and 1990s, to 4 percent after 2001, according to the ProQuest Dissertations and Theses Database.[3]

So, teaching undergraduate courses today in Islamic studies in the second decade of the twenty-first century—often to classes comprised of both Muslim and non-Muslim students—are becoming the norm. *How* the Islam course is taught has been revolutionized by ever new classroom technologies and theories of learning in the digital age. But the issue of *what* we should now teach in the Islamic studies curriculum is less certain it seems to me. We are still trying to make the traditional curriculum in Islamic studies relevant to current events, and I dare say with good reason. It is with this problem that the contributors to this volume have wrestled and shared with readers the results of their own pedagogical thinking and practices.

I would like to close with a comment on a point made by some of the authors. In a very perceptive and nuanced essay, "From Medina to the Media: Engaging the Present in Historically Oriented Undergraduate Courses on Islam," Sabahat F. Adil expresses an important principle for teaching courses on Islam in the Age of ISIS, or any age. She states, "This essay will explore how we can facilitate opportunities for students to grapple with the premodern past while addressing their present and future needs." While some syllabi I have seen in recent years have done away with historical approaches in favor of the purely topical, Islamic history has not become irrelevant to the comprehension of Muslim self-understanding in the modern world. The claim made or assumed by some writers of textbooks that modernity, and not the past, has primarily shaped the recent history of Muslim societies requires intervention and qualification. Modern Islamic history did not begin with Napoleon's invasion of Egypt in 1798. The premodern past of Muslims is still relevant to understanding discourses and debates going on among Muslim intellectuals today.

A few years before I retired, I began asking students in my course on the history of Islamic religious thought to go to the internet and find sites that discussed classical problems in Islamic theology, such as the dispute over whether the Qur'an was created, or eternal, and in what sense. Many students, including non-Muslims, found discussions by students like themselves who knew the classical arguments and found it still relevant today to take a position on problems such as the nature of language and scripture.

In a more profound sense, teaching is about giving students problems to think with. Unlike my own undergraduate days and early teaching about Islam, today's students have more than enough information sources—way too many for even the brightest to grasp. Teaching students to think about the problems that Muslims have faced, resolved, and not resolved—in the past and in the present—should be an important element in Islamic studies curriculums today, as the essays in this book show in several different ways.

November 14, 2016
Creston, North Carolina

Notes

1. Mary Douglas, "The Effects of Modernization on Religious Change," *Daedalus* 1, no. 1 (1982): 1.
2. Martin E. Marty and R. Scott Appleby, eds., *The Fundamentalism Project*, 6 vols. (Chicago: University of Chicago Press, 1994–2004).
3. As reported by Charles Kurzman and Carl W. Ernst, "Islamic Studies in U.S. Universities," *Review of Middle East Studies* 46, no. 1 (2012): 24–46, see 24.

RICHARD C. MARTIN is Professor Emeritus of Religion at Emory University. His books include *Defenders of Reason in Islam: Mutazilism from Medieval School to Modern Symbol* and *Rethinking Islamic Studies: From Orientalism to Cosmopolitanism*, edited with Carl W. Ernst.

TEACHING ISLAMIC STUDIES IN THE AGE OF ISIS, ISLAMOPHOBIA, AND THE INTERNET

INTRODUCTION

Courtney M. Dorroll

I HAVE BEEN TEACHING IN the field of religion and Middle Eastern and North African studies since 2013 at Wofford College, a small liberal arts college in the South. As a new teacher and a southern transplant, I first viewed my students and my classroom as somehow unique to this particular place, but as I began to share stories with scholars in the same field at conferences such as the American Academy of Religion, the Middle East Studies Association, and the American Anthropological Association, I found that the issues related to teaching Islam in the United States are not tied to a particular place. Instead, the national media and general American opinion on Islam and the Middle East is similar from Massachusetts to Colorado to South Carolina. This realization allowed for fruitful conversations and techniques to be passed along from scholars across the United States on the themes that ran through our pedagogical experiences. These conversations revolved around the role of the media (particularly the internet), Islamophobia, and the specific challenges that the age of ISIS had brought to our classroom.

Realizing that scholars in my field of Islamic studies and Middle Eastern studies were confronted with similar challenges was crucial; but it can still be difficult to find empathy for the challenges inside your classroom if you are the only person at your institution who teaches this subject matter. I have had experiences where I felt envious of my colleagues who were teaching Shakespeare or Renaissance art history because I felt that the news media didn't create daily challenges that affected their teaching environment or that top of the moment terrorist attacks did not change the content of their classes or the mood of their students toward their subject matter. This was when I realized I needed a network of other scholars doing Islamic studies and a space to have conversations about the challenges and possible solutions for teaching Islamic studies in contemporary times.

My first step toward making this community a reality was inviting Richard C. Martin to Wofford College, where he agreed to give a talk titled "Teaching Islamic Studies in the Age of ISIS, the Internet and Islamophobia." In his talk, he gave a history of the field and the changes that occurred in the classroom as time and political shifts occurred. His talk was one of the most well attended talks at my small liberal arts college—a room of one hundred seats was packed (and for context we are a school of fifteen hundred students total—so this rarely occurs). The students I informally surveyed all said that the title drew them to the talk.

One year later, when thinking about this issue more, I realized that having a resource for educators about the particularities of teaching Islamic studies today could prove beneficial to my colleagues. It would expand our conversations to a larger audience and add to the literature of Islamic studies pedagogy. I worked with Richard C. Martin to come up with names in the field who have extensive experience teaching Islamic studies and writing on Islamic pedagogy. I also reached out to new professors who have had to face the challenges of our field and adapt quickly before going up for tenure. I wanted this volume to include voices from Muslim and non-Muslim scholars, US and international scholars, US scholars from various regions of the country, and full professors to PhD candidates.

This volume builds off the seminal text *Teaching Islam*, edited by Brannon Wheeler. Rather than supplanting this text, *Teaching Islamic Studies in the Age of ISIS, Islamophobia, and the Internet* works to be a companion piece that addresses issues that occurred after the 2002 publication of *Teaching Islam*. It aims to discuss practical and theoretical debates over the place of the academy and teaching about Islam in the political climate of the last decade. In addition to *Teaching Islam*, a number of articles have addressed the specific pedagogical challenges faced by Islamic studies instructors from the late 1970s to just after 2001. Richard C. Martin's (2010) article "Islamic Studies in the American Academy: A Personal Reflection" describes the process by which Islamic studies scholars felt increasing pressure to adapt their teaching to specifically address politicized and/ or apologetic interpretations of Islamic history in the wake of the 1979 Islamic Revolution in Iran and the terrorist attacks of 9/11. On the other hand, Amir Hussain in his article "Teaching Islam Inside-Out" describes how many of his Muslim students use Islamic studies courses as a space to explore normative and theological concerns because of the lack of Islamic confessional academic institutions in North America. While Martin's and Hussain's reflections have been invaluable in describing seminal developments in the pedagogical challenges of Islamic studies over the years preceding and just following 9/11, there is a need for an up-to-date conversation in an edited volume format about teaching the subject specifically in the contemporary post-George W. Bush era.

Teaching Islamic Studies in the Age of ISIS, Islamophobia, and the Internet has three parts. In Part I, scholars discuss approaches to and theories of Islamic studies pedagogy. This part includes contributions from Muslim and non-Muslim scholars working in the United States, Germany, Switzerland, and Egypt. Topics cover the use of virtual exchanges to connect US students to students in the Middle East (chap. 1), the role of aesthetics in the teaching of and learning about Islam (chap. 2), how certain institutional structures shape the research topics and methods of students doing research abroad (chap. 3), the role of the living context for the historical development of Islamic religious education in Western Europe (chap. 4); how are we critical of "religion making" in our day-to-day teaching (chap. 5), and finally the paradigm shifts within teaching and translating Arabic literature from a scholar who also teaches Islamic studies (chap. 6).

Part II focuses on Islamophobia and Islam and violence. Chapter 7 examines Islam and violence through the lens of an interdisciplinary approach. It encourages scholars to go beyond traditional textbooks or course syllabi to focus on materials that showcase the lives of ordinary people. This teaches students how to critically evaluate Islam both in the lives of ordinary people and in its more radical forms so as to reveal the different contexts of Islam. Chapter 8 approaches this question through the use of comparative legal ethics (the comparison of the US-engineered campaign of "drone warfare" and the jurisprudence surrounding it with the legal discourse on "martyrdom operations" produced by partisan jurists of the Islamic State and al-Qāʿida) to teach students to understand the cyclical nature of the "states of emergency" used by various parties to legitimate what they consider the unique and extraordinary nature of their respective tactics. Chapter 9 explores the significance of teaching about Islamophobia in the age of ISIS and considers whether, pedagogically speaking, a more effective way to address and dismantle stereotypes, biases, and misinformation concerning Islam might not be through introductory Islamic studies courses but rather through an introductory course on Islamophobia.

Part III applies a more hands-on approach and discusses the specifics of how to set up actual courses. Chapter 10 considers what it means to teach Islamic history in the contemporary undergraduate American classroom in a negatively charged sociopolitical climate by exploring the following questions: (1) Should we address contemporary attitudes toward

Islam in a course that is historically oriented, particularly toward premodern history? (2) If so, how do we harness students' preexisting conceptions to create a productive space for learning? Chapter 11 sets out the main learning outcome of an Islamic studies course—to understand that Muslims are people and that Islam is complicated—and gives examples of how this outcome is achieved. Chapter 12 suggests that in order to make the academic goals of the introductory Islam course intelligible in the current American classroom, contemporary political and cultural discourses need to be taken into account when designing and implementing course readings and assignments. Chapter 13 provides step-by-step, guided practices on how to add reflective learning to online courses in Islamic studies and Middle Eastern studies. Lastly, the volume ends with chapter 14, which is devoted to teaching about Islam and gender. It specifically offers various pedagogical strategies (including class debates, dialogues, role plays, and guest speakers) and tips for teaching classes on gender and Islam to diverse groups of students (such as when it would be helpful to contextualize a topic or practice and ways to include the multiplicity of available sources on this topic).

The goal of *Teaching Islamic Studies in the Age of ISIS, Islamophobia, and the Internet* is to help graduate students prepare and current professors to learn about pedagogical approaches and techniques that have helped scholars teach about Islam in the twenty-first century. This pedagogically minded volume can provide hands-on examples and theoretical tools to help alleviate the challenges Islamic studies scholars face in their classrooms. It can also serve as a space for scholars who are the only ones at their institutions working on the Middle East or Islamic studies to engage with other scholars in the same situation. This volume is useful for non-Islamic studies specialists as well, since it focuses on broader issues of pedagogy, the role of teaching vis-à-vis politics, the place of Islam in the general study of religion, and the place of religion in a college curriculum. Eventually, this resource will stand as a historical document testifying to the state of the field at this particular time.

As with all fields of study in the academy, this field is ever-changing and as political and social events change so do our classroom discussions and techniques. Yet let us embrace a space where educators can address their specific time and the state of the field at this moment so that when we look back on this volume in the decades ahead, we can say, yes, times have changed; but perhaps these issues will be affecting another discipline, and this volume can stand as a living memory of the difficult times of a field and how scholars used innovation, empathy, and new technologies from their time to face these challenges and continue to add critical analysis to their field. Do I wish for a day when Islamophobia and ISIS do not afflict my field of Islamic studies? Of course, but I began my teaching career in this environment in order to face these challenges head on and be a voice, though a minority, for my students to hear, and I live with the hope that my students will take away from my courses a new perspective that allows them a more nuanced understanding of the world around them and the mechanisms at play that produce stereotypes, generalizations, and misunderstandings.

I thank my fellow Islamic studies colleagues for being daring, honest, and reflective, and for sharing their success and challenges so that I could make my classroom a bit stronger and personally feel connected to others in my field who face similar adversities and issues in teaching Islamic studies today.

COURTNEY M. DORROLL is Assistant Professor of Middle Eastern and North African Studies at Wofford College.

PART I
APPROACHES AND THEORIES

chapter one

ON TEACHING ISLAM ACROSS CULTURES
Virtual Exchange Pedagogy

Courtney M. Dorroll, Kimberly Hall, and Doaa Baumi

THE VIRTUAL EXCHANGE GIVES TANGIBLE examples of how new media approaches can be used in the classroom. Two of us, Courtney M. Dorroll and Kimberly Hall, teach Middle Eastern studies courses that focus on aspects of Islam at Wofford College, a small liberal arts college in Spartanburg, South Carolina, and Doaa Baumi teaches students at Al-Azhar University in Cairo, Egypt. We have connected the students at Wofford virtually with students at Al-Azhar University and with Jedidiah Anderson's Wofford Introduction to Arabic students at the American University of Beirut, Lebanon; the virtual exchange was a two way project where we worked to connect Wofford students to the American University of Beirut and Wofford students with Al Azhar University.[1] Initially, we created the virtual exchange in order to place US undergraduate students in a space where they could hear from Muslim practitioners firsthand through the use of new media platforms. In recent years, we have linked our students by working together on a virtual exchange where students use Facebook, Skype, WordPress blogs, and other digital media platforms and software to facilitate interaction between the American South, Cairo, and Beirut.

A virtual exchange is valuable in a multitude of classroom settings, as we will illustrate, because it offers students the opportunity to connect with their peers through a variety of online activities. The goal is to help students learn about one another and build trust among themselves, both within the classroom and across cultures. By scaffolding the virtual exchange with a series of reflective activities, we prepare students for the exchange by fostering an understanding of themselves as embedded in a specific cultural context that can be translated for an intercultural audience. We will offer several examples of activities that we have used to develop this perspective. After the initial activities, the virtual exchange takes place via Skype sessions that provide a safe channel for students to discuss topics on religion and culture as a result of the work they have done prior to the virtual exchange. Many different college classroom settings use virtual exchanges because of their benefits, but in this chapter we offer a model for establishing a virtual exchange between Muslim and non-Muslim practitioners in order to foster cross-cultural and cross-religious engagement. We utilize the Association of American Colleges & Universities' rubric on Intercultural Knowledge and Competence to assess our students' growth in intercultural knowledge on completion of the virtual exchange.

MOTIVATION

One of the important motivations for this project was to further cultural understanding between the United States and the Middle East. Many of the students from both Al-Azhar and Wofford have never met followers of other religions. Al-Azhar, located in central Cairo, is one of the oldest Sunni Muslim universities in the Islamic World. The fact that Al-Azhar offers free education (starting from elementary school up to and including undergraduate education) encourages many Egyptians, particularly those who come from rural areas, to join. Many of those students are media targets for conservative Salafi channels. Due to the students' lack of exposure and interest in other religious faiths, teaching in the Department of Comparative Religions is quite challenging for instructors. Many of the students are not really interested in joining this department, and they believe there is no need to explore other religions or to learn about them. Yet, the majority of the students who do join the department think that learning about other religions is only crucial as an avenue to convert people to Islam.

The curriculum also has a great impact on students' understanding of knowing the Other. Because Al-Azhar students of religion only know about other traditions in theory, they do not understand the significant subdivisions that exist within each religious tradition. Furthermore, they do not realize how culture affects and influences different religious practices. For instance, many Al-Azhar students do not know how Christians who live in the United States are different from those living in Europe. In addition, many of the students who join the Department of Comparative Religions do not have a good understanding of the religious diversity within the United States or within the US Christian tradition. When asked about their motivations to learn about other traditions, Al-Azhar students offer a variety of answers. Many are interested in classical Islamic history and the former coexistence between Muslims and non-Muslims during the medieval period. Yet these students realize that they cannot relate the historical harmony and what they read about to the current division in religious cultures and world politics. Others are more interested in learning about the historical theological debates that have existed and continued to take place between Muslims and non-Muslims.

Another important factor that makes Egypt a prime location for this exchange program is the complexity of the Muslim-Christian relations in the country. Despite the fact that there is a high percentage of Christians living in Egypt—about 10 percent—Muslim-Christian relations in Egypt are still precarious. Surprisingly, it is abnormal for average Muslims and average Christians within the Egyptian context to initiate any conversation involving religion. Both Muslims and Christians feel vulnerable asking each other questions about religion. The situation is the same for the students who study comparative religions, meaning that these same tensions and concerns are also mapped onto the academic setting.

US students also face similar gaps in their knowledge of the Other. Wofford College is a Christian Methodist institution. Many Wofford students have never been to the Middle East; their only exposure to Islam and Muslims happens through the news. There are a few students who are Muslims and who are in the Muslim Student Association on campus. Many of them are second-generation immigrants. As a result of their upbringing in the United States, as well as the fact that they speak English as their native language, they are quite dissimilar from Middle Eastern Muslims who appear on the US news. For instance, all the female Muslim students on campus except one international student do not wear the veil, whereas in Egypt most Muslim women do. Therefore, introducing Muslims from the Middle East to Wofford students enables them to gain a more well-rounded understanding of Islam in all its diversity.

The American University of Beirut (AUB) is a private, secular institution in Beirut, Lebanon. The university was chartered in New York in 1863 and is based on the American liberal arts model of higher education. AUB is similar to Wofford in that it is a private institution based on the liberal arts pedagogical approach and both institutions are conducted in English.

ENGAGING THE VIRTUAL CONTEXT

Much of the literature on the use and impact of virtual exchanges in the undergraduate classroom comes from the field of intercultural studies, rather than digital media studies. This is surprising given the prevalence of interest in both implementing innovative teaching by way of technology, as is often cited in the Digital Humanities, and a theoretical interest in virtuality as a concept and construct.[2] The "virtual" is a foundational concept in studies of new media. Pierre Levy defines the "virtual" as "the possible" that operates in tandem with reality, or the actual, whereas N. Katherine Hayles describes it as "the cultural perception that material objects are interpenetrated by information patterns."[3] Both of these definitions figure largely in the pedagogical foundations of a virtual exchange. By using technology to illustrate to students that the horizon of knowledge operates in extension of the classroom, the virtual space becomes an intellectual bridge between everyday life and the structured spaces of learning. Similarly, Hayles's insistence on both the cultural and informational dynamics of the virtual emphasizes that perception is a construct shaped by both the cultural and technological environments in which one is placed. Although neither of these scholars addresses virtual learning environments specifically, these definitions point to the important interfaces between theoretical conceptions of the virtual and its implementation in a pedagogical environment.

Scholars addressing virtual pedagogical environments directly have a similar gap because they typically focus on the fully online, or virtual, classroom and learning environment, rather than the hybrid environment created by the implementation of a virtual component in a traditional classroom. While these studies are important for understanding how tools such as a virtual exchange have operated within a primarily digital environment, what limits their applicability here is the expectation that students bring to the classroom. In a strictly online, or even blended environment, students understand their engagement with these sorts of digital pedagogies as inherent to the delivery of, and engagement with, course content rather than an element that supplements the face-to-face classroom experience. Virtual pedagogy scholars Michele A. Parker, Florence Martin, and Beth Allred Oyarzun identify the outcomes foregrounded in a virtual classroom as interactivity, synchrony, usefulness, and a sense of community. While all these components are present in a traditional classroom, in a virtual environment different "patterns and types" of facilitation, as Parker and Martin term them, are enabled by both the mediation of the screen and the real-time engagement afforded by online learning. While this type of approach offers a useful model for designing outcomes for a virtual exchange, it does not engage with the affective and critical dynamics emphasized in theoretical engagements with virtual environments.[4]

What enters the breach to bridge these two fields is the field of intercultural pedagogy, a fitting interlocutor for our own work. The potential outcomes listed by Parker and Martin are not unique to online learning environments, however, as these are many of the same outcomes cited for intercultural exchange, as Augusta Abrahamse and colleagues note.[5] When time and expense are a barrier to more established means of intercultural facilitation, such as study abroad, virtual exchange becomes an attractive alternative. Jonathan Olsen, Annette Zimmer, and Markus Behr suggest that the desired outcome of the study abroad experience is "the development of students' global understanding and cultural empathy . . . [and] a cultivation of cross-cultural skills."[6] These outcomes are a result of the interactivity, synchrony, usefulness, and sense of community developed while living in a different culture. A virtual exchange, however, offers a version of these benefits combined with the outcomes listed for virtual learning environments. Students engage with their peers in another culture, but they must also engage with the mediation of the technical space. Meaning that in a virtual exchange, students are experiencing the "virtual" as a perceptual horizon of culture and information, as new media theorists have argued; as an interactive, synchronous community, as online learning theorists assert; and as a site for understanding, engagement, and empathy, as intercultural studies emphasizes. Hence, the implementation of a virtual exchange facilitates a rich site of scholarly exploration for both students and instructors.

SCAFFOLDING THE VIRTUAL EXCHANGE
FROM SPARTANBURG TO CAIRO

The inspiration for scaffolding the activities in the virtual exchange came from the emergent field of "virtual ethnography," which Robert Kozinets defines as "a qualitative, interpretive research methodology that adapts the traditional, in-person ethnographic research techniques of anthropology to the study of online cultures and communities formed through computer-mediated communications."[7] The virtual ethnography allows students to curate their identity on social media for a cross-cultural purpose. On both sides, we ask students to represent Cairo or Spartanburg geographically and culturally to connect with the identity of "Egyptian" and "Southerner." Students are empowered to go beyond stereotypes and personally narrate their experiences and identities for the Other. In a semester-long undergraduate course, it is impossible to aim for actual fieldwork abroad, but with social media as a vehicle of communication and connection, we are able to provide a virtual fieldwork experience for our students. In the first implementation of the virtual exchange, the dialogue between these three sets of students flourished, fostering our confidence that the virtual ethnography work paired with the virtual exchange offers a promising new pedagogical tool for broadening students' intercultural understanding.

The virtual ethnography is divided into two interfacing categories of assignments designed to establish a connection between the two groups of students. The first category consists of group activities that are synchronous: all students are required to meet and skype online; the second category of activities are asynchronous, meaning students are able to post at their leisure and then interface via comments on these social media outlets (YouTube, Facebook, and WordPress). Prior to these activities, students also have access to an Online Library Guide that we created to provide contextual information for all students regarding US southern culture, Egyptian culture, Lebanese culture, Christianity, Islam, ethnography, and intercultural sensitivity.

Through the use of Facebook, an Online Library Guide, WordPress, YouTube, and Skype, we link students from a small liberal arts campus in Spartanburg, South Carolina, to students at Al-Azhar University in Cairo, Egypt. They read similar background materials, Skype one another, and share movies, genealogical information, and videos reflecting their hometowns and personal contexts. We link courses and content with everyday lives in order to go beyond East versus West perceptions and instead engage with issues such as family, food, holidays, religious beliefs, and pop culture.

Online Library Guide

One of the most important academic tools scaffolding the virtual exchange is the creation of an Online Library Guide. Research guides at Wofford are web pages that gather links to useful resources for the class, selected by the librarian in consultation with faculty members. Resources selected for research guides include print and electronic books in Wofford's collection or accessible to students through interlibrary loan, scholarly journals, databases, newspapers, scholarly websites, and video or audio sources. With the help of Emily Witsell, Wofford MENA Program librarian, we created an Online Library Guide so that students in both locations could access data such as e-books on subjects pertaining to the cultural context of the American South and Egypt. This sharing of academic resources allows students from both sides to situate the intercultural dynamic of the virtual exchange within a larger academic conversation through shared academic readings. We also added a section on intercultural competency so students could access and utilize sources regarding working across cultures in productive ways.

Facebook

One of the key components for establishing a successful cross-cultural virtual exchange is determining which social media platform works best for producing virtual ethnographies within the virtual exchange. The site must be publicly available, accessible to all students, and easy to use for both creating and responding to the work of others. We use a Facebook group that is managed by the professors and accessible only to students from the exchange in order to maintain the feeling of a shared and unique community within this larger virtual context. This platform is free and easy to use, and provides students with the tools to post videos, ask questions, and chat in real time with one another. The majority of the students already have Facebook accounts established and are well versed on interfacing with the Facebook platform.

As a way to go beyond media or purely academic narratives of the Other, we want students to focus on sharing their lives with one another in order to break down differences through autobiographical discourse. To do this, we ask students to curate a Virtual Genealogy Museum on our Facebook group page. This museum features pictures of individual students' significant life events from their childhood to the present day, highlighting both the context of everyday life and moments of personal significance. We also ask students to upload pictures of their families and write captions documenting their genealogical history. This allows students to be virtual ethnographers where they use their personal context as their field and family and friends as interlocutors. The result of this activity is a virtually curated museum that offers both individual context and community building. The aim of the personal museum is to allow students to get a feel for the specificity of where each student comes from, as well as the shared humanity within families across cultures. By focusing on genealogy, we require students to contextualize the photos and the stories of their family members in order to bring their individual histories to life within the context of the intercultural community. Through the process of curating their family's genealogy for a community exhibit, students experience a sense of agency in creating cultural moments that span time and space.

WordPress

One of the standard experiences of the intercultural classroom is the screening of foreign films to foster intercultural understanding. As part of the virtual exchange scaffolding activities, however, we take this common practice one step further by making it the basis of a shared dialogue. After screening films, we use a WordPress blog to allow students to reflect on and discuss the movies that both groups of students watch. The movies screened for our virtual exchange are about American and Egyptian culture. For example, one semester's film screenings consisted of *A Country Called Amreeka, Cairo Time,* and *Mooz-lum.* The subsequent blog posts allow students on both sides to reflect on the movies and share their opinions with one another. It also creates a space where the standard in-class essay assignment transforms into a meaningful exchange of ideas that their colleagues and virtual exchange partners in Egypt can see and respond to in addition to the grading professor. WordPress offers a robust commenting function, so with this platform students can comment on both the reflections of other students, and the responses to those reflections, facilitating a more in-depth discussion of the films and their relationship to the other scaffolding activities. As a result, the screening events, though viewed in separate locations, act as an additional uniting event because the shared blog allows all voices to be seen and heard, fostering a true virtual discussion.

YouTube

The American video-sharing platform YouTube provides an excellent channel for group scaffolding activities because it provides a reliable and convenient method for connecting students and religious practitioners. The idea of using YouTube was a response to the difficulty of constantly asking Muslim practitioners in the Spartanburg community to come into the classroom to give guest lectures in order to bridge the divide between academic approaches to religious studies and the practice of religion in everyday life. It became cumbersome to ask anew each semester and to take someone's time year after year. In Wofford's case, we are located in a small community with many Christian places of worship but few non-Christian religious institutions. Within the Egyptian context, it can actually be hard to motivate a Coptic Christian to talk at Al-Azhar about their religion because of the stigma and hardships Coptic Christians experience in modern Egypt.[8] These challenges prompted the question of how to offer Wofford and Al-Azhar students a chance to learn from a global perspective of Islam. YouTube provided an easy solution. This new media platform allows for the creation of a private channel where we can upload videos of Muslims and Christians for both groups of students to view. This collection of videos provides a stable and reliable archive of experience that allows the students to learn from a multitude of voices. Creating a YouTube channel is also a resource that can be utilized from semester-to-semester.

Skype

The Skype sessions are designed to help students learn about other faiths and their followers. In order to offer students the opportunity to conduct question and answer sessions with one another, we use Skype for all live virtual exchange sessions. Faculty members from each participating institution facilitate these sessions in order to ensure that their students are prepared with contextual and intellectual information that will fit the Skype session topic. This topic is prepared in class before the Skype session, which allows for the discussion of appropriate questions and time to go over guidelines related to politically sensitive topics.

During each semester, students meet via Skype twice a month. For no less than an hour, students have the chance to raise questions and provide answers. Students have to know in advance the topic they are going to discuss. The Skype session is monitored by two professors, one for each group. The role of the faculty monitor is to make sure the conversation is rooted in contextual information that students have previously read and discussed prior to the Skype session. The monitor also watches the time and divides the questions among students to ensure that there is an equal exchange. The Skype meeting starts with one professor introducing the new topic to the students. Later on, students take part in the conversation. After each session, students must write short, two-page reflections and turn them in to their professor. The professor then discusses the reflections and comments on them in the class.

Scaffolding the Virtual Exchange from Spartanburg to Beirut

The implementation of the virtual exchange between an upper-division global media cultures course at Wofford College and students at AUB uses slightly different scaffolding activities. The focus of the Wofford course is media texts, meaning that students are very interested in the cultural dynamics of media use as both a practice and a form of identity creation. The virtual exchange is implemented as part of a four-week unit on the media cultures of the Middle East and North Africa. The course has one virtual exchange meeting with students at AUB, but we scaffold this meeting with three class sessions devoted to the Lebanese cultural context and the production of two media texts before and after the exchange.

We utilize three distinct scaffolding activities that emphasize both the individual and community context of the exchange. First, students at Wofford work collaboratively to determine a set of questions relevant to their course to help start the conversation during the virtual exchange. Most of these questions revolve around practices and forms of digital media use, with particular interest in the role of social media and access to forms of entertainment such as streaming video and music. The Wofford students then develop two key archival documents that they can share with the

AUB students in order to give them a sense of the digital cultures to which they belong. The first contribution to the Facebook Group page is a curated list of the social media sites that are important to the students in the class. Example sites range from the school-specific, such as the Wofford Athletics website, to the more general, such as Snapchat. Their aim in creating this list is to provide an interactive map of their digital landscape as a basis of conversation and engagement ahead of our Virtual Exchange.

The second and more extensive text that the Wofford students create to share with the AUB students is a collaboratively produced compilation video that depicts a "typical day" in the life of a Wofford student. The inspiration for this project was a class screening of the 2010 Kevin McDonald film *Life in a Day*, which was produced by soliciting individual videos from users around the world in order to depict a typical day on the planet. Reversing this framework, the students in this course create a compilation film as a way to provide the AUB students with the cultural context specific to the United States, the southern region, and their college campus, since those are all the frameworks that shape their identity and media practice. Each student contributes two minutes of video from their own individual day, and we then spend a class period collaboratively editing those clips together to create a short film depicting a typical day in their lives. We post this compilation video on the Facebook group page, and move the individual films to a YouTube channel with a separate link so that AUB students can have access to both the compiled and individual films.

This notion of a student-generated text as the basis of exchange and future learning develops further with the final project in this course, which is a digital textbook created and edited by the students in this course. This textbook takes up the format of cultural theorist Raymond Williams's foundational text *Keywords: A Vocabulary of Culture and Society* (1976). Williams's formulation of cultural studies focused on language in response to his perception of the loss of a shared national language as a result of the cultural schisms that emerged after World War II. Rather than creating a dictionary or encyclopedia, however, Williams chose the keyword format in order to highlight "the available and developing meanings of known words . . . and the explicit but as often implicit connections [that create] particular formations of meaning."[9] So just as the implementation of a virtual exchange is used to ask students to engage with the variety of meanings bound up with that term, "virtual," students are likewise given the opportunity to develop a keyword text that illuminates the definitions and connections between the terms that steer them through the virtual exchange experience and the course as a whole. This emphasis on language and meaning is doubly important in a class engaging with the media worlds of non-Western cultures because it challenges the students to provide context in a variety of formats for an anticipated audience of nonnative English speakers.

Foregrounding this rhetorical dimension of their work, students employ multimodal forms of composition that give readers access to the meaning of the text even if the language itself is inaccessible. Just as their *Life in a Day* video aims to provide cultural context in a visual format for their peers at AUB, the virtual textbook employs sound, image, video, text, and interactivity to make connections between the keywords, as well as to deepen their definition of a single word. The students choose the terms as they proceed through the course, and they develop their scholarly texts in conversation with the variety of media texts and cultures we encounter over the course of the semester. The digital textbook is designed to be annotated, commented upon, and edited by future classes, and by colleagues and peers outside of the class. In their aim of developing connections as a form of meaning making, students also surrender control over the limitations of meaning and design from a place that embraced the other crucial contexts of virtuality in the online classroom: interactivity, usefulness, and a sense of community. Pushing the boundaries of the virtual, however, they embrace asynchronous, rather than synchronous engagement in order to make the text the enduring and living trace of their virtual exchange, allowing it to continue to make meaning and connections long after their claim to authorship expired.

CONCLUSION

Overall the implementation of a virtual exchange, and the assignments used to scaffold it, is very useful for both students and teachers who study other religions and cultures. The virtual exchange provides an important alternative for international classes where there are a variety of students with multicultural and religious backgrounds. While study abroad programs cost a lot of money for both students and universities, the virtual exchange program allows institutions with limited resources to provide their students with a real chance to widen their experience by using the online meetings. It also offers a flexible unit that can be deployed in a variety of courses, making it adaptive and dynamic in addition to cost-effective.

In the age of the internet, the professor teaching Middle Eastern and Islamic studies is given ample opportunity to connect students to the rich cultural contexts of this academic field. Yet this connection must be fostered by a professor who works to help students approach one another with cultural sensitivity and prepares students to go beyond stereotypes and clichés in order to connect at an individual, humanistic level. Without these priming activities, the virtual exchange could actually lead to students to reify stereotypes and leave the process with more animosity than they previously had. Interactions across social media or face-to-face are not enough—the interactions must be contextualized, directed, and purposeful. We utilize cultural sensitivity when creating our exchange and foreground the virtual ethnographic approach to questioning and observing cultures, in the process teaching our students to build trust and be empathetic in order to foster meaningful dialogue across cultures.

This does not mean the exchange is simple, or that all stereotypes are avoided. In many ways, the act of cross-cultural and cross-religious dialogue opens up more issues and problems than it resolves. For instance, making sure the subject of conversation is appropriate in both countries and avoiding possibly illegal or extremely taboo topics in the conversation is a very real concern. We do not speak about LGBTIQ issues, for example, because those discussions are extremely taboo in Egypt. That lesson produced an interesting dialogue among the American students, however, because it offered them a concrete example of international differences that they could compare and contrast with their own national and regional cultural norms, taboos, and legal issues regarding sexuality.

Implementing a virtual exchange takes time and planning, and the key to its success at every step is intercultural sensitivity. Yet the rewards are numerous. Seeing students learn from one another and engage with the Other in order to make connections and identify overarching similarities fosters a real sense of individual agency as a result of the process of explaining their own culture and identity. This transformation allows students to go beyond conversations about which religion is "correct" or which political system is "right" in the virtual exchange. The process of sharing details about celebrations based on specific religious and secular traditions, as well as sharing photos with detailed captions about family genealogy and creating videos to represent the college or university and the city in which one lives, allows students to genuinely as well as virtually connect. The geography of that "Othered" place comes alive, the people become real rather than just symbols utilized in the media or in political speeches. Despite the virtual context, the connections fostered become as real as the aspects of life that are exchanged.

NOTES

1. Funding for this virtual exchange was provided by the Aspen Institute's Stevens Initiative, http://stevensinitiative.org/award-recipients/wofford-mena-virtual-exchange/.

2. Jesse Stommel, "Critical Digital Pedagogy: A Definition," *Hybrid Pedagogy*, November 18, 2014, http://www.digitalpedagogylab.com/hybridped/critical-digital-pedagogy-definition/.

3. Pierre Levy, *Becoming Virtual: Reality in the Digital Age* (New York: Plenum, 1998), 24; N. Katherine Hayles, *How We Became Posthuman: Virtual Bodies in Cybernetics, Literature, and Informatics* (Chicago: University of Chicago Press, 1999), 13.

4. Florence Martin, Michele Parker, and Beth Allred Oyarzun, "A Case Study on the Adoption and Use of Synchronous Virtual Classrooms," *Electronic Journal of e-Learning* 11, no. 2 (2013): 126.

5. Augusta Abrahamse et al., "A Virtual Educational Exchange: A North-South Virtually Shared Class on Sustainable Development," *Journal of Studies in International Education* 19, no. 2 (2015): 141.

6. Jonathan Olsen, Annette Zimmer, and Markus Behr, "Real Success with a Virtual Exchange: The German and American Politics Electronic Classroom," *PS: Political Science and Politics* 39, no. 2 (2006): 352.

7. Robert Kozinets, "Netnography," in *The Sage Dictionary of Social Research Methods*, ed. Victor Jupp (London: Sage, 2006), 135.

8. These experiences have included discrimination in employment, resistance to granting permits to build churches, and prejudice in school teaching materials. See S. S. Hasan, *Christians versus Muslims in Modern Egypt: The Century-Long Struggle for Coptic Equality* (Oxford: Oxford University Press, 2003), 116–117.

9. Raymond Williams, *Keywords: A Vocabulary of Culture and Society* (Oxford: Oxford University Press, 1976), 15.

COURTNEY M. DORROLL is Assistant Professor of Middle Eastern and North African Studies at Wofford College.

KIMBERLY HALL is Assistant Professor of English at Wofford College.

DOAA BAUMI is a PhD student at the University of Birmingham in the Department of Theology and Religion. She is also Assistant Lecturer at Al-Azhar University in the Department of Creed and Philosophy.

chapter two

QUESTIONS OF TASTE
Critical Pedagogy and Aesthetics in Islamic Studies

Manuela Ceballos

INTRODUCTION: SHAPING SENSIBILITIES TOWARD ISLAM
AND MUSLIMS IN SECULAR EDUCATIONAL SETTINGS

The process of ethical formation in certain Islamic discourses is often linked to the concept of *dhawq*—which literally means "taste," but refers to aesthetic sensibility—especially in the work of the influential eleventh-century Muslim theologian Abū Ḥāmid al-Ghazālī (d. 1111 CE). As Ebrahim Moosa states, "Muslim mystics explain *dhawq* as a spiritual condition that follows spiritual ecstasy, when the subject experiences the first steps in witnessing 'true reality.' In other words, *dhawq* is the metaphor for ontological knowledge and experiential wisdom."[1] This aesthetic sensibility is one of the key factors through which education forms and perfects moral judgment. Even though individuals may have certain intuitive predispositions, part of the role of Islamic education is to channel these subjective inclinations and guide the student to appreciate spiritual beauty, to find pleasure in that which is good, and to guide and correct her affective responses to ethical matters. In this view, rational understanding alone is insufficient for the development of a pious self, and therefore, aesthetic disciplining is sought and encouraged as part of a broader spiritual program of learning.

In this discussion of pedagogical issues facing instructors of religious studies in the "age of ISIS," I would like to draw on this Ghazalian notion of "taste" in order to bring attention to the role of aesthetics in the secular teaching of and learning about Islam; or rather, to rethink the relationship between critical pedagogy and aesthetic experience in the discipline of Islamic studies. Even though a customary acknowledgment of the role of images in the formation of public opinion about Islam and Muslims in the United States and Europe is commonplace in introductory courses on

22

Islam, there is not much written on aesthetic theory and pedagogy in Islamic studies, especially beyond visual representation.[2] I argue, however, that recognizing the link between aesthetics and pedagogy, and between ethics and aesthetics, is necessary to formulate and think through important questions, such as: What are the roles of desire and sensorial perception in the production of certain forms of Islam in the university classroom? What kinds of social processes are naturalized through the tools and methods available to scholars and instructors of Islamic studies? What aesthetic experience do university instructors of Islamic studies seek to create and for what purpose?

This process of reflection also leads to an exploration of the aesthetics of anti-Islamic rhetoric and of its seductive power over certain audiences at given moments of time, and more generally, the relationship between aesthetics and ideology. To many of us who have taught courses on Islam, it would seem as if the allure of anti-Islamic rhetoric is stronger and more resilient than those appeals to historical evidence and rational argument designed to counter it. It is important then to examine the aesthetics of different forms of anti-Islamic and anti-Muslim bigotry, their reception by different audiences, and how they shape ethical and political responses. In this light, instructors of Islamic studies are faced with the challenge of deciding what kind of critical intervention is required to counter the aesthetics of prejudice and at what level. We are also called to weigh the benefits of bridging the gap between aesthetic theory and pedagogy (thus consciously engaging with the shaping of sensibilities for specific ethical and political aims), against the potential for negative consequences emerging out of this model of education.

In this chapter, I do not mean to reduce the issues of systemic racism and Islamophobia to simple matters of "(bad) taste." I do, however, want to discuss affective and intellectual investments in Islamophobic and Orientalist representations in the classroom and beyond, as well as the desire for their consumption and pleasure in their reproduction, even when there is awareness of the violence against the bodies of living Muslims that these representations enable. This investment is such that even when instructors are committed, pedagogically and politically, to anti-Islamophobic and anti-Orientalist discourses, we tend to first reproduce them and offer them to our students for dissection and analysis (which inevitably also recreates at least some of the violence that they carry with them), before using historical examples and rational argument as correctives, often without success. I will return to this point at the end of the essay, but first, I wish to discuss the context in which these interventions are taking place, and the challenges that students and communities pose to the assumption that the shaping of ethical sensibilities is part of the role of instructors of religion, specifically of Islamic studies.

Power in Ritual or the Power of Ritual? The Aesthetics of Imagining and Teaching Religion in the "Bible Belt"

As I write this, the Tennessee Board of Education has posted a draft of the new social studies standards for middle school in which the section "Islamic World, 400 A.D./C.E.–1500s" has been eliminated based on the complaints of parents who fear the indoctrination of their children.[3] If this draft is approved, it will significantly reduce instruction about Islam received by students in Tennessee public schools for at least six years after it takes effect, since "world religions" are mostly covered in the sixth and seventh grades (according to the statement of one public official, the unit about Islam in the seventh grade is a week long).[4] Earlier in 2016, concern that having Islam in the curriculum might unduly influence students prompted the passing of a bill against religious proselytism in public schools (the bill's original language used "promotion" instead of "proselytism").[5]

Many concerns about the perceived "pro-Islam" bias in the curriculum centered around a commonly used textbook that contained, along with primary sources relevant to other religious traditions, verses from the Qur'an in translation. A common criticism against the book pointed to the fact that the textbook did not teach students about ISIS (even if the standards only required that students learn about the "Islamic world" up to the sixteenth century) or focus on what the detractors assume is the inherent violence in the Islamic tradition. This debate suggests that, at least in some communities, learning about Islam in contexts other than terrorism, conflict, or militarism (and perhaps, the oppression of women) is taboo.

However, this was not the only point of contention in the discussion over the teaching of religion in Tennessee public schools. Other community members worried about the effect that lessons or tests in which students are asked to write or repeat the *shahāda*, the Islamic declaration of faith, as part of the "Five Pillars" of Islam could have on their religious development.[6] To some of the parents and other interested parties, the assignment was not only a violation of the students' First Amendment rights but also a transgressive act—or rather, a conversion ritual—that threatened their Christianity.[7] That students are asked to state that "there is no god but God, and Muḥammad is His Messenger" even when it is assumed that this phrase is preceded and by the qualification "Muslims believe that . . ." is, to some, a ritual practice and not an academic task (in one version of this assignment, which caused strong reactions once published in local news outlets, a student wrote "Allah is the only God" and added the word "lie" between "is" and "the" in protest).[8] As a ritual practice, writing or repeating the *shahāda* would be unfit for secular, public education (one parent characterized the *shahāda* as the "Islamic conversion prayer").[9] The question that is being asked here, therefore, can be framed in the following way: Is there any instance where memorizing or reciting the *shahāda* is purely informative, rather than formative?

This latter concern is especially interesting, given that some of the Tennessee counties in which parents were most worried about this specific lesson (especially Maury, Sullivan, and Williamson counties) have a statistically negligible Muslim population. In addition, the population's ethnic and racial composition is fairly homogeneous and, according to the census, the vast majority of the inhabitants of all three counties are white. In other words, the fear was not that the teachers (who were not Muslim) were deliberately converting their students, or that the demographics of the region were shifting in such a way that children in public schools would be exposed to different cultural or religious traditions—including Islam—from their peers.

Instead, the parents seemed to acknowledge that repeating the *shahāda*, even outside of an explicitly ritual context, is a powerful speech act; and also that, in some cases, form matters as much as content. To them, the division between theology and religious studies is not always clearly demarcated: teaching "about" religion in the context of Islam was to many of them equivalent to "teaching religion." Without dismissing the bigotry underlying the specific targeting of Islam as a tradition that should not be taught in American public schools (one parent insisted that reciting the *shahāda* would not just make kids "prone to" Islam but also to violence: "All it takes is one seventh-grader to go home and recite the five pillars of Islam, then go to a school with a bomb in their backpack and blow up 10 kids"), it is important to recognize that this struggle over the teaching of "world religions" in the Tennessee standards actually reflects internal debates within the discipline of religious studies in the United States.[10]

As one of the Islamic studies instructors at the state's public, flagship institution, this controversy over how Islam is taught in middle and high schools is worrisome, to say the least. The broader implication inherent in the desire to remove the little that is taught about Islam from the curriculum in middle and high schools is that Islam is essentially dangerous—not only as a religious tradition but also as an object of study. Most of my students at the University of Tennessee are graduates of public elementary, middle, and high schools. When I ask them at the beginning of the year why they have chosen a course on Islam, most of them cite curiosity as a motivating factor. Non-Muslim students want to see if Islam truly is as violent as they have heard that it is. Muslim students—who are in the minority—want to see how Islam is taught in the secular university. They are not studying "Islam"—or what they think Islam is; they are engaging in an ethnographic experiment that focuses on me as a university instructor of Islam and on their classmates as non-Muslims studying the tradition academically.

In both of these cases, there are negative assumptions about the academic study of Islam and suspicions that university professors, to the detriment of their students' education, are not boiling down the tradition to what it "really is," either because the danger supposedly inherent to Islam is not sufficiently highlighted (which, in this view, results in a "watered-down" version in which "true" Islam would be the most violent manifestation of the tradition) or because approaching Islam from a nontheological, nonnormative perspective necessarily means that what is being conveyed is not Islam, but something else. Both arguments about the deficiencies of an "academic Islam" rely on how it fails to produce proper moral sensibilities in students: if Islam is "whitewashed" (no pun intended), students may not be moved to defend their own cultural tradition against it, which results in dishonor. On the other hand, if a theological approach is favored, and the instructor fails to persuade students about the truth of Islam (mostly by ignoring truth as a category), then it must reflect the instructor's fundamental lack of proper *dhawq*, aesthetic disposition. As one of my former students asked me recently, echoing the English poet John Keats's understanding about beauty as truth and truth as beauty, "How can you have heard and read all of the beautiful things that I have heard and read, and not have become a Muslim?" In the worst-case scenario, this evasion of the question of theological truth may reveal that the teacher is transmitting falsehoods about Islam.

That secular knowledge about Islam is somehow forbidden knowledge may be profitable from a market standpoint. However, since I do not see Islam as a commodity to be sold or my students as potential clients, that characterization does not help put me at ease. What is worse, the association between the academic study of Islam and personal rebellion (mostly of non-Muslim, white individuals) reinforces the social and political marginalization of Muslims.

However, as I suggested before, behind the fear of exposing middle-school children to the *shahāda* is the sense that rituals, texts, and objects are, in some contexts, more than vehicles for meaning, more than mere symbols through which essential truths can be uncovered through interpretation.

This understanding of religious ritual and practice is something that I try to explore with my own students in the classroom. In fact, in the 1993 essay "The Construction of Religion as an Anthropological Category" (part of *Genealogies of Religion*, a book often assigned in "theory and method" courses in religious studies), Talal Asad critiques fellow anthropologist Clifford Geertz's influential definition of religion found in "Religion as a Cultural System" because it imagines religion and religious practice as symbolic activities to be read and interpreted, thus "textualizing" them.[11] Whereas Geertz understands religion primarily in terms of symbolic function, Asad focuses on the formation of the pious subject through disciplinary practices.

Exploring this theory in the classroom can be difficult because the examples I offer to elucidate Asad's claims are frequently ones to which students cannot relate. The parents' fear that, unintentionally perhaps, the act of repeating the *shahāda* under the coercive powers of the public school system actually testifies to something sacred, and that this utterance can *do* something even if it is devoid of meaning to a Christian middle-school student from Tennessee, is perhaps a more useful pedagogical example related to the theoretical discussion above, but one that may undermine my own role as an Islamic studies professor at a state university. However, even in the context of East Tennessee, this is not the sole instance in which texts can exert power through mechanisms other than signification alone.

My students, like most other people, have complicated relationships with the hierarchies, rituals, and texts of their own cultural and religious traditions, and not just the traditions of others. Students who self-identify as part of the Christian majority of the state may also find the ways in which their sacred sources are used in the university curriculum challenging or even troubling. Similarly, some Muslim students may find that treating the Qur'an "as literature" in Islamic studies courses or world literature classes is incompatible with their own experience of the text and their expectations about its potential effects (educational, devotional, aesthetic, etc.). In fact, at the same time that this debate over the standards was going on, a very disciplined and thoughtful student in one of my classes told the class during a discussion session that she would not read *The Song of Songs* until she was married. Even if the text did not contain any "information" that would be new to her, she contended that reading it would be transformative in other ways, and that this transformation— even though desirable—was part of a broader process in her sentimental and moral education that could not be rushed. She was not rejecting its erotic content out of principle, but rather wished to use the erotic power in the text in a way that would enhance her piety and affective relationship with her future partner. Even in the context of the secular university, she could not read a sacred text and assume that it would not act upon her in a specific way, even if neither she nor her instructor intended for that to happen.

These two instances of refusal to accept that religious texts operate in ways that are not only symbolic are, of course, not equivalent. The parents who fear that contact with Islamic ritual as portrayed in textbooks will pollute or, in the worst-case scenario, inadvertently change and harm their children, and the student who waits to come into contact with *The Song of Songs* (in translation) for the first time as part of a broader ethical program of affective discipline are differently predisposed toward the texts in question. Furthermore, I should add that the aforementioned student had no problem reading and listening to the Qur'an in the course that she took with me; *The Song of Songs*, on the other hand, was not required reading in that particular class. She was not, as far as I could tell, concerned with how learning about Islam or any other traditions that were not her own would impact her personal devotion, but only about approaching the texts of her own tradition in a secular context before she had had the opportunity to read them as part of a religious and moral program of self-betterment. The assumptions about reading and performance that underlie both cases, assumptions that many of us in the academy find theoretically interesting and pedagogically relevant, actually challenge the possibility of the secular study of religion in the public university. As Amir Hussain notes in his discussion of the personal connection his (Muslim and non-Muslim) students have with Islam, especially after the events of September 11, 2001, "there is the question of teaching Islam. I use a deliberate ambiguity here: although I always strive to teach *about* Islam, I am aware that I also teach Islam."[12]

ANTI-ISLAMIC AESTHETICS

Before returning to this issue of aesthetic sensibilities, moral formation, and the teaching of (or about) religion, I'd like to discuss the types of systems in which judgments about the beauty and morality of Islam are produced. Where and how does the concept of Islam fit into broader conceptions of "taste," and its shaping of moral judgment, in the American context? First, I want to acknowledge that to highlight the role of affect in the Islamic tradition—as I did in the opening of this essay—in a volume on the teaching of Islam in the United States is a problematic endeavor. Portraying religious others as "irrational" or "overly emotional" peoples in need of rational systems and governance has a long history in political and academic discourses that justified empire-building, colonial projects, and control over women as well as other vulnerable populations. However, here I would like to stress three points: (1) making the Islamic tradition "palatable" (once again, speaking of taste) to Western audiences by only emphasizing those aspects of the tradition that they may value as legitimate—in this case, reason—will not change attitudes against Islam and Muslims, but rather, produce a "good" or rational Islam that will be pitted against a "bad" or irrational Islam, (2) aesthetic judgment is not incompatible with reason, nor is it absent from Western or secular educational programs, and (3) the portrayals of Muslims as fundamentally passionate subjects have served to shape Western aesthetic sensibilities.

In other words, representations of Islam and Muslims that center on either lust or violence reflect Western ideals of the good and the beautiful and fit into broader disciplinary structures that target affect in conjunction with moral understanding. When disseminated, these portrayals serve as pedagogical tools that promote the development of desirable aesthetic inclinations through the consumption of the "barbarity" or beauty of others, and also serve as outlets through which to channel socially inappropriate desires. This is not an exclusively American phenomenon: European Romanticism allowed for the simultaneous attraction toward and devaluation of those whose culture was considered inferior. For the Romantics, the interplay of danger and desire in the image of the other could lead to self-understanding. As Edward Said notes in *Orientalism*,

> Why the Orient seems still to suggest not only fecundity but sexual promise and threat, untiring sensuality, unlimited desire, deep generative energies, is something on which one could speculate. . . . Nevertheless one must acknowledge its importance as something eliciting complex responses, sometimes even a frightening self-discovery, in the Orientalists.[13]

Contemporary Islamophobic discourses, though not identical with their Orientalist predecessors, derive generative powers and revelations about the self in the mixture of threat and promise that certain visions of Islam and Muslims provide them.

In the process of creating an Orient to be studied and catalogued, "the imaginative examination of things Oriental was based more or less exclusively upon a sovereign Western consciousness out of whose unchallenged centrality an Oriental world emerged, first according to general ideas about who or what was an Oriental, then according to a detailed logic governed not simply by empirical reality but by a battery of desires, repressions, investments, and projections."[14] Discussing aesthetics and pedagogy within

Western contexts is differently challenging, but following Said's analysis, necessary if Orientalism is to be approached critically as a field of knowledge that reflects Western concerns about other peoples (and *not* concern for other peoples). In the United States, the idea that the ethical cultivation of the student is a main responsibility of the public school or university instructor is usually discouraged, since massive, public programs in aesthetic cultivation are reminiscent of fascist strategies of social control. Thus, the formation of character is meant to be an extra-academic endeavor in student development, and the division between teachers who explicitly engage in the ethical cultivation of students (coaches, counselors, and religious leaders) and those who do not (public school instructors of academic subjects at the middle-school level and above) is strong, even if not always clearly elucidated: grades, which are the avenues through which students are guaranteed or denied admission into college, professional school, and later, professional employment, are not supposed to reflect moral judgment, only academic achievement.

This does not mean that the cultivation of virtues is entirely absent from academic instruction at the university level. In fact, the discourses around student professionalization, for example, are intricately connected to values such as competitiveness, "personal responsibility," respect for hierarchies, and methods of self-presentation that communicate specific class and gender norms as well as other desirable qualities such as proper hygiene, self-confidence, punctuality, originality, and "good taste" in fashion. Civic virtues are also encouraged in public educational settings, and the formation of "good citizens" or "citizens of the world" is an explicit goal of the university. The Romantic legacy of "aestheticizing of morality and politics" is, therefore, not entirely absent from secular practices of education of different ideological strands.[15] Even in Paulo Freire's influential *Pedagogy of the Oppressed*, in which aesthetics initially appears as the antithesis of liberation (it is that which "veils the world" and mystifies oppression), it also plays a fundamental pedagogical role once the "veil is lifted" through the learning process, itself an aesthetic event.[16] In fact, for Freire, proper aesthetic and ethical dispositions, which are inextricably connected, are necessary forces for the oppressed to move beyond fatalism and thus reimagine and remake the world.[17]

CONCLUSION: TEACHING THROUGH AND AGAINST TASTE

It seems to me that, increasingly, I devote more and more sessions to discussions of the *hijāb* (veil or headscarf) in response to prevailing cultural assumptions that Muslim women are especially oppressed while non-Muslim American and European women are especially free.

Therefore, in any given semester, my students and I may read Saba Mahmood's seminal work on agency and piety, Homa Hoodfar's explorations of the multiple meanings and uses of veiling, watch Julia Meltzer and Laura Nix's documentary on Muslim preacher Houda al-Habash's summer Qur'an school in pre-war Syria in which she has a "veiling ceremony" for her students, discuss Fatima Mernissi's critiques of patriarchal interpretations of Islam, and debate the question "Do Muslim women really need saving?" in the context of Lila Abu Lughod's essay of the same title.[18] Despite all this attention and the political and theoretical orientations in which I hope to present the issue of veiling, images of women whose heavily lined eyes are framed by the "prisonlike" weight of their clothing still manage to make it into final essays with astonishing frequency. Most confusingly, the traditionally Orientalist images (and their contemporary reiterations) that students use as illustrations of their projects are accompanied by very sophisticated written analyses that comfortably address the works of the aforementioned scholars with original insights about, say, the ways in which religious oppression is presented as *sui generis*, even if what "religion" is or is not cannot be clearly defined.

The first few times that I received these types of responses, I thought that students had not been paying attention to the material, had not understood the assignment, or that the cognitive (and aesthetic!) dissonance between the Orientalist images of others that they were using to illustrate their critically informed texts reflected the ways in which articles about Islam and books often are "sold" to readers through images chosen by publicists, not the authors themselves. Thus, they were merely "selling" their ideas to me and themselves through an established convention that required this form of "packaging." Some of that may be true. More recently, however, I have come to see that, in this practice, students are also emulating my pedagogical model: I still rely on Orientalist and Islamophobic aesthetics for shock value and as form of seduction (to bring "the lure of Religious Studies" to the forefront, to cite Tazim Kassam).[19] Even though I am critical of this approach, I use these aesthetic systems to invoke desire in my students and to produce certain emotions that I find necessary for engagement, and perhaps even to shape my students' moral and political responses. Later, I "un-teach" these discourses: I reveal their internal contradictions and make visible the racism and misogyny that underlie and sustain them, racism and misogyny that we have all learned not to see. However, in order to do that, I must teach these discourses first and teach them effectively. By "effectively," I mean develop a "taste" for them, if only so that the students can, through emotions such as guilt at their enjoyment, and pleasure in overcoming that enjoyment, move through and past them. That "taste," however, cannot be completely "undone" through deconstruction.

This is an extremely problematic and morally compromised method of engagement with students, not to mention with the traditions for which I am responsible. It may be fair to say that the pedagogical process that I am describing emerges, at least in part, from my own Latin American, Catholic aesthetic sensibilities and therefore, from the ways in which I have myself been taught to understand the world. Despite the fact that there are not many Latin American professors of Islam in North America, I am not the only Islamic studies instructor in the United States to engage students in this way by a long shot. It is also worth mentioning that there are anti-Orientalist and anti-Islamophobic discourses that we could all use as substitutes (and thus reduce student exposure to racist "art" or other aesthetic production) to minimize the instrumentalization and aesthetization of those subjects to whose traditions we owe our livelihoods.

However, some of these counter-Orientalist and counter-Islamophobic aesthetic discourses are either not currently endowed with the social power that would allow them to produce the types of aesthetic responses that I, at least, seek from my students in order to reshape their assumptions about Islam or are so explicitly theological (in that they deploy, in a reformulation of Asad's phrasing, "religious power to produce religious truths") that they may generate the same kind of backlash that I have described in detail in the paragraphs above, regardless of the instructor's own religious background and intent. It is not sufficient, in anti-racist education, to push toward the general appreciation of the beauty of the other, since as the history of Orientalism as a discipline shows, the desire for domination over others can also be manifested through making these others "aesthetically exceptional."[20] Instead, it is important to think about the links between moral understandings and aesthetic judgments—between aesthetics and ethics—in pedagogical practice. Could and should we use methods from within the Islamic tradition to guide students to reject Orientalist and Islamophobic rhetoric? If so, how? I hope that even if the answer to this question escapes the scope of this essay, I have at least persuaded some readers to think about pedagogy in Islamic studies through questions of and about taste.

NOTES

1. Ebrahim Moosa, *Ghazālī and the Poetics of Imagination* (Chapel Hill: University of North Carolina Press, 2005), 176.

2. Relatively recent discussions about the link between Islamic studies in the United States, critical pedagogy, and aesthetics appear in Shahab Ahmed, *What Is Islam: The Importance of Being Islamic* (Princeton: Princeton University Press), 527–529; Mohammad Azadpur and Anita Silvers, "Avicenna on Education in Philosophy and Art," *Arts Education Policy Review* 107, no. 2 (November 2005): 35–39; Abbas Barzegar, "Charisma and Community in the Aesthetics of Political Islam." *Soundings: An Interdisciplinary Journal* 97, no. 3 (2014): 340–48; and Zareena Grewal, *Islam Is a Foreign Country* (New York: New York University Press, 2013), 339–341.

3. Rick Wagner, "Islam Removed from Draft Tenn. 7th Grade Social Studies Standards," *Kingsport Times News*, September 25, 2016, http://www.timesnews.net/Education/2016/09/25 /Islam-removed-from-draft-Tenn-7th-grade-social-studies-standards.

4. Emma Green, "The Fear of Islam in Tennessee Public Schools," *The Atlantic*, December 16, 2015, http://www.theatlantic.com/education/archive/2015/12/fear-islam-tennessee-public -schools/420441/.

5. Melanie Balakit, "State House Passes Anti-Religious Indoctrination Bill," *The Tennessean*, February 29, 2016, http://www.tennessean.com/story/news/2016/02/29/state-house-passes -anti-religious-indoctrination-bill/81107754/.

6. Laura Built, "Tennessee Mother Fights to Remove Textbook from Schools That Teaches about Islam, Claims Her Child's 'Religious Beliefs Were Violated,'" *New York Daily News*, October 6, 2016, http://www.nydailynews.com/news/national/tenn-mom-fights-remove -school-book-teaches-islam-article-1.2819968.

7. Dave Boucher, "Lawmakers Fear Islamic 'Indoctrination' in TN Classes," *The Tennessean*, September 10, 2015, http://www.tennessean.com/story/news/politics/2015/09/10 /blackburn-alludes--islamic-indoctrination--tn-classes/72015122/.

8. Greg Jinkerson, "Maury Parents Angered over Islam Unit," Spring Hill Home Page, September 3, 2015, http://springhillhomepage.com/maury-parents-angered-over-islam-unit/.

9. Todd Starnes, "'There Is No God but Allah'? School Accused of Islamic Indoctrination," Foxnews.com, September 10, 2015, http://www.foxnews.com/opinion/2015/09/10/there-is-no -god-but-allah-school-accused-islamic-indoctrination.html.

10. Melanie Balakit, "White County Group Claims Islamic Indoctrination," *The Tennessean*, October 21, 2016, http://www.tennessean.com/story/news/2015/10/20/white-county-group -claims-islamic-indoctrination/74267142/.

11. Talal Asad, *Genealogies of Religion: Discipline and Reasons of Power in Christianity and Islam* (Baltimore: Johns Hopkins University Press, 1993), 25–54.

12. Amir Hussain, "Teaching Inside Out: On Teaching Islam," *Method & Theory in the Study of Religion* 17, no. 3 (2005): 249.

13. Edward W. Said, *Orientalism* (New York: Random House, 1979), 188.

14. Said, *Orientalism*, 8.

15. Louis Ruprecht, "Caught between Enlightenment and Romanticism: On the Complex Relation of Religious, Ethnic and Civic Identity in a Modern 'Museum Culture,'" in *Rethinking Islamic Studies: From Orientalism to Cosmopolitanism*, ed. Carl W. Ernst and Richard Martin (Columbia: University of South Carolina Press, 2010), 220.

16. Tyson E. Lewis, "Teaching with Pensive Images: Rethinking Curiosity in Paulo Freire's *Pedagogy of the Oppressed*," *Journal of Aesthetic Education* 46, no. 1 (Spring 2012): 42. See also Paulo Freire, *Pedagogy of the Oppressed*, trans. Myra Bergman Ramos (London: Continuum, 2000), and Paulo Freire, *Pedagogy of Freedom*, trans. Patrick Clarke (Lanham, MD: Rowan & Littlefield, 1998).

17. Lewis, "Teaching with Pensive Images," 31.

18. Homa Hoodfar, "The Veil in Their Minds and on Our Heads: Veiling Practices and Muslim Women," in *Women, Gender, Religion: A Reader*, ed. Elizabeth Castelli (New York: Palgrave Macmillan, 2001); Saba Mahmood, *The Politics of Piety* (Princeton: Princeton University Press, 2005); Julia Meltzer and Laura Nix, *The Light in Her Eyes* (New York: Cinema Guild, 2012); Fatima Mernissi, *The veil and the male elite: a feminist interpretation of women's rights in Islam* (Reading, MA:

Addison-Wesley Publishing Co, 1991); Lila Abu-Lughod, "Do Muslim Women Really Need Saving? Anthropological Reflections on Cultural Relativism and its Others," in American Anthropologist 104 (2002): 783–790.

19. Tazim Kassam, "Teaching Religion in the Twenty-First Century," in *Teaching Islam*, ed. Brannon Wheeler (Oxford: Oxford University Press, 2002), 191.

20. Kojin Karatani, "Uses of Aesthetics: After Orientalism," *Boundary 2* 25, no. 2 (1998): 153.

MANUELA CEBALLOS is Assistant Professor of Islam at the University of Tennessee-Knoxville.

chapter three

TRAINING SCHOLARS TO STUDY NON-SCHOLARLY LIFE

Benjamin Geer

IN THE SCHOLASTIC FALLACY, THE researcher explains the actions of people in non-scholarly situations by projecting scholarly thinking onto them. After introducing the concept and discussing a recent example from Islamic studies, I suggest that certain social structures may make this error more likely. Focusing on the case of research in Egypt, I argue that degree programs are not designed to enable students to learn Arabic as a second language well enough to do research that involves talking with people there. Egyptian state institutions also restrict both ethnographic and archival research. These obstacles are likely to deter research on ordinary social practices, on vernacular cultural production, and on archival materials, and to favor research on canonical texts. Moreover, in a field such as Islamic studies, in which researchers can produce work that responds to the demands of nonspecialist audiences, students may be tempted to overgeneralize from these texts (e.g., by relying on them to draw conclusions about Islam in general). I suggest ways for universities and faculty to help students avoid these pitfalls.

THE SCHOLASTIC FALLACY

Aaron W. Hughes criticizes certain scholars in the field of Islamic studies for constructing apologetic accounts of Islam at the expense of sound scholarship. He attributes this to theological stances, as well as to the understandable desire to counter widespread Islamophobia by describing an allegedly authentic liberal Islam.[1] This may be true, but one can also interpret this impulse as an example of a more general phenomenon, by seeing it as an effect of the relationship between the field of Islamic studies and actors outside the field. Unlike a field such as mathematics, where results are mainly of interest to specialists, Islamic studies can produce ideas that respond to the demands of nonspecialists, many of whom are interested in conclusions about Islam in general, whether these conclusions are positive or negative.

There is nothing wrong with trying to make valid generalizations about Islam, as long as they are based on adequate evidence. In contexts where it is difficult or impossible to do research involving direct communication with and observation of people in everyday life, it may be tempting to use texts as a substitute. This is a form of what sociologist Pierre Bourdieu called the scholastic fallacy.[2] For example, to see a work of Islamic philosophy as reflecting the beliefs and practices of Muslims in general, one must ignore the specificity of the social conditions in which philosophical texts are produced, as well as the difference between the theoretical thinking involved in philosophy and the practical thinking employed (even by philosophers) in everyday life.

To produce a work of philosophy, an individual must have a certain "distance from economic and social necessity."[3] This usually requires a privileged social position, which provides enough leisure time to make it possible to engage in philosophical study and writing. This leisure is a necessary, but not sufficient, social condition of the "scholastic disposition which inclines its possessors to suspend the demands of the situation, the constraints of economic and social necessity, and the urgencies it imposes or the ends it proposes." This disposition is what "incites people ... to raise problems for the pleasure of solving them, and not because they arise in the world, under the pressure of urgency, or to treat language not as an instrument but as an object of contemplation, formal invention or analysis."[4]

Moreover, to be accepted and recognized as a philosopher, an individual must have internalized certain dispositions and conceptual schemas as a participant in a field of knowledge production, in which she is in competition with peers for recognition.[5] Each text reflects the shared assumptions of the participants in the field at a given historical moment, which made it possible for them to ask certain questions and not others.[6] A text is also the response of an individual occupying a certain position in the field (e.g., a dominant or dominated position, or a position in a subfield) to the state of play in the field at that moment.[7]

In contrast, "practical sense," which everyone, including off-duty philosophers, relies on in everyday life, is adapted to action rather than contemplation: "This practical sense, which does not burden itself with rules or principles (except in cases of misfiring or failure), still less with calculations or deductions, which are in any case excluded by the urgency of action ... is what makes it possible to appreciate the meaning of the situation instantly, at a glance, in the heat of the action, and to produce at once the opportune response."[8]

Bourdieu argues that, instead of rules or principles, practical sense mobilizes dispositions that "result from a durable modification of the body through its upbringing."[9] In short, in the social worlds of everyday life, we "learn bodily": "The most serious social injunctions are addressed not to the intellect but to the body, treated as a 'memory pad.' The essential part of the learning of masculinity and femininity tends to inscribe the difference between the sexes in bodies . . . in the form of ways of walking, talking, standing, looking, sitting, etc. . . . As much in everyday pedagogic action ('sit up straight,' 'hold your knife in your right hand') as in rites of institution, this psychosomatic action is often exerted through emotion and suffering, psychological or even physical."[10]

When researchers imagine that all thinking is like scholastic thinking, they tend to make the mistake of trying to explain people's actions in non-scholastic situations in terms of scholastic ideas: "Projecting his theoretical thinking into the heads of acting agents, the researcher presents the world as he thinks it (that is, as an object of contemplation, a representation, a spectacle) as if it were the world as it presents itself to those who do not have the leisure (or the desire) to withdraw from it in order to think it. He sets at the origin of their practices, that is to say, in their 'consciousnesses,' his own spontaneous or elaborated representations, or, worse, the models he has had to construct . . . to account for their practices."[11]

Critiques of certain ways of studying and teaching Islam have drawn attention to some of the manifestations of the scholastic fallacy. Edward W. Said's *Orientalism* pointed out the folly of assuming "that the swarming, unpredictable, and problematic mess in which human beings live can be understood on the basis of what books—texts—say" and criticized a type of pedagogy based on "a canon of textual objects passed on from one generation of students to the next."[12] Among anthropologists interested in Islam, there has been a lively debate about whether religious practices can be understood merely as symbols to be interpreted;[13] for Bourdieu, the attempt to read practices as if they were texts is another manifestation of the scholastic fallacy.[14] However, the basic misconception underlying these manifestations (i.e., the confusion between scholarly thinking and practical sense) does not seem to have been a focus of discussion in Islamic studies or in scholarship about teaching Islam.

Recent assessments of the state of Islamic studies observe that the field has made progress in moving beyond the confines of textual sources, by increasingly accommodating social science methods such as ethnography.[15] Still, Carl W. Ernst and Richard C. Martin note that "job descriptions in vacancy announcements still tend to focus narrowly on expertise in classical languages and texts. That is, very frequently a job in Islamic studies is defined exclusively as the study of classical Arabic texts such as the Qur'an and the foundational texts of Islamic law."[16] This no doubt encourages the scholastic inclination to see practices simply as reflections of texts.

One recent example is the much-discussed book *What Is Islam? The Importance of Being Islamic.* Its merits include the author's insistence on constructing a descriptive rather than prescriptive account of Islam, and his rejection of preconstructed categories such as "religion" and "culture." However, like most of the scholarship it critiques, it presents scholastic views of Islam as representative of Islam in general. This is particularly apparent in Shahab Ahmed's discussion of Sufism, which he correctly describes as "a foundational, commonplace and institutionalized conceptual and social phenomenon in societies of Muslims" over a long historical period. While this at first seems as if it might lead him to an exploration of the structures of the social practices involved in Sufism, Ahmed seems to view Sufism merely as the expression of the "higher Sufi thought" of Sufi philosophers and poets such as Muhyi al-Din 'Ibn Arabi and Jalal al-Din Rumi.[17]

Ahmed anticipates the objection that this textual evidence is merely "representative of elite society and culture, and that the society of elites is necessarily unrepresentative of society-at-large." In fact, he argues, the ideas of these elites were disseminated from elite textual sources to a wide audience via "vernacular primers, as well as, and most importantly, the translation, configuration and dramatization of these ideas into poetical and narrative fiction," such as poetry "sung to popular (and, often, illiterate) audiences at Sufi shrines throughout the Indus valley."[18] In his view, such texts are a "means of circulation and mobilization of the ideas, values and norms of high intellectual culture for instruction, contemplation, and criticism in society-at-large": "[T]he vast majority of the population of pre-modern societies of Muslims participated in the normative truth-claims and vocabulary of the hierarchical cosmologies of Sufism. . . . [I]ndeed, an ordinary Muslim's *ziyarah* to obtain the *barakah* that emanates from the tomb of a Sufi in a village or mountain pass in Morocco, India or Indonesia is precisely a *de facto* acknowledgement of an active participation in a cosmos organized and structured and experienced in Neo-Platonic, Avicennan, and Akbarian terms."[19]

This account of Sufism can be contested with ethnographic evidence, particularly since Ahmed has switched from the past tense ("participated") to the present ("is"). For example, in Turkey, Brian Silverstein attended many *sohbets*, which were meetings of a shaykh and his disciples, "structured around the reading and discussion" of hadith:

> Yet there was nothing ostensibly "mystical" about the content of the discussions that took place, occupying roughly 95 per cent of the time of the *sohbet*. I had attended *sohbets* and socialized with *cemaat* members for several months when I realized that almost no one had ever discussed the classic themes of Sufism emphasized in Western literature on the topic, such as "intimate experience of God" and "self-effacement (in the Reality of God)." Not only were these techniques not discussed during *sohbet*, they were not discussed among the many followers outside of *sohbets*. It became quite obvious that the members of the *cemaat* simply were not particularly concerned with these themes on a daily basis.[20]

Similarly, Valerie Hoffman found that philosophy seemed to play little or no role in the lives of the participants in the Sufi orders she studied in Egypt; they were instead focused on obedience to a shaykh, the physical practice of chanting and movement in the *dhikr*, and devotion to the prophet Muhammad and his family. The most widely read Sufi books were "largely collections of brief biographies of Sufi saints," and some shaykhs disdained reading as a way of learning about Sufism, or were illiterate. Most Sufi songs were songs of praise to the prophet Muhammad.[21] While Hoffman does describe a *munshid* who sang "of the mysteries of divine knowledge and longing to enter the presence of God," her skepticism about the audience's reception of these performances is apt: "One is astonished at the density of such songs sung before a largely uneducated audience, sung indeed by a man who lacks much formal education himself. We may well be convinced of the truth that each one will understand only according to his capacity and of the utter impossibility of the average person to appreciate the full import of the words while at the same time doing dhikr."[22]

Even if Ahmed's claim that ordinary Sufis absorb philosophical ideas from vernacular texts were true, his description of Sufism would still miss everything in it that is based on practical sense, rather than on scholastic discourses. When Hoffman asked a shaykh "whether the movements of dhikr help a person come to God," the shaykh replied: "They don't help him get to God, but they help him to train his limbs to do dhikr. Because there is a dhikr of the body and its parts. There is a dhikr of the limbs, of the eye, of the hand. Dhikr must be perfected in the disciple. When all his faculties are doing dhikr, then he recollects nothing but God. All his bodily parts are directed toward one goal—dhikr."[23]

Whether or not this type of physical training imparts any understanding of Sufi philosophy, it establishes the shaykh as a model to be imitated, a model of a particular practical sense that his followers can internalize through physical participation: the shaykh moves and chants in a certain way, and "[a]ll the participants in the *dhikr* imitate these utterances and bodily movements."[24] Thus, Sufi practice is, in a way, like "some universes, such as those of sport, music or dance," which "demand a practical engagement of the body," and in which trainers "seek effective ways of speaking to the body" rather than to the intellect.[25] But it is much more than this, because the shaykh is viewed as a model of Islamic practice, having special knowledge of God. In return for imitation of his practical sense, the shaykh can reward his followers with what Bourdieu describes as "the grace (*charisma*) which saves those it touches from the distress of an existence without justification and which gives them . . . a theodicy of their existence."[26]

It is reasonable to ask whether the shaykh's power over his followers depends at least partly on the fact that the conceptual schemas that they rely on in their perception of him and of themselves have been shaped by the training they have received from him and by their efforts to imitate him (and, if their parents were also Sufis, by the upbringing they received at home). If so, we can interpret this power as an example of what Bourdieu calls "symbolic power": "Symbolic power is exerted only with the collaboration of those who undergo it because they help to construct it as such. . . . This submission is in no way a 'voluntary servitude' and this complicity is not granted by a conscious, deliberate act; it is itself the effect of a power, which is durably inscribed in the bodies of the dominated, in the form of schemes of perception and dispositions (to respect, admire, love, etc.)."[27]

These dispositions manifest themselves in spontaneous physical reactions: the shaykh's followers feel "a mixture of respect and fear" in his presence and lower their eyes; one said, "When I found myself in the presence of the shaykh . . . I was overcome by a feeling of fear, as if I had unwittingly done something wrong."[28] Such reactions are typical reflections of the relation of symbolic power: "The practical recognition through which the dominated, often unwittingly, contribute to their own domination by tacitly accepting, in advance, the limits imposed on them, often takes the form of *bodily emotion* (shame, timidity, anxiety, guilt). . . . It is betrayed in visible manifestations, such as blushing, inarticulacy, clumsiness, trembling, all ways of submitting, however reluctantly, to the dominant judgement."[29]

In turn, shaykhs display their power in a variety of ways: they "regularly test their disciples by ignoring them, keep them waiting, assigning humiliating tasks to them, and treating them rudely."[30] The physical act of making someone wait, for example, is one of the most common ways of manifesting power.[31] Most important, the social relation of domination between the shaykh and his followers serves practical purposes:

> But it is especially to seek his help in arbitration that people come to see the shaykh.... The shaykh is also a political notable, even though he would not describe himself as such. He holds local power as a result of his political connections with the government, due to which he can intervene effectively on behalf of the community. He is a member of the ruling party.... Government officials often have recourse to him for taking care of problems in the village.... Once the followers have recognized the presence of *walaya* in the shaykh, they establish a relationship of allegiance with him that sociologically takes the form of a patron-client relationship.... The relations of patronage that we have noted in the Egyptian case, where the shaykh takes care of the needs of the community, are inherent in the very concept of *walaya*: proximity to God implies patronage.... The people of the village experience their relationship with the shaykh as one of exchange and mutual benefits, which they exploit themselves.[32]

Thus, it is not surprising that Rachida Chih found that the relationship between the shaykh and his followers overshadows everything else in their experience of Sufism: "When one asks Sufis what distinguishes them from those who are not Sufis, one receives answers such as 'love of the shaykh' (*mahabba li-l-shaykh*), 'attachment to the shaykh' (*mulazamat al-shaykh*), or 'putting oneself at the shaykh's service' (*khidmat al-shaykh*)."[33]

These practices of domination and patronage are part of Sufism, just as much as the philosophy of Ibn 'Arabi is part of Sufism. One can have some chance of understanding these practices only by observing them in everyday life, rather than by reading theoretical or normative texts. This is not a matter of making a distinction between "elite Islam" and "popular Islam." Scholars, too, rely on practical sense in everyday life whenever they are not actually doing scholarship. Instead, the scholar must distinguish between two ways of understanding the world: "the scholastic one which he tacitly sets up as the norm, and the practical one which he has in common with men and women seemingly very distant from him in time and social space," and which he, too, uses "in the most ordinary acts and experiences (those of jealousy, for example) of ordinary existence."[34]

THE NEGLECT OF TRAINING IN SPOKEN ARABIC

A researcher wishing to observe and listen to people in everyday life in Arabic-speaking countries must be proficient in spoken Arabic. But outside the Arab world, most universities that offer courses in Arabic as a second language teach only standard Arabic, a variety that is reserved for written communication and a small number of very formal or official contexts.

Although surveys indicate that conversing with native speakers is a high priority for students, instruction in spoken varieties of Arabic is rare. Most degree programs offer a maximum of two semesters of spoken Arabic. Students who study only standard Arabic "often experience frustration and embarrassment when trying to communicate with Arabic speakers" and are, in effect, excluded from everyday social practices.[35]

The main opportunity for students to learn spoken Arabic as a second language is in study-abroad programs. However, these programs are also, at most, two semesters long,[36] and "study abroad sojourns are becoming ever shorter—a semester, summer, or even just a few weeks, rather than an entire academic year."[37] Studies have found that a longer period of immersion is correlated with greater gains in oral proficiency, but degree programs do not give students the opportunity to take advantage of this.[38]

After only one year of immersion, most students will struggle to do research that involves talking with people or studying vernacular media such as film and television, especially if they have had little previous training in spoken Arabic. In my own experience, the nonnative speakers who have reached an advanced level in Egyptian colloquial Arabic, enabling them to use it extensively and with ease in their research, have devoted a minimum of two years in Egypt to language training and immersion. Some have managed to do this by, in effect, creating their own study-abroad program, using their own financial resources, but this is not feasible for most students. Others have progressed to an advanced level in spoken Arabic while at the same time doing field research for a graduate degree, but this is clearly not ideal.

Faced with such limited opportunities to learn spoken Arabic, students have an incentive to choose research topics that involve only written sources. They may therefore refrain from asking research questions that can be answered only through ethnography, interviews, or the study of vernacular media. Or they may try to answer those questions using written sources alone, and thus fall into the scholastic fallacy.

Since Egyptian anthropologists produce high-quality research using their native language, one might well ask whether, given scarce resources, it would be more efficient if only native speakers did this type of research. However, as Hania Sholkamy observes, favoring local researchers over foreign ones "promotes a kind of nationalism that cannot further understanding per se."[39] In another undesirable scenario, foreign researchers, who do not speak the local language, treat local researchers as mere "'service providers' for research assistants, for translating, and newspaper summaries, for first hand testimonies, and time and again as providers of experts."[40] Instead, "anthropologists at home and abroad need to stay on shared intellectual territory. Ideally we should all work at home and work abroad and thus have a greater sensitivity to one another."[41]

The Risks of Research in Authoritarian States

Field research in authoritarian states involves particular methodological and ethical problems. In a survey of researchers who did fieldwork in authoritarian states in northern Africa and western Asia, many respondents described "a pervasive 'culture of suspicion,' as evidenced by interviewees' mistrust and nervousness in speaking frankly to researchers for fear of political repercussions," and reported "the common perception that American researchers in general may be connected with the CIA or other intelligence agencies."[42] Sheila Carapico notes that laypeople without university degrees are likely to have the impression that research is something akin to spying. Moreover, it can put both the researcher and the participants at risk: "More pernicious than neighborhood gossip, however, is the fact that security agents, secret police, and ordinary snitches may indeed track a foreigner's moves and conversations.... In many Arab countries it is common knowledge that telephones are tapped, for instance, and dialing a number, perhaps especially from abroad, may bring that phone line under surveillance. Mail is opened and read by censors. The principled quandary under these circumstances is whether one's colleagues will become targets of police scrutiny—or worse."[43]

In the context of survey-based research, the problem of respondent self-censorship (known as "preference falsification") is well-known, but "survey-based research on public opinion in authoritarian regimes . . . has mostly tried to avoid a direct discussion of this issue."[44] Janine A. Clark found that this made some researchers wonder whether "the fear of answering survey questions honestly may have invalidated the survey results," but it is not clear how this problem can be solved.[45]

Sholkamy describes how both bureaucratic and security obstacles discourage ethnographic research in Egypt. Social scientists cannot legally carry out research in Egypt without a permit from the Center for Public Mobilization and Statistics (CAPMAS), which can reject applications without explanation. Moreover, CAPMAS recognizes only survey research, not ethnographic research, and requires the researcher to submit the written questionnaire that will be used in the survey. Some anthropologists have found no alternative to inventing a fake questionnaire in the hope of obtaining a permit.[46]

Before the uprising of 2011, it was common for researchers to carry out interview-based or ethnographic studies in Egypt without permits, perhaps with a letter from their home institution, taking the chance that the authorities would not notice or care. The risks of this approach seem to have increased since then. In a context of increased xenophobia, in which the media have regularly portrayed foreigners as spies or agents seeking to destabilize Egypt, several foreign researchers have been arrested, deported, and/or banned from entering the country, with no official explanation.[47] In January 2016, Giulio Regeni, a Cambridge University PhD student who had been doing fieldwork on trade unions in Egypt, disappeared in Cairo; his body was found by a roadside nine days later, bearing extensive signs of torture. As of this writing, Egyptian human rights groups and Italian investigators suspect that Egyptian security services may be responsible, but the case remains unsolved.[48] At the very least, it suggests that the risks of doing research that involves talking to people in Egypt have increased considerably in recent years.

In some cases, a researcher might be tempted to carry out interviews from abroad using video calls transmitted over the internet. While this reduces the risk for the researcher, it is much more difficult to protect the interviewee. Authoritarian states have sophisticated surveillance technology, and even if the call is encrypted to prevent interception in transit, an intelligence agency may find other ways to monitor it.[49]

Research in archives is perhaps safer but can be no less daunting. In the wake of the revolutionary uprisings that took place in several countries in northern Africa and western Asia starting in 2010, archival research has become more difficult in some countries and impossible in others, and historians now "face the prospect of ever-diminishing access to archives and national libraries in the region."[50] In the case of Egypt, the obstacles to archival research are considerable: "Unlike other world-class document repositories . . . the National Archives of Egypt are not open to the public. Access is limited to those with permits, and it is the state's repressive security apparatus that acts as arbiter. . . . [S]tate security viciously restricts access to all but a privileged few; these people tend to be professional historians whose research is perceived as nonsubversive to the state and its narratives, which are overwhelmingly nationalist."[51]

Many official documents remain unavailable, their whereabouts unknown. In particular, there is almost no access to official documents dating from after the 1952 military coup; historians have therefore had to rely "almost entirely on foreign archives, the press, interviews and personal memoirs."[52]

The periodicals section of the Egyptian National Library has offered unrestricted access, but it has no digitized materials (only bound volumes and microfilm, many of which are missing), there is no electronic catalog and no index of any kind, and the process of obtaining each item is very slow.

Therefore, a researcher must either know in advance exactly which materials he wants, or have a great deal of time to spend reading volume after volume in the hope of finding something of interest. In practice, this means that there are many research questions that cannot be asked or are unlikely to be asked.

The state of audiovisual archives in Egypt is even worse. Egypt has had the most prolific Arabic film industry since the early twentieth century, and Egyptian films have long been popular throughout the Arabic-speaking world.[53] Egyptian cinema is thus an important record of interaction between cultural producers and a wide audience over a long period of time. However, preservation at Egypt's National Film Center is utterly inadequate, and hundreds of films have been lost because of neglect.[54] Many films that have been preserved cannot be viewed, unless their distribution via television or DVD is still considered commercially viable.

Given these obstacles, it is not surprising that "[r]esearch agendas, instead of being problem-driven, are often guided by what material is available or even accessible."[55] This is a problem in itself because the narrowing of available materials impoverishes research by narrowing the range of questions that can be asked. A less obvious risk is the temptation to overgeneralize from limited sources, to make them say things that they cannot really say. I have discussed above how this can happen with canonical texts, but it also affects the increasingly common attempts to use social media as a substitute for surveys based on probability sampling. Social media users are not representative of the broader population, fake accounts are often created to spread propaganda, and automated sentiment analysis is poorly equipped to recognize sarcasm and irony.[56]

CONCLUSION

Degree programs that involve training in Arabic should give spoken Arabic at least as high a priority as standard Arabic, for example, by integrating them in the same course of instruction, using spoken Arabic for oral communication in the classroom, and standard Arabic for reading and writing.[57] At more advanced levels, it would seem reasonable to emphasize content-based instruction (otherwise known as content and language integrated learning). It is common for French departments outside the Francophone world to teach courses in literature, history, and philosophy in French, but only a few universities outside the Arab world offer any content courses in Arabic, and this approach should be more widely used.

Study-abroad programs of at least two years should be offered as part of degree programs. The structure of such programs is as important as their duration because mere presence in a country is not enough to guarantee language immersion. One way to improve language immersion while at the same time promoting ethnographic research is to integrate ethnography into the study-abroad program: "In these types of programs, students receive substantial pre-departure training in conducting ethnographic research. . . . While abroad, they conduct a small ethnography connected to their local environment. This connects their more general knowledge to the local context they encounter, promotes interactions with locals via data collection, helps them overcome ethnocentric orientations, and assists linguistic development through the need to collect and analyze information in the target language beyond superficial interactions."[58]

Research in an authoritarian state should always be designed so that it can be adapted if the situation there makes the fieldwork impossible or too risky. One way to do this is to design a project involving two or more countries (e.g., a comparative study), thus making it less dependent on the situation in any particular country.

A number of universities and national libraries around the world have collections of rare books, periodicals, and other materials that, to some extent, overlap with the contents of hard-to-access libraries and archives in authoritarian states. By digitizing these materials and making them freely accessible on the internet, these institutions can help shield research from the interference of internal security services in those states. Better still, by providing full-text and other search capabilities, they can make it possible to carry out research that would not otherwise be feasible. It is especially valuable to create open-access digital archives of noncanonical texts, such as correspondence, commercial and legal documents, newspapers, popular magazines, and school textbooks, which can provide glimpses of everyday social practices.

Finally, when students carry out research on canonical texts, they should be encouraged to historicize those texts, understanding each one as a stance taken in relation to the state of a particular field at a particular historical moment, by an author occupying a particular position in that field, rather than as a timeless expression of broader social phenomena. This approach requires humility based on the recognition that, with only texts as evidence, one can try to answer some questions but not others.

NOTES

1. Aaron W. Hughes, *Theorizing Islam: Disciplinary Deconstruction and Reconstruction* (New York: Routledge, 2014), 2–3, 34, 66.

2. Pierre Bourdieu, *Pascalian Meditations*, trans. Richard Nice (Stanford, CA: Stanford University Press, 1997), 49–84.

3. Bourdieu, *Pascalian Meditations*, 15.

4. Bourdieu, *Pascalian Meditations*, 12–13.

5. Bourdieu, *Pascalian Meditations*, 10–11.

6. Bourdieu, *Pascalian Meditations*, 96–97.

7. Pierre Bourdieu, *The Rules of Art*, trans. Susan Emanuel (Cambridge: Polity Press, 1996), 87–88.

8. Pierre Bourdieu, *The Logic of Practice*, trans. Richard Nice (Stanford, CA: Stanford University Press, 1990), 103–104.

9. Bourdieu, *Pascalian Meditations*, 139.

10. Bourdieu, *Pascalian Meditations*, 141.

11. Bourdieu, *Pascalian Meditations*, 51.

12. Edward W. Said, *Orientalism* (New York: Random House, 1979), 93, 129.

13. See, for example, Stephen S. Bush, "Are Meanings the Name of the Game? Religion as Symbolic Meaning and Religion as Power," *Religion Compass* 6 (2012): 525–533.

14. Bourdieu, *Pascalian Meditations*, 52.

15. Charles Kurzman, and Carl W. Ernst, "Islamic Studies in U.S. Universities," *Review of Middle East Studies* 46, no. 1 (2012): 31; Hatsuki Aishima, "Contesting Public Images of 'Abd al-Halim Mahmud (1910–78): Who is an Authentic Scholar?," in *Ethnographies of Islam: Ritual Performances and Everyday Practices*, ed. Baudouin Dupret, Thomas Pierret, Paulo G. Pinto, and Kathryn Spellman-Poots (Edinburgh: Edinburgh University Press, 2012), 170; Clinton Bennett, "New Directions: The Who, Why, What, How, and Where of Studying Islam," in *The Bloomsbury Companion to Islamic Studies*, ed. Clinton Bennett (New York: Bloomsbury, 2013), 261.

16. Carl W. Ernst and Richard C. Martin, "Introduction: Toward a Post-Orientalist Approach to Islamic Religious Studies," in *Rethinking Islamic Studies: From Orientalism to Cosmopolitanism*, ed. Carl W. Ernst and Richard C. Martin (Columbia: University of South Carolina Press, 2010), 13.

17. Shahab Ahmed, *What Is Islam? The Importance of Being Islamic* (Princeton, NJ: Princeton University Press, 2016), 20–22.

18. Ahmed, *What Is Islam?*, 85–88.

19. Ahmed, *What Is Islam?*, 92.

20. Brian Silverstein, "Sufism and Modernity in Turkey: From the Authenticity of Experience to the Practice of Discipline," in *Sufism and the Modern in Islam*, ed. Martin van Bruinessen and Julia Day Howell (London: I. B. Tauris, 2007), 42.

21. Valerie Hoffman, *Sufism, Mystics, and Saints in Modern Egypt* (Columbia: University of South Carolina Press, 1995), 22–23, 64, 137.

22. Hoffman, *Sufism, Mystics, and Saints in Modern Egypt*, 175–176.

23. Hoffman, *Sufism, Mystics, and Saints in Modern Egypt*, 167.

24. Paulo G. Pinto, "Creativity and Stability in the Making of Sufi Tradition: The Tariqa Qadiriyya in Aleppo, Syria," in *Sufism Today: Heritage and Tradition in the Global Community*, ed. Catharina Raudvere and Leif Stenberg (New York: I. B. Tauris, 2009), 130.

25. Bourdieu, *Pascalian Meditations*, 144.

26. Bourdieu, *Pascalian Meditations*, 241.

27. Bourdieu, *Pascalian Meditations*, 171.

28. Rachida Chih, "What Is a Sufi Order?," in *Sufism and the Modern in Islam*, ed. Martin van Bruinessen and Julia Day Howell (London: I. B. Tauris, 2007), 31.

29. Bourdieu, *Pascalian Meditations*, 169.

30. Hoffman, *Sufism, Mystics, and Saints in Modern Egypt*, 144.

31. Bourdieu, *Pascalian Meditations*, 228.

32. Chih, "What Is a Sufi Order?," 32–33.

33. Chih, "What Is a Sufi Order?," 27.

34. Bourdieu, *Pascalian Meditations*, 51.

35. Jeremy Palmer, "Arabic Diglossia: Teaching Only the Standard Variety Is a Disservice to Students," *Arizona Working Papers in SLA and Teaching* 14 (2007): 111–112; David Wilmsen, "What Is Communicative Arabic?," in *Handbook for Arabic Language Teaching Professionals in the 21st Century*, ed. Kassem M. Wahba, Zainab A. Taha, and Liz England (New York: Routledge, 2013), 133.

36. Julia Jensen and Martin Howard, "The Effects of Time in the Development of Complexity and Accuracy during Study Abroad: A Study of French and Chinese Learners of English," *EUROSLA Yearbook* 14, no. 1 (2014): 32.

37. Emma Trentman, "Arabic and English during Study Abroad in Cairo, Egypt: Issues of Access and Use," *Modern Language Journal* 97, no. 2 (2013): 457.

38. Michael Vande Berg, Jeffrey Connor-Linton, and R. Michael Paige, "The Georgetown Consortium Project: Interventions for Student Learning Abroad," *Frontiers: The Interdisciplinary Journal of Study Abroad* 18 (2009): 1–75; Dan E. Davidson, "Study Abroad: When, How Long, and with What Results? New Data from the Russian Front," *Foreign Language Annals* 43, no. 1 (2010): 6–26.

39. Hania Sholkamy, "Why Is Anthropology So Hard in Egypt?," in *Between Field and Text: Emerging Voices in Egyptian Social Science*, ed. Seteney Shami and Linda Herrera (Cairo: American University in Cairo Press, 1999), 134.

40. Mona Abaza, "Academic Tourists Sight-Seeing the Arab Spring," *Ahram Online*, September 26, 2011, http://english.ahram.org.eg/News/22373.aspx.

41. Sholkamy, "Why Is Anthropology So Hard in Egypt?," 134.

42. Janine A. Clark, "Field Research Methods in the Middle East," *PS: Political Science and Politics* 39, no. 3 (2006.): 418. See also Courtney Radsch, "From Cell Phones to Coffee: Issues of Access in Egypt and Lebanon," in *Surviving Field Research: Working in Violent and Difficult Situations*, ed. Chandra Lekha Sriram, John C. King, Julie A. Mertus, Olga Martin-Ortega, and Johanna Herman (New York: Routledge, 2009), 98.

43. Sheila Carapico, "No Easy Answers: The Ethics of Field Research in the Arab World," *PS: Political Science and Politics* 39, no. 3 (2006): 430.

44. Junyan Jiang and Dali L. Yang, "Lying or Believing? Measuring Preference Falsification from a Political Purge in China," *Comparative Political Studies* 49, no. 5 (2016): 601–602.

45. Clark, "Field Research Methods in the Middle East," 418.

46. Sholkamy, "Why Is Anthropology So Hard in Egypt?," 127–129.

47. Brian Rohan and Maram Mazen, "In Egypt, Clamp on Academic Freedoms Sparks Scholar Backlash," Associated Press, February 18, 2016, http://bigstory.ap.org/article/c47ae f5e5eb24f988779bd8e410a4d84/egypt-clamp-academic-freedoms-sparks-scholar-backlash.

48. Alexander Stille, "Who Murdered Giulio Regeni?," *The Guardian*, October 4, 2016, https://www.theguardian.com/world/2016/oct/04/egypt-murder-giulio-regeni.

49. Stuart Deibert, "Lawfulness of a Lethal Operation Directed against a U.S. Citizen Who Is a Senior Operational Leader of al-Qaʿida or an Associated Force," Department of Justice White Paper, November 8, 2011, 65–69.

50. Omnia El Shakry, "'History Without Documents': The Vexed Archives of Decolonization in the Middle East," *American Historical Review* 120, no. 3 (2015): 922.

51. Hussein Omar, "The State of the Archive: Manipulating Memory in Modern Egypt and the Writing of Egyptological Histories," in *Histories of Egyptology: Interdisciplinary Measures*, ed. William Carruthers (New York: Routledge, 2015), 176.

52. Anthony Gorman, *Historians, State and Politics in Twentieth Century Egypt: Contesting the Nation* (New York: Routledge, 2003), 74.

53. Viola Shafik, *Popular Egyptian Cinema: Gender, Class, and Nation* (Cairo: American University in Cairo Press, 2007), 4–5.

54. Sayed Badreya, "Saving Egyptian Film Classics," in *This Film Is Dangerous: A Celebration of Nitrate Film*, ed. Roger Smither and Catherine A. Surowiec (Brussels: International Federation of Film Archives, 2002), 417–419; Jay Weissberg, "Fires, Heat Trouble Egyptian Film Preservation," *Variety*, July 31, 2010.

55. Omar, "The State of the Archive," 177.

56. Daniel Gayo-Avello, "A Meta-Analysis of State-of-the-Art Electoral Prediction from Twitter Data," *Social Science Computer Review* 31, no. 6 (2013): 649–679; David Bamman and Noah A. Smith, "Contextualized Sarcasm Detection on Twitter," *Proceedings of the Ninth*

International AAAI Conference on Web and Social Media, 2015, http://www.aaai.org/ocs/index .php/ICWSM/ICWSM15/paper/view/10538.

57. See Munther Younes, *The Integrated Approach to Arabic Instruction* (New York: Routledge, 2015).

58. Trentman, "Arabic and English during Study Abroad in Cairo, Egypt," 469.

BENJAMIN GEER is Research Fellow at the Digital Humanities Lab, University of Basel.

chapter four

ISLAMIC RELIGIOUS EDUCATION AND CRITICAL THOUGHT IN EUROPEAN PLURAL SOCIETIES

Mouez Khalfaoui

ISLAMIC RELIGIOUS EDUCATION CURRENTLY TAKES place in both secular and confessional forms; it is being taught at religious schools (madrassas) and mosques as well as primary and secondary schools throughout the world. In both the Muslim and European context, the reform of Islamic education remains the subject of continuous debate and controversy. Being markedly shaped by different social and cultural environments, the specificities of ongoing discussions vary. Both educational staff and educational experts in Muslim-majority societies and in non-Muslim countries are complaining about present teaching methods as well as teaching concepts, teaching materials, and predominant conditions of teaching.[1] In spite of the fact that many reform attempts turned out to be fruitless,[2] a number of them are still in operation today. This is because reform projects within the sector of Islamic education involve not only politicians but also sociologists, historians, and scholars of the Islamic faith.

In Muslim-majority societies, the so-called reform of Islamic education is debated within the context of modernizing Muslim society as a whole. Already in 1977, during the first Islamic Conference for Islamic Education, participants agreed that the best way to reform Islamic education would be to integrate it into the international system of education, which again was dominated by the West.[3] While reforms in the field of Islamic education were long inspired by an overall wish for transformation and modernization in the Muslim world, motivations changed after September 11. Since the terrorist attack of 2001, the fear of religious radicalism has driven reforms of Islamic education in Muslim countries. Accordingly, classical teaching institutions were strongly criticized and described as "terror factories." In recent years, the curricula and teaching methodologies of these institutions have been under continuous "reform."[4]

In Western Europe, the reform of Islamic education has long been shaped by the multiethnic and multi-religious specificities of European societies. Those debates have taken place in an environment where Muslims were, and still are, a minority, peacefully coexisting with a broad range of "believers" and "nonbelievers." In its European context, Islamic education has thus always emphasized respect for "the other." Contrary to many regions of the Muslim world, Islam is taught in Europe on both a confessional and a secular-scientific level. Secular teaching methods that are currently used can be subdivided into at least three categories: (1) anti-dogmatic, (2) analytical, and (3) phenomenological. New methods of teaching religious education are continuously being developed and tested, often falling outside the schemata introduced above, leading to considerable plurality in the teaching of Islamic content in Europe. Thus, contemporary teaching approaches vary in their respective focus, goal, as well as their use of teaching material and sources.

Recently, the teaching of Islamic religious education in Western Europe has been shaped by the establishment of new Muslim teaching institutions—namely the faculties of Islamic theology, which train not only teachers of Islamic theology but also religion experts and researchers. Although scholars at European universities have a long history of studying Islam and Oriental Cultures (Orientalism), as well as teaching about Islamic religion and culture, they do not have the capacity to teach Islam from an "insider perspective" (Islamic theology). This makes the task of establishing Islamic theology as an academic discipline very challenging both for the Muslim minorities and the European stakeholders. In addition to the academic difficulties, there are social and political difficulties that have to be considered when dealing with Islamic theology in Europe.

In this regard, I would like to deal only with the situation of the Muslim minorities in Western Europe. There, the social and political debates surrounding Muslim minorities are characterized by several difficulties.[5] The establishment of Islamic theological institutions in Germany, England, Sweden, The Netherlands, Belgium, and so on is meant to be a solution to these problems. In this regard, Islamic religious education aims to:

- Promote integration and political participation of and among Muslims,
- Reduce extremism,
- "Produce" a new moderate Islam and "Muslims,"
- Solve social and religious problems that Muslims are facing in Europe,
- Help Muslims to gain a better understanding of their own religion, and
- Improve the dialog between the majority of the population and the Muslim minority.

In this issue, I would argue that most European countries share the same situation. Both the mass media and several scientific studies depict a very dark situation; they speak of the "Islamization of Europe" through conservative Muslims and depict Europe as the first place where Muslims will be the majority of the population. This new Muslim majority will "Islamize" their surroundings by applying shari'a and Islamic law. The image of the Muslim minority in Europe is in many cases exclusively depicted from a negative perspective. There are certainly many positive aspects regarding the existence of minorities in Europe; however, it is not the appropriate moment to speak of these aspects now. These controversial interpretations prove that there is a lack of well-founded research about Muslim minorities and that Islamic religious education has an important role to play in changing the negative image of Muslims.

CONCEPTS OF REFORMING ISLAMIC EDUCATION

Both in Muslim and non-Muslim common wisdom, the current debate on Islamic religious education is mostly shaped by the idea of reform. In this chapter, I will deal with this issue from two perspectives: on the one hand, I will deal with the issue of terminology; on the other hand, I will deal with the concepts of reform that have been debated in regard to Islamic religious education.

The term "Islamic education" is currently used in a number of ways and in different contexts, yet there is no precise and uniformly agreed on definition of it. A lot of teaching material and curricula both in the Muslim world and in the West explicitly or implicitly suggest that "Islamic education" is a transcendental and holy activity and as such a very religious concept. In both Muslim and European contexts, Islamic education is expected to maintain norms of rationality and the human experience and to strengthen the deep-rooted values of morality and religiosity. The role of the geographical, sociocultural, and political contexts in the development of new teaching concepts for this field are under debate with regard to this point. While universalists and essentialists argue that Islamic education is universal and that it should be universal, since the moral principles have the same roots, another point of view underlines the idea that education should also have a local dimension that relates it to the lived context. These different opinions are reflected in the debate about the "reform" of Islamic education.

In Muslim-majority societies, the term used for reform includes *Islah*, which also means "correction" and "rehabilitation."[6] These two expressions reflect a key characteristic of the ongoing debate in Muslim societies, which stands in direct contrast to the West. Reforms are being discussed and placed in opposition or in agreement with the international system, which is full of Western teaching methods and concepts. While many "reformists" think that Islamic educational reform is best achieved by incorporating Western ideas as much as possible, so-called conservatives or traditionalists argue that the reform of Islamic education requires the emphasis to be on classical methods and concepts of teaching. Between those two camps, a middle way has developed, with scholars trying to combine aspects of "Islam" and Western educational concepts.

Within the European context, the discussion about Islamic education is focused on the implications that the multiethnic, multi-religious, and pluralistic European society may have on the teaching of Islamic content. Conscious of their existence in a multi-religious society, and of the religious heterogeneity within the Muslim community itself, people involved in contemporary Islamic education in Europe are in constant disagreement with one another. A main topic of debate relates to the question of how multi-religiosity and multiethnicity can be combined without the alienation of Muslim students from their faith and their Islamic cultural background.

Furthermore, the debate about the reform of Islamic education is not only shaped by its context but also by different political and social agendas. For European politicians, for example, the reform of Islamic religious education means, in many ways, the disconnection of European Muslims from religious streams and schools that are considered "radical" and "foreign." That way, they hope to establish a "European Islam," which is expected to be moderate and modern, especially in comparison to more conservative religious interpretations and practices. The goals of European politicians regarding this alleged reform education are undermined by technological advancements that facilitate the global communication between Muslims. This access to communication strengthens the relationship of European Muslims to their homeland and connects Muslim youth with ultraconservative groups worldwide. Mass media and social media, as well as affordable means of transportation, allow Muslims to join worldwide networks, visit Islamic teaching institutes, and, generally speaking, exchange ideas without the limitation of national boundaries. This is also due to the Muslim concept of *Umma* that underlines the unity of all believers so that the global *Umma* (Muslim community) transcends Muslims' respective homelands.

Thus, in the debate about Islamic education in Europe, there are two tendencies among Muslim communities that also find support in European minority politics. These two tendencies can be identified as globalization versus de-globalization.[7] Overall, it seems that the reform of Islamic religious education in Muslim majority societies and European countries either follows the goal of further globalization or the opposite aim of de-globalization. The leading question in both contexts of discussion remains: Is there any theory of Islamic religious education that meets the needs of changing ways of living in both Muslim countries and in the West? In other words, one could ask: What are the roots of Islamic education, which parts can be changed and adapted to changing contexts, and how (through which media) does the context influence the concepts of Islamic religious education? An underlying question is also whether the context should be treated as the main determinant in the development of Islamic religious education.

ISLAMIC RELIGIOUS EDUCATION AS PART OF RELIGIOUS EDUCATION

The discussion about the reform of Islamic education in Western societies is currently debated within the broader framework of reforming religious education in general. The latter involves two types of religious education:

1. *Confessional education.* This category seeks to deepen the religious faith of children.
2. *Non-confessional education.*[8] This category has the following three subcategories:
   a. *Anti-dogmatic religious education.* This claims to be neutral and objective. The religious teaching in this form consists of informing students about the main religions of this world. The aim is to inform them about important facts and interesting human religious phenomena and to understand the role of religions in human history.
   b. *Analytical teaching.* This type of education seeks to explore religion with regard to its implicit and spiritual aspects. Students learn how to analyze and to interpret aspects of the human condition and the beauty of nature. In the process, religion is explained.
   c. *Phenomenological religious education.* In this form of education, students are expected to not only know about their religion but to also practice it.

According to the main tenets of contemporary education theory, there are three goals of religious education. First, religious education strives to search for the truth. This requires that students learn to criticize religious content and express their doubts about it. This seems very difficult to do in confessional religious education. The second goal is based on comparison. This method helps students to find different and common points between various faiths (it can consist of comparing Schism with Sunnism, etc.). This method is non-confessional per se. Third, religious education helps students to know their own religion and reflect on it; it teaches them to be believers of their own religion and, at the same time, respect the beliefs of others.

To summarize, the discussion stresses the evidence that Islamic religious education is currently in a phase of transition from classical to modern era, from private to public sphere, and from homogeneous to heterogeneous societies. Therefore, the concepts and aims of the research in this area need to be renewed too.

CURRENT SITUATION OF ISLAMIC RELIGIOUS EDUCATION IN FOUR EUROPEAN STATES

Both in Muslim states and the West, the existence of a number of research projects on Islamic education reflects the importance ascribed to this subject. In the following, I will present the current situation in four Western European states regarding the teaching and the aims of Islamic religious education.

As far as Islamic education in modern European societies is concerned, the debate is shaped by the following questions:

- How should Islamic education be taught and which concepts should be used?
- How should Islamic education be reformed in order to adapt to the new contexts of living?
- Is there an appropriate form of religious education in multi-religious and multiethnic societies?
- What does the reform of Islamic education mean to Muslim-majority societies and to Muslim-minority societies in the West, and how is it taking place?
- What should be taken into consideration when teaching Islam in different contexts and what influence does Muslims' living environment have on it?

Furthermore, the situation depends on the following factors:

- The general level of education and the importance that the state ascribes to educational matters (this is usually reflected by literacy rates, enrollment ratios, and public spending on education),
- The cultural environment and whether it favors reform of Islamic education,
- The existence of experience in reforming Islamic education, and
- The existence of an appropriate sociocultural and political context for new concepts of teaching.

TEACHING ISLAM IN GERMANY

Towards Islamic Religious Education III

This part of the essay is based on a report titled "Towards Islamic Religious Education III: Pupil's Personal Living Environments, Religious Identities and Society" (*Auf dem Weg zum IRU III*) presented at a conference that was held in Stuttgart in southern Germany, between March 16 and March 8, 2009. Among the religious education teachers were some that taught Christian ethics and religion. Various representatives of religious groups such as the Islamic Federation of Berlin attended the conference. The media and public were only allowed to attend the last public meeting.

The conference had four parts. The first part was related to the Muslim pupils and their identities. In this part, findings of the empirical research on classroom instruction and supporting survey studies were presented. The second part was related to religion and identity and examining the relationship between them. The topic of the third part was religious identity and society. The subthemes were the experiences in the classroom and concepts of religious pedagogy and theology. Finally, the fourth part dealt with topics of standardized civil religion or pluralism. In this part, the focus was on socially effective identities through religious education.

In the conference, reports pertinent to various states of Germany were presented, and some reports, especially those from the federal states of Bavaria and Baden-Württemberg, received particular attention. The speakers highlighted the findings of empirical surveys and stated that Muslim parents and pupils were satisfied with the level of education. Moreover, there is increasing interest in and attention to Islamic religious education.

Three researchers presented their studies and discussed Muslim pupils' question of identity in the second part of the conference. These researchers included Irka-Christin Mohr, a specialist of Islamic religious education from the University of Erfurt, Martin Engelbrecht who is a sociologist from the University of Erlangen-Nuremberg, and Annette Treibel from the University of Karlsruhe.

In total, four workshops were organized. In these workshops, teachers, academics, and education policy experts dedicated their efforts to analyzing and evaluating practical experience. Mistrust of colleagues, the lack of teaching materials, and misgivings of the public were the main problems identified by the Islam teachers, who came from all over the country. The participants also debated new school textbooks such as *Mein Islambuch* and *Saphir 5/6*. Apart from this, didactic and pedagogical aspects of Islam lessons were also discussed.

The results of different work groups were shared at the final public meeting during the conference, which sparked hot discussion between authors of school textbooks and various Islamic religious groups. One of the most important discussion topics was the usage of different pictures in the textbooks. For instance, in textbook *Saphir 5/6*, one author used a picture of an angel with wings. The participants of the public meeting were clearly divided into two groups. One group opposed the use of such of pictures and stated the argument that they are prohibited in Islam.

However, the second group justified the use of the picture by arguing that the purpose was merely pedagogical and didactic.

In short, the conference provided an opportunity and reinforced the objectives of the Islamic religious education, debated the drawbacks, and also explored the future in an optimistic way. It is worth mentioning that the majority of the conference participants concluded that in the case of Islamic religion lessons, there is clearly a lack of expertise from an independent institution.

Pedagogy of Islam as a New Field in Germany

Islamic religious education was introduced as a regular subject in German schools as late as the beginning of the twenty-first century. This undertaking started with limited regional projects in a few areas.[9] Within the last decade, it has been expanded and established as a subject of learning in almost all the states of the German federal republic. Besides the political debate and agenda of this project,[10] the main focus of debate and research continues to be on pedagogical aspects of Islamic education. The abundant literature on Islamic pedagogy has three different aspects: (1) teaching materials, (2) teaching methods, and (3) and teaching personnel. In the following I will focus on the first two aspects; the arguments regarding the third are largely covered in the first two.

Teaching Materials

Several new books have been published in Germany in the last ten years. They consist of innovative teaching materials that present a new understanding of religion and of pedagogy. The new textbooks are all written by authors who are currently teaching the subject of Islamic education either at schools or at university. These new materials bear witness to the pedagogical and didactical approaches and paradigms within the field.[11] Indeed, these new books reflect a contestable shift from classical teaching pedagogy to a new one that takes into consideration the context of Muslim students' lives, as well as their social and cultural situation.[12] The textbook entitled *Saphir* also illustrates this new teaching concept.[13] *Saphir* has many volumes that go from primary to secondary schools. The book is compiled by a team of authors who are all Muslim teachers. Most of them have practical experience in the field of teaching, while some others are members of university faculty in Germany and are chairs of Islamic pedagogy. The book aims to make Muslim pupils feel integrated in the European context in which they live. The pictures of the book, the texts used for the teaching, and the contents are taken from the point of view of Muslims living in Europe.[14] Compared to other textbooks that were produced in the 1980s in Austria, for example, where the references and pictures mainly concentrated on strengthening the spirit of belonging to the land of origin, *Saphir* sees Europe as the only homeland for Muslim students and tries to help them understand this context. Of course, the book refers to Islamic states but sees the focus of life as being in Europe; in short, it speaks of European Muslims, not of Muslim migrants. Besides the subjects of Islamic faith, *Saphir* presents several aspects of interreligious dialogue, relationships to a non-Muslim neighborhood, and the concepts of living together in a secular society. When it comes to didactic issues, the book presents many similarities with the textbooks of Christian religious education; it insists on what we can call the comprehensive approach,[15] a leading concept in German academia. The didactic method of this textbook differs from what used to be known as the Islamic classical teaching method. While the classical method was based on memorization and teacher-oriented learning,[16] the new approach is based on modern teaching methods such as teamwork and weekly projects. In this regard, the Islamic education textbooks strengthen the general conceptions of Islamic education that are incarnated in the curricula of Islamic education.

The Curriculum of Islamic Education

Besides textbooks, the curricula of Islamic education in Germany have been an interesting subject of research for the last decade. The research of Irka-Christin Mohr and Michael Kiefer gives an overview of the development of Islamic pedagogy, as well as insight into how the curricula of Islamic education are being produced and the debate about them within Muslim communities in the German state.[17] Starting from the fact that the German regional states have approached the subject of teaching Islam at school differently according to their own regional or local situation, Mohr and Kiefer spent several years conducting field research in their own areas. While Mohr focused on taking part in teaching classes and interviewing teachers of Islamic education, Kiefer concentrated his research more on following the political and legal debate on the subject. Both researchers show how complicated the issue of Islamic education in Germany is. Due to the differences between Muslim-majority societies and the regional specificities of the German and European context, the curricula of Islamic education aim to give Muslim students a new understanding of their Muslim identity, of the context where they live, and how to cope with secular concepts. As a case in point, Mohr addresses how the curricula understand the issue of Muslim community (*umma*).[18]

German Muslims have believed until very recently that Austria is a role model in dealing with issues related to the Muslim community and the teaching of Islam. There are some issues in European countries, particularly in Germany, which could be called "primitive issues." These are related to the theoretical aspects such as the headscarf, if and how the teaching of Islam could or should take place in public schools, and which kind of methods can be used to teach Islam. In Austria, the government has provided space for the Muslim community for the proper integration of teaching Islam in everyday school settings. Since 1912, Islam has been a recognized religion and Muslims are allowed to perform their basic religious rituals. Moreover, Muslim women are allowed to wear headscarves. It is interesting to note that Muslims living in other European countries, but especially German Muslims, also wish to gain as much religious freedom as Muslims living in Austria have achieved. Without any doubt, by and large the Muslim community of Austria is very proud of their religious tolerance and peace of mind. For instance, in Austria, teachings of Islam officially started during the 1980s. A short time after this development, textbooks were printed and used. Moreover, Islamic education teachers were trained in two academic institutions, and Muslims had emphasized the perfect delivery and instruction of this subject. Ednan Aslan, a professor and the head of the Austrian Islamic pedagogical academy at the University of Vienna applauded this development. For instance, in a paper published in 2009, Aslan argues that the Islamic instruction experience exercised in Austria should be considered a model of beneficial collaboration between Muslim communities and a non-Muslim secular state. This collaboration has resulted in better organization and integration of the Muslim community. Moreover, the teachings of Islam are carried out in a smooth manner without complications.[19] On the other hand, in Germany, the situation is opposite to that in Austria. For instance, Bülent Ucar, a German professor and chair of the Islamic pedagogical center at the University of Osnabrück has highlighted this issue and stated that the situation in Germany is backward and conservative in the same book in which Ednan Aslan published a paper.[20] This shows the contrasting situations in two neighboring countries. Ucar has also mentioned that things have developed quickly in Austria. During the last few years, many German Muslims have taken "refuge" in Austria mainly because of the "comfortable situation of Muslims in Austria." These German Muslims did not feel happy or a part of German society. It is important to mention that the issue of the headscarf is not the sole reason. In 2009, as a result of challenging discussion about

Islamic education in Austria, several measures were taken. For example, the curriculum and textbooks were revised. Moreover, the Austrian state encouraged Muslims to take more preventative measures in regard to issues of democracy and human rights. This development showed a change in the policy of the state as the Austrian state has remained neutral for such a long period of time.

Contrary to what many people think, the reforms and changes in Austria have not been accidental. Specialists of both Islam and education have highlighted a few issues with regards to textbooks or teacher training, despite there being no obvious problems in Austria in the last few decades. Some Islamic community leaders of Austrian Muslims have also drawn attention to some problems. For instance, Anes Shakfeh, the former head of the IGGÖ (Islamische Glaubensgemeinschaft in Österreich) in Austria has pointed out these problems and has also hoped to rectify them soon.

There are several factors that led the change and reform process in Austria. However, one of the most important was the publication of a book by the Austrian sociologist Mouhanad Khorchide. The findings of this book pushed the Austrian state to get involved in debate about Islamic education in Austria. Khourchide conducted research on teachers of Islam in public schools in Austria and highlighted the following findings:

- 75 percent of the Austrian teachers of Islam are open-minded,
- 25.3 percent of the teachers want to stay in a closed society,
- 21 percent of them see democracy as a threat to Islam,
- 14.7 percent of the teachers believe Islam does not conform with Austrian legislation,
- 18 percent of the teachers support killing heretics,
- 23 percent of them consider Shia as non-Muslims, and
- 31 percent of the teachers have patriarchal thought processes.[21]

It is important to discuss the consequences of this research. The Austrian state obliged teachers of Islamic education to sign a contract in which they accept the Austrian constitution, democracy, and human rights.

The examples in Germany and Austria show that Muslims in these countries are working hard toward the perfection of Islamic instruction. This process has also highlighted some important elements that still need to be developed. For instance, in Austria, Muslims have done well in their efforts to make Islamic teaching perfect; however, there is a need to revise the content. In a time when Austrian Muslims were doing these things, the German Muslims were occupied with establishing instruction.

I would like to share my personal experiences in Germany and Austria and even teaching and doing research in a number of both Muslim and non-Muslim countries including the United States, India, and other

European countries. I have observed that one of the most important challenges associated with the teaching of Islam in present times is related to the teaching of content. There are two aspects of this challenge. The first challenge concerns teaching of the students and factors affecting the actual life of the pupils. The second challenge is how the teaching of Islam in secular schools can occur and gain freedom from the religious dominance. This situation can also be looked at from another perspective. The actual question concerns finding an available solution that removes the contradiction and conflict that exists between the methods of teaching Islam in schools and the methods used by the religious scholars in mosques and madrassas. Until recently, there have been no efforts made to study this important research subject.

TEACHING ISLAM IN GREAT BRITAIN

In Great Britain, religious education at public schools is constitutionally defined as a non-confessional and multi-faith subject. In the United Kingdom, there are currently nine principal religions and among them, Muslims constitute the second largest confessional group, due to 4.8 percent of the country's overall population being Muslim.[22] There has been a noticeable increase in the Muslim population in the United Kingdom since the 1950s mainly due to immigrants who arrived in search of better economic opportunities. Despite this, the overwhelming majority of British citizens remain Christian. Muslim immigrants are now well integrated in the society, but they refer to and consider themselves as British Muslims.

The majority of Muslim immigrants came from countries such as Pakistan, India, Kenya, Uganda, and Balkan States, which posed a challenge to the British educational system as the educational system proposed to reform itself in order to cater to the specific religious needs of Muslims.[23] One of the most important questions concerned the religious education of the Muslims. Other questions such as Muslims' dress code, food requirements, and sexual education were also highlighted, but religious education remained the topmost discussion subject. One researcher was also motivated to study the evolving public discourse regarding the integration of religious minorities and the role of Islam in the United Kingdom—in particular, the "Rushdie affair" of 1989.[24] As far as religious education in the United Kingdom is concerned, it takes place both in private and public institutions. In public schools, children are exposed to different confessions existing in the world. Thus, the nature of religious education is nondenominational. This shows that children gain Islamic education from a general and "external" standpoint rather than from a particular denominational "insider position." In the United Kingdom, religious education has been included in nationwide curriculum in primary schools; however, at the high school level, it is only a voluntary module.[25] Apart from the general form of public religious education, there are six types of institutions offering confessional Islamic religious education to students:[26]

- Madrassas,
- Homeschooling,
- Religious education offered at mosques and other Islamic institutions in the evenings or during the weekends,
- Private Muslim schools,
- State-sponsored Muslim schools, and
- Institutions of higher education.

The method of teaching Islam is a religiously specific "insider perspective" in the aforementioned institutions. It is possible that the content of teaching varies, but all teachers are Muslims. Some adopt traditional methods of teaching, and some may use modern learning approaches.

In the United Kingdom, madrassas still play an important role in imparting religious education because these are the oldest forms of education.[27] A madrassa can be defined as an all-day school that has a somewhat "exclusive character." It is worth mentioning that it is usually attended by Muslims of Indian origin and generally classical Islamic themes are taught.

In the last few years, madrassas have taken a few reform steps. For instance, courses such as Math or English have been added to the curriculum. This development raises a few questions. One question is: What is the level of compliance of the education offered at madrassas with the national educational standards? However, some experts argue that the comparison of public schools with madrassas is not possible because madrassas put strong emphasis on metaphysical aspects.

In the United Kingdom, homeschooling similar to madrassas forms an alternative to public education. This is usually located in private homes or mosques and is generally operated by parents or community leaders. Moreover, it has so far not been linked to or affiliated with the public educational system, like the Department of Education and Skills. Teaching at these homeschools is to be considered of an "exclusive nature," similar to the madrassa. This could have consequences for proper integration of children with a migrant background into British society. Apart from this, there are several other issues, including the standard of teaching, qualification of teachers, and the material they teach to the students.[28]

Additive teaching is another form of sectarian religious education, which is normally given in mosques and Islamic centers during the weekends or in the evenings. This kind of education is of a traditional nature and is particularly used to complement a student's regular classes at public schools. The purpose of such teaching is to provide religious education about Islam, as in private schools such content is not covered.[29]

Other kinds of schools are the publicly sponsored and private Muslim schools in the United Kingdom. The objective of Muslim community schools is to provide a holistic Islamic education that is based on Islamic principles.[30] Moreover, such schools also try to accommodate the education of Muslim students to the higher standards of public schools. The number of Muslim schools has risen to more than one hundred since the 1980s, but only eleven of them are publicly funded.[31]

It is worth mentioning that publicly funded Muslim schools such as the one run by Yusuf Islam in London fall under the administrative jurisdiction of the school authority. Moreover, like public schools, publicly funded schools also come under the supervision of municipalities and local authorities. In such schools, there is a greater emphasis on the teaching of Islamic content and their curriculum matches the general state or pubic curriculum in the United Kingdom. These schools exclusively hire Muslim teachers who have obtained qualified training. The privately funded schools sole financing source is the support and donations from respective communities, unlike publicly sponsored Muslim schools. Privately funded schools have developed their own curriculum, which does not differ entirely from public schools. However, these schools do not fall under the administrative jurisdiction of school authorities, thus they can exercise a greater degree of freedom and independence. The Association of Muslim Schools, commonly known as AMS, is generally responsible for protecting the interests of such schools and managing coordination activities.[32]

The academic standard and qualification of teachers plays the most important role irrespective of the type and nature of the aforementioned institutions. In 1991 the University of Birmingham became the first university in the United Kingdom to establish a bachelor degree program offering special courses for Muslim students. This four-year program was aimed to equip students to teach Islamic studies at primary schools. Moreover, their education is complemented by courses on Christian studies. Chris Hewer stated that other than the Bachelor's program, a College of Higher Education and the AMS jointly developed a program especially for trained teachers of Islam who are looking to enhance their qualifications.[33]

There are several other organizations that offer higher learning opportunities, including the Muslim College, the Markfield Institute of Higher Education, and the HawzahIlmiya. The Islamic studies education provided by the British universities cannot be compared with the Islamic theology taught by the German universities. However, universities of both countries still bear resemblance in areas such as "Islamic sciences" (Islamwissenschaften) or "Oriental Studies" (Orientalistik). In the United Kingdom, the content of Islamic studies has been taught from an "external" or "outsider perspective." There are some other examples where Islamic studies have been taught "from within" or an "insider perspective," for example, the Muslim College that was established by Dr. Zawi Badawi. This teaching approach is contrary to that of British universities. The curriculum of the college is based on classical Islamic content; however, critical thinking, the study of different world religions, and also Western philosophy are an integral part of the curriculum. Successful students receive Master's degrees in Islamic studies.[34] Contrary to the Muslim College, the Markfield Institute of Higher Education also offers a number of modules that are not directly related to classical Islamic tenets including "Islam and Pluralism," "Islam in Europe," and "Islam, Women and Feminism."[35] HawzahIlmiya, which is a traditional learning institution, mainly provides education to Shia students and its curriculum offers courses of a secular nature, such as human psychology or sociology. The students have two choices to obtain in-depth knowledge and complete their studies in Oom (Iran) and Damascus (Syria).[36]

TEACHING ISLAM IN FRANCE

Muslims in France are about 6–8.5 percent of the overall population and the majority of them are descendants of Muslims who migrated from former French colonies during the nineteenth century.[37] France is a secular country, which makes the relationship between school and religion a highly sensitive topic. In 1882 compulsory education was established in France, and in 1886 separation of religion from education was made through legislation mandating secular staff in schools. These developments paved the way for the law passed in 1905 regarding the separation of church and state. Since then, religious education has been primarily the responsibility of families and religious institutions. Moreover, parents are provided with an opportunity to organize a once a week course on religion outside of school.[38]

Public schools in France do not provide teaching on Islamic religious content. However, the parents may send their children to mosques or other private Islamic organizations for such kinds of learning in the afternoon or during the weekends.

In France, religious education does not constitute an independently taught subject; however, since 2001, different religious topics have been combined within the teaching of subjects such as history, history of art, or philosophy. These reforms were the result of recommendations furnished in a report on the status of religion for the French Ministry of Education by the philosopher Régis Debray. Jenny Berglund states that in French schools emphasis is currently placed on the different historical influences of religion, for example, the linking of the religion of Islam with the development of areas such as agriculture, art, medicine, geography, and algebra.[39]

The teachers have been facing a lack of adequate qualifications to impart knowledge about Islam, especially teachers of history.[40] Generally, teachers feel reluctant to teach about Islam mainly for two reasons: (1) religion is not normally discussed in ordinary life, and (2) French society has negative perception of Islam-related matters.

A number of schools coexist in France such as Catholic, private, and public schools. Some schools have been established for Muslims and a few private schools receive financial support from the state to meet their costs like payment of salaries to teaching staff. These schools (such as Averroes High School based in Lille, which is considered one of the high-ranking schools) also implement the national curriculum.

In short, Berglund describes how there has been a change in the perception and public discourse in France that shows the significance and indispensability of religious education at schools, as highlighted in the above-mentioned Debray report.[41] There has been a shortage of well-qualified teachers; however, the establishment of the European Institute of Religious Sciences (IESR) and the École Pratique des Hautes Études in Paris/Sorbonne in 2006 are expected to make valuable contributions in this context in future.

CONCLUSION

The purpose of this essay was to study the Islamic religious education at a school level in a comparative manner in four different secular European countries—namely Germany, Austria, Great Britain, and France. These countries share one common characteristic: they have a Muslim-minority population. These countries have varying history and political practices, and all have developed different approaches in an attempt to offer Islamic education to Muslim children. The differences among these countries are based on factors such as the state's neutrality and the relationship between the state and religion. Germany and Austria are two countries where there is close cooperation between public and religious institutions. However, in the United Kingdom, contrary to Austria and Germany, an influential "state church" prevails and public schools only offer nondenominational teaching on various important religions. It is important to mention that due to strict division between church and state, France prohibits any religious education at public schools.

Immigration and integration are also two important aspects that should be thoroughly studied when comparing the four aforementioned countries. The civil social unrest that took place in the 1990s played an important role in the society's "social cohesion," drawing attention toward the integration of Muslims. Islamophobia, fundamentalism, and radicalization have been the main topics of discussion. Many scholars see religious education as a litmus test to the social cohesion of Western European societies with Muslim minorities. Meanwhile one of the most important challenges for the Muslim minority is the preservation of Muslim identity while at the same time becoming active members of European societies and playing an important role in democratic states.

NOTES

1. Harry H. Behr, *Curriculum Islamunterricht: Analyse von Lehrplanentwürfen für islamischen Religionsunterricht in der Grundschule. Ein Beitrag zur Lehrplantheorie des Islamunterrichts im Kontext der praxeologischen Dimension islamisch-theologischen Denkens* (Bayreuth: Universität Bayreuth Kulturwissenschaftliche Fakultät, 2005), 403–404.

2. The projects of reform and rehabilitation are countless in the Muslim world, dating back to the nineteenth century. Nevertheless, the majority of them are considered to be misleading.

3. Behr, *Curriculum Islamunterricht*, 395–397.

4. Mouez Khalfaoui, "Medrese: Religiöse Wissensvermittlung in der islamisch geprägten Welt und darüber hinaus," *Schweizerische Zeitschrift für Religions- und Kulturgeschichte* 108 (2014): 449–440.

5. The alleged issues of Muslim minorities in Western societies are failure of integration and political participation, difficulties in matters of education, the increasing role of political Islam, and Islamic radicalism. Besides these negative aspects there exist several positive ones, but they are less relevant for mass media and political discourse.

6. Roxanne Euben, "Premodern, Antimodern or Postmodern?: Islamic and Western Critiques of Modernity: Islamic and Western Critiques of Modernity," *Review of Politics* 59, no. 3 (1997): 430–432.

7. For a discussion of these two contrasting tendencies, see Hartmut Kaelble, *Sozialgeschichte Europas: 1945 bis zur Gegenwart* (Munich: C. H. Beck, 2007), 14–16.

8. Jenny Berglund, *Teaching Islam: Islamic Religious Education in Sweden* (Münster: Waxmann, 2010), 19–20.

9. The book edited by Wolfgang Bock gives an overview of the different experiences of Islamic education in Germany in the last decade, see Wolfgang Bock, ed., *Islamischer Religionsunterricht?: Rechtsfragen, Länderberichte, Hintergründe* (Tübingen: Mohr Siebeck, 2006).

10. Bock, *Islamischer Religionsunterricht?*, 151–153.

11. Irka-Christin Mohr, *Islamischer Religionsunterricht in Europa: Lehrtexte als Instrumente muslimischer Selbstverortung im Vergleich* (Bielefeld: Transcript, 2006), 68.

12. Mohr, *Islamischer Religionsunterricht in Europa*, 68–70.

13. This textbook has several volumes dedicated to classes going from fifth to tenth grade of the German school system. See Rabeya Müller, Lamya Kaddor, and Harry H. Behr, eds., *Saphir 5/6: Religionsbuch für junge Musliminnen und Muslime* (Munich: Kösel, 2008).

14. Mouez Khalfaoui, "Islamunterricht im europäischen Kontext: Gibt es einen 'Euro-Islam' in der Schule?," in *Kindheit und Jugend in muslimischen Lebenswelten: Aufwachen und Bildung in deutscher und internationaler Perspektive*, ed. Sabine Andresen and Christine Hunner-Kreisel (Wiesbaden: SV Verlag, 2010), 237.

15. This approach concentrates on understanding all aspects of a phenomenon without taking any position pro or con.

16. For a deep view of the modern turn of Islamic pedagogy, see Wilna A. J. Meijer, *Tradition and Future of Islamic Education* (Münster: Waxmann, 2009), 63–65.

17. Michael Kiefer and Irka-Christin Mohr, eds., *Islamunterricht, Islamischer Religionsunterricht, Islamkunde: Viele Titel—Ein Fach?* (Bielefeld: Transcript, 2009), 37–54.

18. Kiefer and Mohr, *Islamunterricht, Islamischer Religionsunterricht, Islamkunde,* 28.

19. Ednan Aslan, ed., *Islamische Erziehung in Europa* (Vienna: Böhlau, 2009), 326.

20. Bülent Ucar, "Der Islamische Religionsunterricht in Deutschland: Aktuelle Debatten, Projekte und Reaktionen," in Aslan, *Islamische Erziehung in Europa,* 88.

21. Mouhanad Khorchide, "Der islamische Religionsunterricht in Österreich," in *Österreichischer Integrationsfond* 5 (2009).

22. Brian Gates and Robert Jackson, "Religion and Education in England," in *Religious Education at Schools in Europe, Part 2: Western Europe,* ed. Robert Jackson, Martin Jäggle, and Martin Rothgangel (Göttingen: V&R Unipress, 2014), 72–74.

23. Tariq Modood, Anna Triandafyllidou, and Barrero Zapata, *Multiculturalism, Muslims and Citizenship: A European Approach* (London: Routledge, 2006), 166.

24. Berglund, *Teaching Islam,* 19–20.

25. Marie Parker-Jenkins, *Children of Islam: A Teacher's Guide to Meeting the Needs of Muslim Pupils* (London: Trentham Books, 1995), 46.

26. Maszlee Malik, "Islamische Bildung in Großbritannien: Ein Überblick," in *Religionen in der Schule und die Bedeutung des islamischen Religionsunterrichts,* ed. Ucar Bülent, Martina Blasberg-Kuhnke, and Arnulf Scheliha (Osnabrück: Universitätsverlag Osnabrück, 2010), 295.

27. Malik, "Islamische Bildung in Großbritannien: Ein Überblick," 296.

28. Malik, "Islamische Bildung in Großbritannien: Ein Überblick," 292.

29. Malik, "Islamische Bildung in Großbritannien: Ein Überblick," 299.

30. Chris Hewer, "Schools for Muslims," *Oxford Review of Education* 27, no. 4 (2001): 519.

31. Berglund, *Teaching Islam,* 19–20.

32. Hewer, "Schools for Muslims," 519.

33. Hewer, "Schools for Muslims," 517.

34. Hewer, "Schools for Muslims," 524.

35. Hewer, "Schools for Muslims," 524.

36. Hewer, "Schools for Muslims," 523.

37. Berglund, *Teaching Islam,* 19–20.

38. Jean Paul Willaime, "Religious Education at Schools in Europe," in Jackson, Jäggle, and Rothgangel, *Religious Education at Schools in Europe,* 104.

39. Berglund, *Teaching Islam,* 19–20.

40. Berglund, *Teaching Islam,* 19–20.

41. Berglund, *Teaching Islam,* 19–20.

MOUEZ KHALFAOUI is Professor of Islamic Jurisprudence at the University of Tübingen.

chapter five

STUDYING ISLAM AND THE AMBIVALENCE OF THE CONCEPT "RELIGION"

Alfons H. Teipen

THE DENIGRATION OF MUSLIMS AND mischaracterizations of Islam have been a part of Western and American discursive practice for a long time.[1] Yet, such "othering" of Islam has become particularly pronounced in the aftermath of 9/11 and has intensified even more in recent years with the rise of ISIS and the 2016 US presidential election, in which then-candidate Donald Trump called for a "ban" on Muslims. The intensity with which Muslims are vilified by some segments[2] of the evangelical Christian Right is at points reminiscent of anti-Semitism. Eerily similar to anti-Semitic accusations against "untrustworthy Jews," based on a misrepresentation of the *kol nidrei* prayer of the traditional Jewish Yom Kippur service,[3] evangelical Christians have accused Muslims of untrustworthiness based on a misrepresentation of the Shi'a doctrine of *taqiyya*.[4] Prejudice against Islam among many evangelical Christians has produced a sizeable Islamophobia industry[5] that peddles its wares in "Christian Family" bookstores. Insinuations that President Barack Obama is a crypto-Muslim are only part of a much larger complex that portrays Islam not only as essentialized but also racializes and demonizes it in colors reminiscent of the *Protocols of the Elders of Zion*. Some Evangelicals have rehashed medieval polemic accusations, rendering Islam as the barbarous, uncivilized "wholly other," most famously in the assertion of Southern Baptist preacher Jerry Vines that Muhammad "is a demon-possessed pedophile," and Rev. Franklin Graham, son of famous Christian preacher Billy Graham, who claimed that Islam is a religion of war and an "evil and wicked" religion.[6]

Just as in medieval polemics, many of these portrayals of the other take on gendered and sexualized tones: evangelical Christians routinely depict Muslim males as shameless and Muslim females as helpless victims of male sexual aggression. Harem imaginations and rescue fantasies of Orientalist art[7] that were built on colonialist-racist theories of the nineteenth century[8] find their modern counterpart in the topos of the oppressed veiled woman[9] and post-9/11 American calls for "a rescue from the veil."[10] American evangelical discourses after 9/11 have utilized such rescue fantasies in their portrayal of missionary successes, where conversion of Muslim women is depicted as a rescue from the veil.

At the same time, conservative political post-9/11 American discourse has raised concerns about a supposed "shari'a creep" in the United States, arguing that the US legal system is under threat from shari'a law.[11] In these shari'a debates, accusations of Muslim women's "plight" again play a dominant role.

Yet, while Islamophobic voices appear to be dominating in theological discourses, one also occasionally encounters Islamophile moments not only of mutual respect but sometimes outright admiration from evangelical Christians toward Muslims and vice versa. Instead of "othering," such moments suggest that conservative and "fundamentalist" adherents of both religions can appreciate the religious other. Two anecdotes may illustrate this point.

In the years since 9/11, many of us "Islam specialists" in the United States have been invited to civic groups, synagogues, and churches to talk about Islam. I distinctly remember one experience in a conservative Protestant church in my hometown, Greenville, SC—which sometimes is referred to as the "buckle of the Bible Belt." A woman in her midfifties came up to me before my first of three sessions for her congregation and asked me point-blank whether I had been "saved by Jesus Christ, our Lord and Savior." My somewhat timid response that I had grown up Catholic was probably not quite what she had hoped for. The same woman came back to talk to me after finishing the last session in the congregation. As I had done in many other cases, I had suggested to the pastor of the church that two Muslim pupils of mine, a male and female college student from my institution, could be part of the last session, so that congregants could also gain a little access to the "insider's perspective," rather than just learning about the religion from an outsider like myself. After the last session, the woman in question told me that she wished her own kids had grown up Muslim. When I inquired why, she told me that both her by now adult children had struggled with alcohol and drugs, and had engaged in premarital sex leading to pregnancy in one case. She was impressed by these two young Muslims she had just met, who apparently struggled neither with alcohol, nor drugs, nor with premarital sex, and were very devoted to their religion. While I briefly contemplated correcting this woman's misperceptions and pointing out that many Muslim teens struggle with similar issues, I chose to move on to answer other questions.

Another memorable moment involves a very religious Muslim taxi driver from Greenville, who shared with me his admiration for a female student from the formerly self-described "fundamentalist" Bob Jones University.[12] As a leading member of the Greenville mosque that had been set on fire in 1995, this Muslim was highly critical of extremist ideologies. Surprisingly, however, he was particularly warmhearted toward one Bob Jones University woman student, who worked at a local supermarket: often, when the taxi driver was in the vicinity of that supermarket during prayer time, he would stop there, as this fundamentalist Christian woman, dressed in conservative clothing, would offer him a quiet corner in the supermarket where he could pray without interruption. Being a deeply religious woman herself, she—more so than any of her nonreligious colleagues—understood how important religious practice can be for a fellow human being.

In an antagonistic environment, where one would not expect evangelical Christians to show admiration for Muslims or conservative Muslims to show admiration for fundamentalist Christians, these two anecdotes seem to suggest otherwise. Traditional characterizations and perceptions of the "other" that focus on apparently incompatible belief systems are encountered quite frequently in the Deep South, yet these two anecdotes appear not just to contradict such binary thinking, but suggest the opposite— namely, that adherents of seemingly incommensurable traditions can appreciate each other.

Our ordinary taxonomy that divides humans into adherents of different religious traditions is not always very helpful for viewing significant similarities between adherents of different traditions.

How do we, who are teaching courses on Islam in the so-called Bible Belt, talk about Islam in such a fashion that we neither repeat traditional stereotypes in a discourse of alterity nor pretend that there are no significant differences between Islam and Christianity? How does one responsibly raise the level of discourse about Islam in the world of ISIS and Trump neither oversimplifying along the lines of President George W. Bush that "Islam is a religion of peace" (or Rev. Franklin Graham's counteraccusation that Islam is a religion of war) nor suggesting that 9/11, ISIS, and other Islamist phenomena have nothing to do with religion at all?

Teaching religion at an institution in a very conservative, Protestant southern part of the United States involves challenges of a particular sort: students will need to appreciate that Islam and Christianity are not polar opposites, that "religion" is not limited to faith and doctrine, Martin Luther's *sola fide* notwithstanding, and that "religion" is not standing in opposition to "the secular," but both are mutually interdependent and constructed through each other.

I am arguing that discussion about Islam in this environment suffers from a triple misunderstanding: First, with roots in medieval discourses of alterity, students often perceive Islam to be a polar opposite to Christianity. Second, definitions of religion based on Protestant Christonormativity suggest that religions must be centered and focused on faith (what I call the *sola fide* fallacy) and thus lead to major misunderstandings of the complexity of religious phenomena. Third, the presumption that religion can be understood independent of the secular, based on a mistaken understanding of the separation of church and state, fails to recognize the interconnectedness of the religious and the secular.

As correctives to these misunderstandings, I use Ninian Smart's dimensions of religion (discussed below) to redress mischaracterizations of alterity and Islamophobic accusations against Islam, to overcome the *sola fide* fallacy, and to demonstrate the permeability between the "secular" and "religious" (and ultimately the logical inconsistency of the "secular/religious" dichotomy). Due to time limitations, I do this without burdening undergraduate students with lengthy readings in postcolonial theory and theoretical reflections on the construction of religion as a category, but by focusing on practical examples through which students can reflect on their own embeddedness in knowledge regimes. In the process, students will achieve not only a more differentiated understanding of the "religious other" but will also see their own lives, enmeshed as they are in religious-ideological structures of the Deep South, in a more self-reflective fashion.

Brannon Wheeler's 2003 edited volume *Teaching Islam* has laid much of the groundwork at the beginning of the twenty-first century for thinking about the teaching of Islam as a religion in American institutions of higher education. While not explicitly referencing Smart, Wheeler's introductory essay is addressing some of his dimensions of religion.[13] Yet, the intensity of negative sentiments toward Islam has increased since the early 2000s, and theoretical reflections about the subject matter of "religion" have undergone significant development, particularly in the work of Gil Anidjar and John Thatamanil. Whereas the essays in Wheeler's volume are referencing some "negative stereotypes" about Islam, such stereotypes are now recognized as symptoms of a deeper seated Islamophobia; and whereas essays in the 2003 volume were using the term "religion" largely uncritically, in recent years postcolonial thinkers have helped us scrutinize the shortcomings of the term "religion."

NINIAN SMART'S DIMENSIONS OF RELIGION

Ninian Smart's dimensions of religion are a particularly useful way to address many students' misperceptions about religion in general and Islam in particular. Smart's work on the dimensions spans several decades but is most clearly and accessibly articulated in the introduction to his 1996 book *Dimensions of the Sacred: An Anatomy of the World's Beliefs.*[14]

Smart suggests that many Western approaches to the comparative study of religion have been guided by the tacit assumption that Christianity is the norm(ative) religion against which others were to be compared. Such "comparison" often takes Christian church histories, with their emphasis on development of doctrine and church organizations, as the blueprint to understand other religions. Smart instead has proposed that "religions and comparable worldviews should be studied at least as much through their practices as through their beliefs," since they are "incarnate worldview(s), where the values and beliefs are embedded in practice. That is, they are expressed in action, laws, symbols, organizations."[15] Smart's dimensions of religion thus are tools through which these actions, symbols, organizations, as well as other aspects expressing religion can be better brought into view.

Such "worldview analysis" is particularly helpful for a mainly Protestant student body that is understanding "religion" primarily as a matter of faith, to demonstrate how "religion" is a multidimensional reality that suffuses various aspects of an adherent's life. Smart's later observation "that there are sufficient affinities between religious and secular worldviews (such as applied Marxism and nationalisms)" allows me to draw on the students' own experiences so as to bring into view not just the broad spectrum within which religion works but also the expression of equivalent phenomena in everyday life, thus being able to interrogate the dichotomy between "religion" and "the secular."[16] In my introductory class, I illustrate both the complexity and ordinary everydayness of "religion" by using Smart's dimensions of religion to critically reflect on how the "data" of religion compares and contrasts with "data" of a person's everyday experiences, thus problematizing both simplistic and unidimensional understandings of religion, as well as stark differentiations between religious and secular phenomena.

Smart suggests a list of seven dimensions, the names of which are mostly self-explanatory (ritual/practical, doctrinal/philosophical, mythic/narrative, experiential/emotional, ethical/legal, organizational/social, and material/artistic), that point to different ways in which religion finds its expression in various aspects of an adherent's life.

The following examples are intended to illustrate how I use some of these dimensions to interrogate perceptions of alterity, elucidate the complexity of Islam, and question the dichotomous differentiation between the secular and religion.

Doctrinal/Philosophical

Many students in the American South tend to be from conservative evangelical Christian backgrounds, surrounded by, and often immersed in an oversimplified discourse about Islam. Perusing the "Islam section" of a "Christian Family" bookstore one finds a smorgasbord of literatures decrying the evils of Islam, and many of my students have grown up with parents, relatives, or neighbors from "fundamentalist" (or "preservationist"[17]) institutions like Bob Jones University, that regard Islam as a threat to civilization.

At the beginning of a class, students appear most comfortable with looking at religion through what Smart calls "the philosophical-doctrinal dimension." When asked how they themselves would define religion, most students raised in the Protestant Christian environs of the Deep South immediately reference faith (in one God) as the unquestionable pinnacle of religion, what I would call the *sola fide* fallacy, without which religion would not be religion. In a southern Christonormative context, where it is assumed that everyone goes to church, and where the question of salvation hangs thick in the air, such a reference is understandable. Not only is faith central in many students' minds, but faith for many appears to be the only criterion: "Have you accepted Jesus as your Lord and Savior" (as the earlier anecdote indicates) is not merely a polite exchange of ideas, but for many conservative evangelical Christians it is the one question that determines your fate in the afterlife—it is a life-and-death question.

Many of my students understand the God of Islam to be radically different from the God of Christianity. Following Rev. Franklin Graham, they often agree that "(t)he God of Islam is not the same God of the Christian or Judeo-Christian faith. It is a different God, and I believe [Islam is] a very evil and very wicked religion."[18] Using anti-Muslim rhetoric that characterizes Islam as belief in a very different God can serve as a starting point to discuss Qur'anic theology. After reading excerpts from the Qur'an, students quickly realize that Allah is not portrayed as an indigenous Arabian deity, but rather is described as the God of Abraham, Ishmael, and other prophets familiar from biblical Scriptures and claimed to be the same God as the one worshipped by Jews and Christians.

When invited to think about whether Christians and Jews could agree with that claim, students quickly become aware of the intricacy of the question. To complicate the question, I invite students to look at the suggestion of the Dutch Roman-Catholic bishop Tiny Muskens, who suggested that Western Christians should use the word Allah to indicate that they are worshipping the same God as Muslims.[19] To further discussion even more, I introduce Walter Cronkite's comments on Rev. Jerry Falwell's reactions to 9/11: Falwell had blamed the attacks of 9/11 on "the ACLU . . . , the Pagans, and the abortionists, and the feminists, and the gays and the lesbians,"[20] which prompted Cronkite to suggest that Falwell could be "worshipping the same God as the people who bombed the Trade Center and the Pentagon."[21] The question whether Jews, Christians, and Muslims do indeed worship the same God finds different answers with students, yet, when adding the question as to whether the God in question may be a God worth dying or killing for, discussions can become even more interesting.

Going a step further, in class we begin discussing other strongly held faiths and beliefs to problematize our understanding of "religion." In what ways are other teleological expectations (in market forces, in scientific progress, in the goodness of humankind, etc.) religious in nature? Are there "secular" beliefs that can be also regarded as "religious"? Are American patriotic "messianic" or "eschatological" beliefs (in "Manifest Destiny," the "American Dream," or Dr. Martin Luther King Jr.'s "Dream") religious or secular in nature? Lastly, just as "life-and-death questions" of Christian faith and the question of martyrdom, or dying for a God is deeply religious in nature, the question of dying, or "sacrificing oneself" for a concept or an ideology (such as "the nation" or patriotism) helps to problematize simplistic differentiations between the religious and the secular: are (US) soldiers dying on a battlefield "martyrs"? How do they differ from Muslim "martyrs" dying in "jihad"?

While these discussions help students realize the problematic nature of simplistic understandings of Islam, as well as simplistic definitions of religion, they also help to make meaningful Smart's other dimensions of "religion."

Practical/Ritual (and Emotional/Experiential) Dimension

Many of our students are deeply affected by news coverage of anti-Western sentiments in Muslim majority countries. For example, when discussing media portrayals of Muslim reactions to the threatened or actual desecration of copies of the Qur'an, such as the threat of Florida Pastor Terry Jones to publicly burn a copy of the Qur'an in 2010 or accusations that US troops had desecrated the Qur'an, students often are bewildered about these perceived "extremely emotional" reactions of Muslims. Students do not understand the high regard that some Muslims have toward the physical artifact—the typical reaction, when discussing such incidents is a student observing: "It's just a book." Media coverage of Muslim reactions to such incidents often reinforces the stereotype that Muslims react "irrationally" to such perceived, threatened, or actual desecrations. Such stereotypes are an extension of Orientalist accusations that Muslims are often "irrational and childlike" as opposed to "the European (who) is rational, ... mature."[22]

Yet, the desecration of objects is not limited to "religious" contexts. One brief exercise that helps students obtain a better appreciation of notions of desecration and proper and improper use of "sacred" objects is to explore American attitudes toward the national flag. In an experiment, the basic outline of which I borrowed from a former colleague of mine, I bring two large envelopes to class: one contains a basic cloth handkerchief or bandanna with red, white and blue as the basic colors, while the second one contains the American flag. I ask for student volunteers (and try to ascertain that the volunteer for the second envelope is an ROTC student or a student with military family background). I ask the first student to open the envelope, unfold the cloth, put it on the ground, and then jump on it a few times. When I ask the second student to do the same, he or she will hesitate, and (particularly if the student is member of ROTC) I can try to "bribe" that student with a good grade for the class, without danger that the student actually will "harm" the flag. Discussions about the proper use of a flag, including how to fold it, and how to dispose of it should it become desecrated, help students realize that rituals surrounding the American flag are taken very seriously by many, and feelings can run high when the flag itself gets "threatened" or "abused." The exercise is an easy entry point into a discussion about sacred artifacts, ritually proper actions, as well as the emotional/experiential dimension of religion. Discussions about more recent experiences with American traditions around the national anthem, such as recent kneeling protests during the singing of the anthem at NFL games help students perceive the sacrality of such symbols, the emotional/experiential dimension (or how upset adherents can become when ritual prescriptions are "violated") and students become more aware of their own embeddedness in ritual and sacrality.

Ethical/Legal Dimension: Shari'a and Anti-Shari'a Legislation

Conservative American media over the past few years have reported extensively on a perceived "shari'a creep," accusing various Muslim individuals or groups of wanting to introduce shari'a law in the United States, in violation of secular law and the US constitutional order.[23] Such "shari'a creep" accusations build on Orientalist accusations against non-Christian religions in general, and Judaism[24] in particular, as being "religions of the law" rather than the "spirit."[25]

Yet, while most Protestant theological voices emphasize a separation between church and state, leaving legislation to state authorities, public discourse among evangelical Christians in the United States suggests that proper legislation is central to the success of the community. Evangelical Christian voices on questions of abortion and LGBTQI issues suggest that evangelical Christianity is not as antinomian in practice as it purports to be in theory. Conservative Christian voices that raise concerns about reproductive rights, regulation of sexuality and marriage, and most recently rules about gender and restrictions on bathroom usage demonstrate this.

John Esposito and Dalia Mogahed's book, *Who Speaks for Islam*, provides a good entry point for students to think about similarities between majority Muslim countries and the United States in terms of the intersection between religious guidelines and law. Based upon data from Gallup's World Poll, the authors argue that traditional Muslim attitudes toward shari'a are comparable to American attitudes toward the Bible and legislation: similar to many Muslim majority countries, where a majority of the population would like to see shari'a as a source of legislation, according to a 2006 Gallup poll, "Forty-six percent of Americans say that the Bible should be 'a' source for legislation."[26]

Social/Institutional Dimension and Gender

Gender relations, the "role of women in Islam," and Orientalist characterizations of Islam as a particularly misogynist religion provide the background against which the course approaches issues of gender, representation, and power. Students often perceive women's dress, hijab, chador, burqa, and niqab as expressions of oppression of women, and, in line with Orientalist "rescue fantasies,"[27] want to liberate Muslim women from such oppression.

Before introducing students to the vast variety of different attitudes toward and expressions of hijab and "women's dress" and discussing Islamic fashion, the burqini, and various attempts at banning the veil in Muslim majority countries as well as "the West," I explore my students' own experiences with "dress codes."

When asked how many students in class have lived under some type of sartorial restriction in the past themselves, I occasionally have a student or two who went to private (often religious) schools with a specific dress code. I sometimes share excerpts from the student handbook of neighboring Bob Jones University, as it contains not only an elaborate, very conservative dress code but also has an explicit statement on sexual immorality that condemns "adultery, fornication, homosexuality, bisexual conduct, bestiality, incest, pornography, or any attempt to change one's biological sex," set limits on dating, and does not permit mixed (gender) swimming.[28]

Yet, probing further in discussions about appropriate dress, I inquire about dress codes that students may have experienced in middle school or high school. It is often only at this point that students remember that they also have been affected by sartorial regimes. Bringing these experiences into discussions about "Islamic dress" assists students to understand the complexity of the question and helps them to think more critically not only about religiously inspired sartorial regimes of power but also "secular" and everyday experiences with sartorial regimes, sexed bodies, including "peer-pressures," power, and "subjectification." Such discussions allow us to get into view different institutional regimes of control and think more broadly about the social/institutional dimension of religion.

Other Dimensions: Material/Artistic and Narrative/Mythical

The remaining dimensions of Smart's taxonomy can be used in a similar fashion. Using the "material dimension" students can compare the ideology of space of national monuments (e.g., the White House, the US Capitol Building, and the Liberty Bell in Philadelphia) with religious architecture to observe how architecture "works" to evoke a shared narrative or how it impacts its viewer. Likewise, in the narrative/mythic dimension, comparing and contrasting the intertextuality of religious /ideological narratives helps students to think about the complex relationship of texts and narratives: How does the Qur'an's supposed "indebtedness" or "dependence" on prior Scripture relate to the New Testament's "dependence" on the "Old Testament," or how does the Qur'an's insistence that Jesus prophesied the coming of Muhammad relate to the New Testament's insistence that Jesus' coming was predicted in Hebrew Scripture?

CONCLUSION

The above examples demonstrate that discourses of alterity, be it the presumed otherness of Islam vis-à-vis Christianity or the otherness of the religious from the secular, are often overdrawn. Claims of utter alterity often function to help construct an identity against "the other." As Roger Ballard has shown, Islam (and Judaism) served as "wholly alien" to a Christian Europe, which was constructed upon that alterity.[29] While most popular discourse of the late twentieth century has abandoned claims of an utter alterity of Judaism, Islam is often still portrayed in terms diametrically opposed to "Judeo-Christian" civilization.[30] Yet, as the above examples indicate, a closer look at underlying similarities can help to problematize strongly dichotomized assertions of alterity.

José Ignacio Cabezón discusses this dialectic of self and other in the academic study of religion. For him, religious studies should be "an interminable quest to critically challenge the structures that cultures erect to separate Self and Other; an unending program to destabilize and denaturalize categories that have previously stood as obstacle to a real and substantive engagement with the Other, to 'relativize difference.'"[31]

Similarly, Thatamanil has argued that the category of religion "has a provincial origin in the West but has come to be employed universally," yet with little awareness that "from the outset . . . no tradition itself is pure, singular, homogenous."[32] While Cabezón's and Thatamanil's projects, to relativize difference and to think theologically "after religion," involve theoretical reflections that are not easily accomplished in an introductory course on Islam that is already heavily overburdened with a large quantity of highly unfamiliar materials, some of the practical correlates of their observations can be made fruitful in such course: they can guide the way in which even a basic introductory class can scrutinize rhetorical constructions of the "religious other." As we have seen in the examples above, students will be able to perceive the multiple overlaps and similarities among religious traditions that problematize assertions of an essentialized alterity. Not only are religions often much closer in their doctrines than the discourse of alterity would suggest, but they are more than just doctrines and organizations: in their various dimensions they reveal broader similarities that exhibit a very complex picture.

Yet not only is the question of an essentialized alterity being challenged in such comparative reading, but the very question of a neat division between the religious and "the secular" is opened to scrutiny. Commonalities between the religious and "the secular" highlight the conceptual problems of the construction of religion as binary opposite to "the secular." Religion and the secular do not only mutually constitute each other, as Anidjar reminds us, but the secular itself may be no more than a child of European Enlightenment, itself nothing more than Western Christianity in disguise.

Taking as his cue Edward Said's ambivalence about the "secular," Anidjar traces the birth of "the (western) secular" to Christianity: "Christianity it is, then, that actively disenchanted its own world by dividing itself into private and public, politics and economics, indeed, religious and secular. . . . Munchhausen-like, it attempted to liberate itself, to extricate itself from its own conditions: it *judged* itself no longer Christian, no longer 'religious.' Christianity (that is, to clarify this one last time, Western Christendom) judged and named itself, reincarnated itself, as "secular.'"[33]

Anidjar's summary of the process of "Western Enlightenment" suggests that Christianity (Christendom) of medieval Europe split itself into private and public spheres, and while only the private "religious" sphere retained the name, the public/political/economic in essence remained Christian, while changing its label to "the secular." Anidjar's analysis not only suggests the dependence of the secular on the religious, but it also points to the role of rhetoric in the construction of identity and alterity: assertions of alterity and identity are not dependent on a "real" other, rather, a constructed, imagined rhetorical other does the job. While Anidjar's observations at large may not be fully appreciable by students in an undergraduate introductory class to Islam, some of the concrete examples of the intersection between the religious and the secular may help those students become more critical thinkers not just about various religions but also about simplistic dichotomies between the religious and the secular.

NOTES

1. See Norman Daniel, *Islam and the West: The Making of an Image* (1960; repr., Oxford: Oneworld Publishing, 2000). See also David L. Johnston, "American Evangelical Islamophobia: A History of Continuity with a Hope for Change," *Journal of Ecumenical Studies* 51, no. 2 (2016): 224–235.

2. According to a 2014 report by the PEW Research Center, negative attitudes toward Islam are particularly pronounced among white American evangelical Protestant Republicans ("How Americans Feel about Religious Groups," July 2014, http://www.pewforum.org/2014/07/16/how -americans-feel-about-religious-groups/). Of course, not all members of the groups described in the above share the same sentiment. The above group intersects with others, such as the Teavangelicals (see David Brody, *The Teavangelicals: The Inside Story of How the Evangelicals and the Tea Party are Taking Back America* [Grand Rapids, MI: Zondervan, 2012]) or Christian Zionists. In the following, I will use the phrase "many evangelical Protestants" and similar phrases to refer to the segment of Evangelicals who espouse more negative sentiments toward Islam and Muslims.

3. See David Charles Smith, "Protestant Anti-Judaism in the German Emancipation Era," *Jewish Social Studies* 36, no. 3-4 (1974): 203–219.

4. See Yarden Mariuma, "Taqiyya as Polemic, Law and Knowledge: Following an Islamic Legal Term through the Worlds of Islamic Scholars, Ethnographers, Polemicist and Military Men," *Muslim World* 104, no. 1-2 (2014): 89–108.

5. See Nathan Lean, *The Islamophobia Industry: How the Right Manufactures Fear of Muslims* (New York: Pluto Press, 2012).

6. Richard Cimono, "'No God in Common': American Evangelical Discourse on Islam after 9/11," *Review of Religious Research* 47, no. 2 (2005): 163.

7. See Ella Shohat, "Gender in Hollywood's Orient," *Middle East Report* 162 (1990): 40–42.

8. See Juergen Osterhammel, *Colonialism: A Theoretical Overview* (Princeton, NJ: Marcus Wiener, 1997).

9. See Leila Ahmed, *Women and Gender in Islam* (New Haven, CT: Yale University Press, 1992).

10. See Lila Abu Lughod, *Do Muslim Women Need Saving?* (Cambridge, MA: Harvard University Press, 2013); see also Kevin J. Ayotte and Mary E. Husain, "Securing Afghan Women: Neocolonialism, Epistemic Violence, and the Rhetoric of the Veil," *NWSA Journal* 17, no. 3 (2005): 112–133.

11. Cyra Akila Choudhury, "Shariah Law as National Security Threat?," *Akron Law Review* 46 (2012): 51, 61ff.

12. See David Gibson, "Bob Jones University Questions 'Fundamentalist' Label," *Huffington Post*, November 11, 2011, http://www.huffingtonpost.com/2011/11/21/bob-jones-university -fundamentalist_n_1106276.html.

13. Brannon Wheeler, ed., *Teaching Islam* (New York: Oxford University Press, 2003), 4–10.

14. Ninian Smart, *Dimensions of the Sacred: An Anatomy of the World's Beliefs* (Berkeley: University of California Press, 1996).

15. Smart, *Dimensions of the Sacred*, 2f.

16. Smart, *Dimensions of the Sacred*, 2.

17. In the aftermath of the attacks of 2001, then president of Bob Jones University suggested that the word "preservationist" may be better suited to capture the character of the university, as the word "fundamentalist" "now carries overtones of radicalism and terrorism." See "Bob Jones III Wants to Shed Fundamentalist Label," *Peninsula Clarion*, March 15, 2002.

18. Franklin Graham, Interview on *Now with Bill Moyers*, PBS, January 3, 2003.

19. "Dutch Bishop: Call God 'Allah' to Ease Relations," Europe on NBC News.com, August 15, 2017, http://www.nbcnews.com/id/20279326/#.V-_jpYgrLIU.

20. Simone Schweber, "Fundamentally 9/11: The Fashioning of Collective Memory in a Christian School," *American Journal of Education* 112, no. 3 (2006): 393.

21. Schweber, "Fundamentally 9/11," 393. Whereas Walter Cronkite's comment on the Buchanan/Robertson remarks after 9/11 had been somewhat cynical, Pat Buchanan's observations on conservative Muslim perceptions of the United States appear to be more earnest: radical Muslims hate us because "(w)e pollute their culture and countries with drugs, alcohol, abortions, blasphemous books, filthy magazines, dirty movies and hellish music that capture and corrupt their young" (quoted in Carl Horowitz, "Immigration and the Culture War," *Social Contract* 12, no. 2 [Winter 2002]: 144).

22. Edward W. Said, *Orientalism* (New York: Random House, 1979), 40; cf. Deepa Kumar, "Framing Islam: The Resurgence of Orientalism during the Bush II Era," *Journal of Communication Inquiry* 34, no. 3 (2010): 254–277.

23. See Choudhury, "Shariah Law as National Security Threat?"

24. James Pasto has pointed out that medieval anti-Judaism shares a good number of similarities with medieval "Orientalism." See "Islam's 'Strange Secret Sharer': Orientalism, Judaism, and the Jewish Question," *Comparative Studies in Society and History* 40, no. 3 (July 1998): 437–474.

25. For traditional Christian dichotomies between Judaism and Christianity such as "religion of law" vs. "religion of spirit," see Harris Franklin Rall, *The Life of Jesus* (New York: Abington Press, 1917).

26. John Esposito and Dahlia Mogahed, *Who Speaks for Islam? What a Billion Muslims Really Think* (New York: Gallup Press, 2007), 49.

27. See Shohat, "Gender in Hollywood's Orient."

28. Bob Jones University, *Student Handbook 16–17*, 2016, http://www.bju.edu/life-faith/student-handbook.pdf, 28–32, 57, 21f, 63.

29. Roger Ballard, "Islam and the Construction of Europe," in *Muslims in the Margin: Political Responses to the Presence of Islam in Western Europe*, ed. W. A. R. Shadid and P. S. van Koningsveld (Kampen: Kok Pharos, 1996), 28.

30. See Richard Bulliett, *The Case for Islamo-Christian Civilization* (New York: Columbia University Press, 2004).

31. José Ignacio Cabezón, "The Dialectic of Alterity in the Study of Religion," *JAAR* 74, no. 1 (2006): 26.

32. John Thatamanil, "Comparative Religion after 'Religion,'" in *Planetary Loves: Spivak, Postcoloniality and Theology*, ed. Stephen D. Moore and Mayra Rivera (New York: Fordham University Press, 2011), 243, 251.

33. Gil Anidjar, "Secularism," *Critical Inquiry* 33, no. 1 (Autumn 2006): 60.

ALFONS H. TEIPEN is Associate Professor of Religion at Furman University.

chapter six

PARADIGM SHIFTS FOR TRANSLATION
AND TEACHING

William Maynard Hutchins

DURING MY YEARS OF TEACHING in religion, Arabic, and history programs, I have typically assigned at least one translated work of Middle Eastern literature. I think this is an important way of humanizing the Middle East for American students, especially in the tumultuous period since 9/11. In courses, paradoxically, translated fiction provides a reality check of daily life for students awash in a popular culture of prejudice against Muslims. Contrasts between preached Islam and lived Islam can be illuminated with the judicious use of fiction and films. Women's voices are typically lost when attention is focused on the pulpit rather than on a novel.

There are distinguished Muslim and Middle Eastern authors who write in English, and their works deserve attention. For use in a course, however, I advocate the use of translated works written for a Middle Eastern audience, if only because members of a family are usually more candid when discussing family issues among themselves. Translated literature helps to ward off the "animated *National Geographic*" syndrome by adding invitations to emotional involvement. Facts and values are often intertwined, and this becomes apparent in a good translated novel. Excellent literature encourages not only suspension of disbelief but also suspension of cultural difference as well. Finally, translated literature earns a place in a course on the Middle East because religions are complicated cultural systems that incorporate storytelling and metaphors.

Pedagogical resources for incorporating translated fiction into courses include the following: *Arabic Literature for the Classroom: Teaching Methods, Theories, Themes and Texts*, edited by Mushin J. al-Musawi,[1] *Resources for Modern Arabic Literature (Middle Eastern & Islamic Studies)*, compiled by Walaa Al-Salmi,[2] *Literature in Translation: Teaching Issues and Reading Practices*, by Carol Maier and Françoise Massardier-Kenney,[3] the WWB

Campus initiative of Words Without Borders,[4] and the extensive index of contributors of *Banipal: Magazine of Modern Arabic Literature.*[5]

Paradigm Shifts for Translation

In an email dated July 20, 2015, Bilal Sayaheen announced a study of "The Reception of Arabic-Language Works Translated into English and Published in the U.S. before and after September 11." His proposal sounded eminently sensible, since 9/11 was a watershed event. My experience for the past four decades, however, has been that this event was not one of the five most significant paradigm shifts affecting me as a translator of contemporary Arabic literature.[6]

I think the first important paradigm shift was from an Orientalist to a social science or Islamic civilization approach for Arabic and Middle Eastern studies. The second was the award of the Nobel Prize for Literature to Naguib Mahfouz in 1988. The third was the development of the internet. The fourth has been the disintegration of the Middle East as we once knew it and the subsequent flight of huge numbers of people—including authors—from their homelands. The fifth is the current popularity of the "Global" novel.

The first paradigm shift, I claim, was from Orientalism to Islamic Civ. Young scholars may discuss Orientalism in the abstract, and it is a huge topic with a vast literature; I write from my personal experience. I began my career in the 1960s with an Orientalist training in the University of Chicago's Oriental Institute, which was established in 1919,[7] and regularly crossed the street to converse with other students in the lounge of the Center for Middle Eastern Studies, which was founded in 1965.[8]

This first paradigm shift was, for example, heralded by the establishment of an "Islamic Civ" course at the University of Chicago in 1956 by Marshall Hodgson,[9] the founding of Centers for Middle Eastern Studies at multiple American universities, and the offering of the NDEA Title VI critical language fellowships starting in 1958. These last two initiatives became part of the federal government's Great Society programs in 1965.

After a couple of terms that I paid for, my PhD program was funded by an NDEA Title VI fellowship for Arabic, and I could not have afforded it otherwise—even at the bargain-basement prices of the 1960s. I finished my PhD in the Oriental Institute of the University of Chicago in the Arabic and Islam section. When I was a student there, the department hired a philologist to teach Arabic and then a graduate of a "modern" linguistics program. That generational shift occurred in less than a decade. The philologist was also part of a transitional generation and introduced me to both al-Jahiz from the ninth century CE and Tawfiq al-Hakim from the twentieth. They became two of my literary heroes.[10]

The website of the Center for Middle Eastern Studies at the University of Chicago states: "The educational aims of the Center are to assist students in acquiring: (1) firm grounding in an academic discipline or a professional field; and (2) specialist knowledge of the languages and civilizations of the Middle East."[11] The first aim is clearly supportive of an Islamic Civ approach while the second harks back to Orientalism. I feel that I embodied both aims by apprenticing for a year as a postdoctoral fellow with the Islamic Civ course at the University of Chicago, after Hodgson's death, and then by teaching first-year Arabic in the Oriental Institute for another year.

One assumption of the Orientalist tradition as I experienced it was that only classics ought to be translated and then only after a Western Orientalist had produced a definitive edition. Since I wrote my dissertation on the theory of knowledge of Fakhr al-Din al-Razi, at my defense I was asked which text by him I planned to edit.

In addition to classic texts, the adventures of Europeans in the Middle East might also be worth noting. This second assumption was exemplified by an African history course I audited at the London School of Economics in 1965; it was devoted to lectures on the European penetration of Africa. Two years earlier at Yale University, though, I had taken Harry R. Rudin's African Civ course, although at the time I did not realize that this was the wave of the future or that I would teach "African Thought" at Appalachian State University.

One small but important shift away from Orientalism in my translation practice has been use of the author's own spelling of her name in English transliteration—instead of the "correct" (library catalogue/Orientalist) transliteration. At one time, library cataloguers defaced the title pages of translated Arabic novels by changing the spelling of the author's name if it did not match the "scholarly" spelling. Back then, this seemed a sufficient incentive for me (especially after several years of transliteration training) to change an author's spelling of his name. I regret doing that. Today Arab authors commonly move between various cultures and alphabets, but Tewfik El Hakim also did that, decades ago. Even today, to use www.worldcat.org, a searcher needs to type in the "correct" library spelling of an author's name. Google is more accommodating, even accepting searches in Arabic.

It is not uncommon for cross-disciplinary Islamic Civilization courses to use translations of contemporary novels or short stories. To meet this need, the Center for Middle Eastern Studies of the University of Texas at

Austin started a Modern Middle East Literatures in Translation series,[12] and Donald Herdeck launched Three Continents Press.[13] At approximately the same time, Professor M. M. Badawi began lecturing on contemporary Arabic literature in the United Kingdom[14] and Denys Johnson-Davies began publishing excellent English translations from works of contemporary Arabic literature, such as *Modern Arabic Short Stories* in 1967. In 1966, Khayats, in Beirut, published Trevor Le Gassick's translation of *Midaq Alley, Cairo* by Naguib Mahfouz.

The paradigm shift from Orientalism to Area Studies, however, did not eliminate hubris. Scholars of my generation no longer aspired to edit yet another medieval text better than an Egyptian scholar, but some still sought to write the definitive history of, say, Yemen or the definitive biography of an Arab luminary. A friend of mine in graduate school considered anyone who attempted to write Middle East history on the basis of an ability to read original texts in Arabic or Farsi to be an Orientalist; in fact, this was virtually his definition of an Orientalist. Even so, he aspired to write the definitive history of an Arab country. I propose as a Golden Rule of Cross-cultural Studies this maxim: do not conduct research overseas you would not pursue at home, and vice versa. Why study the argot of prostitutes in Sanaa, for example, if you would choose not to do a comparable study in London because "that would be too dangerous"?

My concern for heeding this maxim was a major factor in my decision to focus on the translation of Arabic literature rather than on research endeavors that placed me in competition with Arab scholars. The general rule of thumb for literary translation is that a person should translate into her mother tongue. Admittedly, to obtain a fellowship to conduct research in Egypt, after failing to obtain a fellowship for translation, I applied for and received a grant to write a biography of Tawfiq al-Hakim. That year, though, the force of circumstance proved too strong for me, and I chose and translated most of the stories for *Egyptian Tales and Short Stories of the 1970s and the 1980s*, which was published by the American University of Cairo Press in 1987. After Lynne Rienner Publishing purchased Three Continents Press, I finally wrote *Tawfiq al-Hakim: A Reader's Guide*, with considerable guidance from editors of the firm. The book contains some biographical sections but mainly consists of literary criticism together with consideration of al-Hakim's use of religious and spiritual themes. The book was published in 2003.

Oddly enough, after teaching for years in a religious studies program, I feel I have stumbled on a comparable phenomenon. Some of my colleagues assert that a religious studies department needs a sociologist of religion, an anthropologist of religion, a psychologist of religion, and so on to explain (away?) religion, which they consider to be a single—though complex—entity. These scholars with their wide assortment of specialties can all come from the same divinity school and need never have enrolled in a course in the department bearing the name of their specialization. Their students can then be sent back for advanced training at the mother (secular) divinity school to become a sociologist (etc.) of religion, without themselves ever passing through a sociology department. But, then, they "know" religion. If you substitute the word "Arabic" for "religion," you circle back to Orientalism while waving the banner of the Social Sciences.

The second paradigm shift was the announcement of Naguib Mahfouz as the Nobel Laureate for Literature in 1988. Donald Herdeck, various editors at the American University in Cairo Press, Professor Roger Allen, and others had struggled for years to interest major Western publishers in Arab authors, including Naguib Mahfouz. The award of the Nobel Prize for Literature to him and the subsequent purchase of fourteen of his titles by Jacqueline Kennedy Onassis for Doubleday were followed by a generally favorable reception for his works in English translation, notably for *The Cairo Trilogy*, which was published in individual volumes, one a year, starting with *Palace Walk* in 1990. Mrs. Onassis was at that time Doubleday's celebrity editor, handling Michael Jackson's autobiography, for example. She, however, did the line-by-line pencil editing for all the volumes of my translation of *The Cairo Trilogy* in a perceptive, polite, and professional manner.

The Nobel Prize for Mahfouz and the success of *The Cairo Trilogy* has, I claim, meant that major publishers no longer reject submissions merely on the once common excuse that a novel has been translated from Arabic. "Who would be the audience for that?" Income from the deal has also allowed the American University in Cairo Press to offer the Naguib Mahfouz Medal for Literature (since 1996) to the best untranslated Arabic-language novel of the year and to increase the quantity and quality of its publications of Arabic literature in translation. Egypt's current economy and the decline in tourism there, however, have severely impacted this press. Although my translation of the volumes of *The Cairo Trilogy* was well received, an editor of the AUC Press told me to my face back then that I would never translate Mahfouz again. I had to wait several years to find more opportunities as a translator of Arabic literature.

The third paradigm shift has been open internet access for the general public from approximately 1995. When Jacqueline Kennedy Onassis edited individual volumes of *The Cairo Trilogy*, corrected sections of the manuscript, in approximately eighty-page packets, were sent back and forth by postal service between North Carolina and New York and also to Cairo, because the American University in Cairo Press had brokered the deal.

The internet has made it possible for a translator to correspond, even several times a day with an Arab author or a publisher almost anywhere in the world, including Yemen during a nasty civil war. It has also facilitated the research necessary for translation. Think Google. Think Wikipedia. The internet has brought new publication venues too—sites like those of Words Without Borders and InTranslation of *The Brooklyn Rail*. *Banipal Magazine of Modern Arab Literature,* although a print journal, also has a major online presence and influence. Its regular publication would hardly be possible without the internet. Samuel Shimon, Margaret Obank, and their publication *Banipal* have been extremely important for me, introducing me to a stream of new Arab authors whom I have been asked to translate. All these venues have been important for me whether by publishing my translations of short stories or excerpts from novels by Arab authors and by introducing me to new authors. They are also valuable resources for instructors who wish to add translated works of Middle Eastern literature to their courses.

Before the internet widened my horizons, I confined my translation efforts to my comfort zone, which is Egypt, and even so to obtain an author's permission to translate back then I had to visit her in Cairo or send a friend or some other emissary. There is a direct correlation between access to the internet and my ability and willingness to translate non-Egyptian authors. I now also hear occasionally from Arab graduate students interested in an author I translate or in one of my translations considered as a translation. For my 2012 revision of my translation of *Return of the Spirit* by Tawfiq al-Hakim, I benefited from access to portions of the MA thesis of Amira Salah El-Deen Askar of Zagazig University in Egypt, after she contacted me online.

I keep hoping to fall in love with an internet Arabic dictionary, but perhaps my ignorance is to blame for my failure to date in this regard. I occasionally google words in Arabic if only to see what image comes up. I am tired, though, of hearing in the locker room from friends, who brag about their connoisseurship of artisanal beer, cheese, and bread, that Google will translate my texts for me. My response is: "Literary translation is by definition an artisanal craft, Guys."

The fourth paradigm shift, by my calculations, came with the series of political and military disasters during which autocratic governments in the Middle East crashed into the Arab Spring—and the subsequent dispersal of large populations including authors to all parts of the world. Clyde Edgerton, who is known to some as a "North Carolina author" and who has fittingly been recently inducted into the North Carolina Literary Hall of Fame,[15] has complained of the difficulty of making deals with New York editors, who do not know, for example, what a "doublewide" is. Many Arab authors, especially Arab women authors, have struggled for decades to find a market, especially if they do not have ready access to Cairo or Beirut or some similar publishing center and to the "right" literary elites. Now that many Arab authors are either in external or internal exile, in prison, and/or under some type of significant threat, translators bear an additional responsibility to offer them at least the flimsy lifeline represented by an English translation of their works. Mahmoud Saeed's repeated attempts to publish in Iraq, for example, led to incarcerations there, and he was subsequently asked to leave a Gulf country. At least four of the authors I have translated have been imprisoned. Sadly, some Arab authors find an Arab audience in their country of origin only after finding an audience for their works in translation. I have translated and do still translate quite a few Arab women authors, but my attempts to find publishers for their works beyond literary journals and websites has to date been in vain. My translation of Munira al-Fadhel's novella *For the Voice, For the Fragile Echo*, however, was serialized in the print edition of *The Brooklyn Rail*.

The previously liberating influence of the area-studies approach to Arabic instruction shows its limitations here, if only because a novel by an author who has lived for decades in exile in Europe may be regarded as inauthentic, especially if his novel is set in Europe or written in a European language. I was attending a conference with a distinguished Western scholar of Arabic literature when he put some books by an Arab author back on the sales table, once he realized they had been written in French, not Arabic. Should he have? Some Arab authors also mistakenly, I believe, assume that an American audience will want a novel with American themes or one dedicated to Chelsea Manning (formerly known as Bradley Manning). The process of selecting works to be translated into English remains chaotic, and there are many lapses of communication between potentially interested parties on both sides of the Arabic/English language divide and the publisher/translator chasm.

The fifth paradigm shift has been heralded by the new or renewed— think of Kahlil Gibran or Gibran Khalil Gibran, and the success of *The Prophet*, published in 1923—success of literature written in English by Middle Eastern authors. "Publication in English," including in English translation is becoming comparable to "Written in English" for some awards like the Caine Prize, the Man Booker International Prize, and the

Emerging Voices Prize. (This goes a step beyond the eligibility require-ment for the Nobel Prize for Literature that "enough" works by an author be available in some Western language or languages—either originally or by translation.) Ibrahim al-Koni was, for example, shortlisted for the Man Booker International Prize in 2015 on the basis of the English translations of some of his works.[16] English translations are being judged not merely as translations (for translation awards) but as an alternative transcription—like a glass harmonica piece transcribed for harp, at times even by their own author. The Iranian author Amir Hassan Cheheltan, for example, has written: "The new collection of stories is the first of my books to appear in Persian since 2005. In the intervening nine years, four new novels of mine have been translated and published in German, English, and Norwe-gian without first having had a chance to appear in Persian, their original language."[17]

This paradigm shift is related to the phenomenon of the "global" novel written in English, whether by an Arab author or not. The success of some Arab authors who write global novels in English, has, I feel, done little to lift the fortunes of Arab authors who write primarily in Arabic, even though some authors writing in Arabic perhaps aspire to become the Arab equivalent of Haruki Murakami and to write Arabic that will easily trans-late into *New Yorker* English.

One editorial committee for a Middle East publication series was reported to have become "more and more anxious about book sales" by 2016.[18] Fair enough, one might say, but what would be interesting is if this attitude reflected some jealousy for the success of Global novels written by Arab authors in English or French.

A perceptive and professional (third) reader for one of my translations wrote: "If there is an audience looking for 'news' from 'there,' this novel requires too much work in between the fast-moving sections.... The novel also would be a difficult teach . . . and the whole text would make a long read for students."

This reader appealed here to the Islamic Civ paradigm but then, I feel, transitioned to the Global novel perspective: "Although it creates an interesting composite portrait, and is a compelling innovation in Arabic literature, it would be difficult to open this book up to English-language audiences—not in its referents, but its form."[19]

The good news is that the American Literary Translators Association awarded their 2015 prize for English prose translation to *New Waw* by Ibra-him al-Koni, a Tuareg author who writes in Arabic. Perhaps it also became, with that award, an Arabic-language Global novel in a good way?

The first, third, and fourth paradigm shifts also affect teaching about Islam and Islamic culture. To these three categories I would add two additional, somewhat paradoxical paradigm shifts for teaching. First, the American invasions of Afghanistan and then Iraq brought to my classroom soldiers training for deployment to Iraq or Afghanistan and veterans of those wars. Their genuine interest in the subject matter—whether prompted by a desire to stay alive or by puzzlement about: "Why were/are they shooting at us?"—helped calm Islamophobia in the classroom. With them have come, even to the mountains of North Carolina, a number of Muslim students, who contribute by their very presence. Second, Wikipedia and YouTube—so the internet again—have changed the way I teach a "content" class. Instead of arriving in the classroom with a power-point or list of notes for the blackboard, I can pull up a series of Wikipedia articles on the people and topics I plan to discuss and then spice these up with music and interviews from YouTube. This approach, I hope, allows me to respond more spontaneously to my students in the classroom.

As a teacher, I am also a consumer of translated literature, using either assigned texts or works archived by language and country at www.words withoutborders.org. At the most general level, whether as a translator or a teacher, I look for works of Arabic literature I hope will engage a student emotionally rather than for works that bring "news from there." I often try to pair a novel with a feature or documentary film to heighten the emotional impact and thus balance Islamophobia's emotional appeal. Admittedly, the use of fiction as a reality check seems as paradoxical as benefiting from the presence of soldiers and veterans in the classroom to assuage free-floating prejudice against Islam. Translated literature also brings an everyday-life approach to the classroom, precisely because it tends to focus "on what is going on in ordinary people's lives rather than on abstract theories of social action."[20]

Marwa al-Sabouni in her elegant and engrossing book *The Battle for Home* writes that Western scholars who study Islamic architecture have "overlooked discussion of the *architectural experience*."[21] In the same chapter, she provides the example of a tree: "You can enhance your experience and take it to a deeper level if you wish: you can focus on its bark, on the insects that march on it.... On each level of experience there is a new world of 'design' to be discovered and enjoyed. It is exactly that effect at which the old Islamic architecture aimed."[22]

She suggests turning architectural instruction "in a new direction, so as to study the small things, the real things, the things that people relate to in their daily lives."[23]

In my quiet way, I hope my work as a translator of Arabic literature and as a teacher of Islamic culture has moved in the direction that Marwa al-Sabouni recommends in these passages. A novel or short story written for a Middle Eastern readership and translated from an Middle Eastern language into English (or French, or German, etc.) can provide readers, including students, the vicarious experience of things Middle Eastern people encounter in daily life, even if they currently live in Denmark.

For years before and after 9/11, I deplored the contrast between the frequent, front-page coverage of turmoil in the Middle East and the minimal coverage of the region on arts and lifestyle pages. A novelist from Georgia suggested astutely several years ago that if there were more coverage of the Middle East on the culture pages there might be less violence to cover on the news pages. In 2015, though, the *New York Times* did finally run a big spread in color about eating dates and another on yummy foods for Ramadan *iftars* and four months later published a signed, laudatory obituary for the courageous and distinguished Egyptian author Gamal al-Ghitani.[24]

Notes

1. Mushin J. al-Musawi, ed., *Arabic Literature for the Classroom: Teaching Methods, Theories, Themes and Texts* (New York: Routledge, 2017). Contents: Introduction: Arabic Literature for the Classroom, Part I: Theory and Method, 1. Proxidistant Reading: Toward a Critical Pedagogy of the Nahḍah in U.S. Comparative Literary Studies—Shaden M. Tageldin, 2. Teaching Arab Women's Letters—Boutheina Khaldi, 3. Arab Women Writers 1980-2010—Miriam Cooke, 4. Teaching Francophone Algerian Women's Literature in a Bilingual French-English Context: Creative Voices, Dissident Texts—Brinda Mehta, 5. Teaching Classical Arabic Literature in English Translation—Jocelyn Sharlet, 6. Classical and Post-Classical Arabic Literary Delights—Nizar Hermes, 7. Language through Literature—Taoufik Ben Amor, Part II: Theme, 8. Lessons from the Maghreb—Hoda el Shakry, 9. Teaching Humor in Arabic Literature and Film—Tarek El-Ariss, 10. The Art of Teaching Arab Traumas Triumphantly—Hanadi Al-Samman, 11. The Urban Gateway: Teaching the City in Modern Arabic Literature—Ghenwa Hayek, 12. Teaching Mahmud Darwish—Jeff Sacks, 13. Teaching the Modernist Arabic Poem in Translation—Muhsin al-Musawi, 14. Lessons from a Revolution—Nathaniel Greenberg, Part III: Text, 15. Teaching the Maqamat in Translation—Roger Allen, 16. Ibn Hazm: Friendship, Love and the Quest for Justice—A. Terri L De Young, 17. The Story of Zahra and its Critics—Elizabeth M. Holt, 18. The Arabic Frametale and Two European Offspring—James Monroe, 19. Teaching the Arabian Nights—Muhsin al-Musawi.

2. Resources for Modern Arabic Literature (Middle Eastern & Islamic Studies), compiled by Walaa Al-Salmi (March 2009) [last updated August 2014], https://libraries.indiana.edu/resources-modern-arabic-literature-middle-eastern-islamic-studies.

3. Carol Maier and Françoise Massardier-Kenney, *Literature in Translation: Teaching Issues and Reading Practices* (Kent, OH: Kent State University Press, 2010).

4. "WWB Campus: Bringing International Literature into the Classroom," Words without Borders, accessed July 5, 2018, http://www.wordswithoutborders.org/education/.

5. "Contributors," *Banipal: Magazine of Modern Arab Literature*, accessed July 5, 2018, http://www.banipal.co.uk/contributors/.

6. My first publication of a translation from Arabic literature appeared in *Playboy Magazine* in 1975. It was an excerpt from al-Jahiz (d. 868/869 CE), "Boasting Match over Maids and Youths."

7. "History of the Oriental Institute," Oriental Institute, University of Chicago, accessed July 5, 2018, https://oi.uchicago.edu/about/history-oriental-institute.

8. "About Us," Center for Middle Eastern Studies, University of Chicago, accessed July 5, 2018, https://cmes.uchicago.edu/page/about-us.

9. John Boyer, *The University of Chicago: A History* (Chicago: University of Chicago Press, 2015), 466.

10. "Established in 1965, the CMES has been supported by the Divisions of Humanities and Social Sciences at the University of Chicago and by grants from the U.S. Department of Education and the Mellon Foundation for more than forty years." https://cmes.uchicago.edu/page/about-us. "The University of Texas at Austin has a long history of academic focus on the Middle East. The Center for Middle Eastern Studies, established in 1960, offers some 300 Middle East language and area studies courses each year. The Center provides a supportive environment for faculty researching and teaching on the Middle East throughout the University, which are carried out by 150 scholars with faculty appointments in 22 departments. The Center offers an interdisciplinary program in Middle Eastern Studies at both the undergraduate and graduate levels," https://liberalarts.utexas.edu/mes/center/index1.php.

11. "About Us," Center for Middle Eastern Studies, University of Chicago, accessed July 5, 2018, https://cmes.uchicago.edu/page/about-us.

12. "Modern Middle East Literatures in Translation," University of Texas at Austin, accessed July 5, 2018, http://www.utexas.edu/cola/mes/center/publications/literature.php.

13. "Donald Herdeck's Three Continents Press: An Interview," *Gargoyle Magazine*, accessed July 5, 2018, http://www.gargoylemagazine.com/gargoyle/Issues/scanned/issue15/herdeck _interview.htm.

14. Roger Allen "obtained his doctoral degree in modern Arabic literature from Oxford University in 1968, the first student to obtain a doctoral degree in that field at Oxford, under the supervision of Dr. M. M. Badawi," http://ccat.sas.upenn.edu/~rallen/.

15. https://theseahawk.org/3091/lifestyles/uncws-clyde-edgerton-to-be-inducted-into-the -north-carolina-literary-hall-of-fame/.

16. https://themanbookerprize.com/international/backlist/2015.

17. Amir Hassan Cheheltan, "Writing Is a Dangerous Act: The Situation of Writer in Iran," *Art & Thought on Literature* 103 (2015): 38–40.

18. Email to the author, March 22, 2016.

19. Editor's email containing the anonymous reader's report, May 20, 2016.

20. Donna Lee Bowen, Evelyn A. Early, and Becky Schulthies, eds., *Everyday Life in the Muslim Middle East*, 3rd ed. (Bloomington: Indiana University Press, 2014), 2.

21. Marwa al-Sabouni, *The Battle for Homs: The Vision of a Young Architect in Syria* (New York: Thames & Hudson, 2016), 142.

22. al-Sabouni, *The Battle for Homs*, 168.

23. al-Sabouni, *The Battle for Homs*, 176.

24. Julia Moskin, "During Ramadan, Dates Are a Unifying Staple," *New York Times*, June 16, 2015; Sam Roberts, "Gamal al-Ghitani, Egyptian Novelist with a Political Bent, Dies at 70," *New York Times*, October 21, 2015.

WILLIAM MAYNARD HUTCHINS is Professor of Philosophy and Religion at Appalachian State University. He is best known for translating *Palace Walk*, *Palace of Desire*, and *Sugar Street* by Naguib Mahfouz.

PART II
ISLAMOPHOBIA AND VIOLENCE

chapter seven

INTERDISCIPLINARY EDUCATION FOR TEACHING CHALLENGING SUBJECTS
The Case of Islam and Violence

Laila Hussein Moustafa

THE SUBJECT OF THE ALLEGED relationship between religion and violence comes up as a particularly sensitive area in today's social and political climate. This topic arises for instructors who teach religion in general and Islam in particular. Educators who find themselves challenged in classroom discussions by the prospect of dealing with such sensitive subjects, including topics such as racism, sexual violence, and suicide, should not have to struggle with deciding whether to address such controversial issues, to create a safe space for discussion, or to skip the discussion entirely. The task can be made easier by being aware of how those in other disciplines address similar pedagogical issues.

TEACHING RELIGION IN COLLEGE

In *Teaching Religion and Violence,* edited by Brian K. Pennington, various instructors describe what pedagogical strategies they used for teaching about the role of violence in particular religious traditions, including Hindu, Jewish, Buddhist, Christian, Sikh and Islam.[1] The book was written by a group of faculty members who are teaching religion in colleges and universities in the United States and Canada. In this volume, Michael Dobkowski, addressing the issue of teaching about religion and violence in the Jewish tradition, recommended using collaborative learning strategies with students.[2] He also advocated engagement with the Talmud to draw the students into rabbinic reasoning on war and the role of unity and peace. In another essay, William Morrow described his pedagogical method of problem-solving when teaching about Christianity and violence. He used a comparative approach that helped students discover similarities and differences between religious systems.[3] Other authors in the volume focused on the influence of popular media on various groups. Professor Amir Hussain, concerned about the shift in American public discourse after 9/11 "from a pervasive Islamophobia to a more pronounced hatred," started to use materials that described how television news works and also how religious groups use the media. He wanted to show students the power of the media and to help students learn how to analyze the information they received from the media.[4] Randal Cummings, in "Teaching Religion, Violence, and Pop Culture," explained that he used contemporary music, advertising, and film in his class to illustrate that religion and violence are all around.[5] Along these lines, Ken Derry discussed how he used film to explain the "semantic tension and ambiguity" that relates to religious tradition. Derry discussed how students would analyze and interpret film in a way that they might not do with texts. His pedagogical strategies showed that film might activate students' learning.[6]

Catherine Caufield, in "The Agency Paradigm: A Pedagogical Tool to Facilitate Nuanced Thinking on Sensitive Issues," addressed the pedagogical challenge of teaching a sensitive topic because it touches part of the students' religious beliefs.[7] Caufield shared her experience of teaching a "Women in World Religions" course and, specifically, how she created tools to help students ask questions about the historical context of religions. The tools helped the students to ask questions about religious interpretations of sacred texts and how women could choose to exercise their power. Caufield's goal was to help the students understand complex ideas and reduce confusion. For example, when students see the complexity of an issue, they can be actively engaged and take positions in discussion. Caufield called the tools the "Agency Paradigm." She asserted that the tools helped students to understand the complicated characteristics, dynamics, and interrelationships that women experience in their daily lives and their individual faith traditions.

Barbara E. Walvoord, in Teaching and Learning in College Introductory Religion, argued that scholarship on teaching religion must challenge the conventions of teaching and learning.[8] Walvoord rejected the idea of using lectures as a way of communicating ideas. Her conversations with faculty revealed that instructors sometimes do not know where the boundary between church and state exists. Faculty also feared being seen as trying to pressure students toward a particular religion. Walvoord conducted a survey to study introductory courses in religious studies and theology. She targeted public, private nonsectarian, and religiously affiliated colleges throughout the United States of America. The survey participants included 12,463 students enrolled in 533 courses at 109 colleges and universities.[9]

Walvoord also gathered qualitative data from 66 classes that she selected because the instructors' supervisors considered their classes highly effective. According to the survey, some students take the classes with the expectation that class will resemble the religious instruction in their church, mosque, or temple. Some students think religion is a matter of personal feeling. Some believe that their own communities are always right and that critical thinking is dangerous if applied to their own beliefs. Some students thought they would be unofficially required to agree with the teacher's point of view. Walvoord suggested that faculty should deal with these issues by clarifying to their students that the course is an academic class, not religious instruction.

Walvoord identified different methods and tools the faculty used to create environments in which students could grow and change. Two-thirds of the students who responded to the survey reported progress after they used analytical tools and critical thinking. Three-fourths of the students reported that they developed their own values, acquired critical thinking tools, learned to consider the historical and rhetorical contexts of sacred texts, and learned to question and search for answers. Students reported they became less judgmental and listened to other viewpoints. Walvoord suggested that faculty should find ways to help students adopt critical thinking tools for their own questions so they can identify their values and develop their spiritual journey.

Walvoord argued that faculty and students must question their goals for learning. Faculty must ask themselves if they are planning to challenge the students' beliefs and how they are going to address the challenges that arise. According to the author, instructors must be thoughtful and clear about their own goals to help students develop their thoughts and address challenges. The instructors' goal is to understand the students' needs, to nurture the students' spiritual journeys, and to not force students to have particular beliefs but help them develop tools to answer their questions.

The individual instructors in the examples above were trained to teach religion itself as a subject, but may not have had any training in subjects such as linguistics, film, popular culture, or literature. In fact, instructors with one area of expertise, looking for effective ways to explain to students the complex root causes of religiously associated violence, may find themselves discussing topics outside their area of specialty, such as politics, religious identification, globalization, nationalism, colonialism, and poverty.[10] This limitation suggests that it is worth exploring team teaching as an interdisciplinary approach to the subject, where the more diverse expertise of teams can provide complementary instruction.

This essay presents my argument for team teaching as a model for an interdisciplinary teaching approach to a controversial issue or current sensitive events. I base this argument on my experience while participating as an observer in a team-taught course titled "Exploring Sustainable International Development." First, I examine different types of interdisciplinary education in general and interdisciplinary teaching approaches to controversial issues in particular. Second, the case study illustrates how students can learn to solve challenges in a real-world context by addressing the needs of an international community. At the end of the essay, I suggest a model that can be implemented in teaching about Islam and violence. The proposed teaching model can be used by instructors to move beyond discipline-specific approaches and put interdisciplinary teaching into practice to help solve issues that should not be solved by one discipline.

INTERDISCIPLINARY EDUCATION

In this part, I investigate the definition and the rational for interdisciplinary education, and I also explain the dynamic of team teaching and the challenges that it produces. The concept of interdisciplinary education has been defined in multiple ways. According to Julie Thompson Klein, interdisciplinary education "is a means of solving problems and answering questions that cannot be satisfactorily addressed using single disciplinary approaches."[11] Klein emphasizes interdisciplinary education as the synthesis of two or more disciplines, and one that establishes a new level of discourse and integration of knowledge.[12] Klein and William H. Newell describe interdisciplinarity as an educational approach that incorporates the perspectives of more than one discipline and integrates their insights through construction of a more wide-ranging viewpoint.[13] According to the *Dictionary of Education,* an interdisciplinary approach to organizing a curriculum "cuts across subject matter lines to focus upon comprehensive life problems or broad areas of study that bring together the various segments of curriculum to meaningful association."[14] Geoffrey Squires defines an interdisciplinary course as "one in which two or more disciplines are taught in conscious relation to one another."[15]

What these various definitions share is the idea that this style of instruction combines different disciplines under one umbrella in order to develop learning in one or more of the disciplines, and it often can accomplish this through team teaching.[16] Interdisciplinarity means going beyond established practices to create or develop new methods to exceed the discipline in order to solve a problem.[17] In particular, it is a means of solving problems and answering questions that cannot be answered by using one disciplinary approach.[18] Interdisciplinary approaches should enhance learning and complex social problem-solving. Hence, an interdisciplinary teaching approach brings together insights from distinct fields of study, which can offer radical new contributions to creating solutions to difficult problems facing society. In some cases, an interdisciplinary approach may even lead to the development of new disciplines.[19]

Interdisciplinary education has been recognized as important because it allows instructors and students to address challenging issues from multiple perspectives.[20] Instructors concerned with interdisciplinary education have recognized that one of the major problems in classrooms today is the separate "subject" approach to knowledge and skills.[21] By sharing perspectives from different fields, instructors can help students to think beyond how a single discipline would approach a problem.[22] Students engage in discussions that consider different perspectives; this allows them to discover the limitations of any single discipline and encourages them to be engaged in the learning experience.[23]

The interdisciplinary teaching approach helps leverage the different perspectives and skills of participants. W. G. Bennis has noted that complex problems can be solved by temporary groups who may be relative strangers and represent diverse disciplines.[24] Each person in a problem-solving team will possess unique skills and knowledge that others do not have. The assumption is that certain problems cannot be solved or adequately addressed by individuals acting in isolation; instead, groups acting together can produce a unified solution or technique. According to Charlotte Woods, global problems require an interdisciplinary teaching approach that can help prepare students for working in a multi-professional setting.[25]

INTERDISCIPLINARY APPROACH TO COMPLEX ISSUES

A central benefit to interdisciplinary education is its fostering of critical thinking, a skill that is almost universally valued today for not only understanding controversial issues, like those surrounding Islam and violence, but also any other challenging issues.[26] According to Marije van Amelsvoort and colleagues, interdisciplinary classes encouraged students to think independently about multiple solutions to a single issue or task and in this way supported critical thinking.[27] While student voices must always be respected in the classroom, the need for respectful engagement is especially pronounced in an interdisciplinary curriculum that deals with multiple perspectives and individuals who may have deep-seated opinions and feelings about complex and controversial subjects. Developing an ability to reasonably articulate one's position on a subject appropriately complements critical thinking skills.

Dealing with controversial issues does present special challenges. Instructors must make efforts to ensure that true debate and discussion take place in class and that different ways of learning are respected.[28] Research shows that adequately addressing a controversial issue requires some special skills, for example, in running discussions.[29] Many instructors try to avoid controversy entirely, believing they should keep their political opinions to themselves.[30] It is well worth the effort to engage, however. It develops experience in debate that can benefit all participants. The challenge of such teaching often means instructors may need extensive professional development. This may include training in facilitating a large or small group learning process. It might also entail practice in the use of the constructivist-oriented pedagogy commonly associated with this approach.[31]

TYPES OF COLLABORATIVE TEACHING MODELS

Collaborative teaching models are well suited to interdisciplinary education. There are three models of collaborative teaching: (a) traditional team teaching, which involves two or more instructors teaching the same course; (b) a linked course model, which involves two or three courses that are linked by a theme and taught by different subject specialists; and (c) the connected course, where instructors arrange for all course sections to meet together at the same time so that instructors can illustrate the interdisciplinarity of certain topics.[32] In this essay, I focus on team teaching because I have experienced it personally, as I discuss in more detail below.

The Team Teaching Model

Team teaching involves two or more instructors working together to teach one course. More specifically, team teaching has been defined as "two or more instructors collaborating over the design and/or implementation and evolution of the same course or courses."[33] The instructors typically must collaborate throughout the entire course, share the same responsibility, and meet every class.[34] Team teaching, which has come to be associated with interdisciplinary education, had its origins in US high schools in the 1960s.[35] William Alexander was the first to point to team teaching. The initial idea behind the use of team teaching was simply to have better control of large groups of students.[36] According to Pamela Morris, team teaching has three forms: parallel, rotational, and interactive.[37] In the rotational form, two instructors work together to create the course and split the lecture content. The interactive teaching form involves a group of instructors who work together to blend content and create a course to teach.[38] Team teaching requires a special way of organizing and managing the class. For example, it requires careful planning in order to avoid disagreements in relation to the students, such as disagreements around teaching strategies and grading.[39]

A team teaching approach possesses many of the advantages of interdisciplinary education discussed earlier. Team teaching gives the students the opportunity to learn from multiple perspectives from different disciplines.[40] Team teaching promotes dialogue and increases multiple perspectives because students have the opportunity to hear two or more instructors with different viewpoints, which might give the students the opportunity to disagree about something without being hostile.[41] Thus, the team teaching environment encourages students to be more active in the learning process, and students are more likely to feel they can add to the discussions.[42] This can help improve the relationships between the instructors and the students.[43] Team teaching that includes experts from different disciplines also can help students to develop critical thinking skills by synthesizing diverse perspectives and relating the knowledge to a larger theoretical framework.[44] It improves the students' social and communication skills as they develop their skills in how to evaluate and implement critical thinking. Bakken and Clark, and also Thompson, point out that team teaching helps instructors to design collaborative techniques.[45] For example, team teaching can help instructors to learn and hear about new ideas from their colleagues and can give the instructors a chance to be engaged in deep discussions about the course materials.

Every teaching method has its challenges. In the case of team teaching, team members need to support each other and share leadership and ideas.[46] So, a down side of team teaching is the loss of autonomy. The team members may have difficulty managing each other's behavior in some cases, for example, if one of the team members is slow in responding to students' emails or is not available to answer students' questions. Team teaching also may require more updating and constant examination to support innovative pedagogical changes.[47]

Interdisciplinary Case Study—Sustainable Development

The goal in presenting the following case study is to give an example of how the interdisciplinary team teaching approach is used to encourage students to engage in solving complex issues.

In fall 2016, I attended a one-semester course entitled "Exploring Sustainable International Development." The course was an international engineering design course for communities-in-need and was designed as a yearlong course. Part of the motivation for the course was a concern that, although academic programs in engineering should create a sense of civic engagement, students often lack vision because projects are created without plans for sustainability. The course brought together a group of instructors from Urban Planning, Engineering, Anthropology, Sociology, and Community Health to examine international sustainable development. The course goal was to focus on the skills needed to plan and implement internally supported community development projects and to evaluate the impact of the projects over time. The course engaged the students in nontraditional learning experiences and helped them to learn by introducing them to reading materials and lectures from different disciplines. The students were divided into groups, and each group was assigned to submit a project by the end of the course.

I attended the course to observe the dynamics among the instructors and the interactions between the students and instructors. I also wanted to learn about the team teaching model. I wanted to learn how team teaching was perceived, and under what conditions students felt comfortable to ask questions and learn. As a librarian, I offered some outside sources to instructors to help students learn how to find information about the community they planned to serve.

The main instructor was Ann-Perry Witmer, a civil engineer who initiated the course because she wanted to break with "rigid engineering thinking." She wished to turn the course into an interdisciplinary one to solve an issue that faced engineers trying to help communities in need of clean water. The instructors attended almost all the classes, even if they were not developing a lecture. Almost every week one of the instructors would develop a lecture, assign reading, and ask questions to generate a meaningful response. The main instructor was always in the class observing the dynamic between the instructor and the students, and also that between the students and each other. Each instructor developed a lecture in his or her area of specialization. Each also interacted with the students during class by helping students to better understand how to do the exercises. Instructors were never observed to disagree in class and always displayed respect for each other and a commitment to the team-teaching learning environment. Soon students were interested and engaged in the learning process. One interesting exercise involved engaging students in an interdisciplinary debate during class. The instructors were very helpful, as they taught the students not only to engage in the debate but also to respect the views held by others, especially those with whom they disagreed. The students were encouraged to learn critical thinking tools to find solutions to challenges that they might face. For example, students were taught to design a survey to collect information from the community they planned to visit and help in Ecuador. Creating the survey required the students to learn and think about how to ask questions and conduct interviews. The class had almost twenty-five students, both graduate and undergraduate, from different disciplines, including engineering, accounting, anthropology, architecture, community health, education, global studies, and urban planning. Alumni who completed at least one year of the course volunteered their time and skills to mentor new students and help them to understand their role in the project and determine appropriate methods and actions.[48]

The course was designed to prepare students for working with local residents in a town in Ecuador to provide the town with a sustainable supply of clean water that they can maintain in the future. The general objective of the course was to have students deal with the challenges of assessing the needs of a farming community and coming up with alternative solutions. Solutions had to be sustainable and affordable for the community. The course emphasized the skills needed to plan and implement internationally supported community development projects in a sustainable manner, as well as skills to evaluate the impact of the project over time. Instructors did not recommend any specific solution; instead, they encouraged students to explore their options.

The class was set up in groups of five to eight students from different disciplines. Each student team was asked to design a project, present their ongoing progress on their projects, and to present their design to the other groups at the end of the semester. During the course, students were expected to create a vision and gain experience and skills that could help them in the real world. The students' presentations addressed their project problem and their proposed solutions.

The course had many governing principles that defined a successful project. These were developed by the main instructor, Ann-Perry Witmer, drawing upon her time working in international projects in Latin America and Western Africa.[49] The governing principles included community empowerment, investment by the recipient community in the system both financially and in terms of labor, cultural appropriateness of the project, consultation with the community, and partnership with NGOs by the course designers. The governing principles helped the course's instructors to identify potential projects in collaboration with the community and NGOs, and they helped to form the course objectives. Most of the students in the class were not familiar with the team teaching approach, but they were provided with information to help them understand team teaching.

INTERDISCIPLINARY TEACHING: TEACHING ABOUT ISLAM AND VIOLENCE

In this part, I propose an interdisciplinary team teaching model that might be used to develop a course that meets the need of those who teach an Islamic subject and have to address the issue of violence.

An instructor who teaches Islam is usually trained to teach about religion but may not have had training in teaching or explaining violence as a subject. Educators need to see Islam and violence as two distinct subject areas of expertise, not one. This idea should help educators to see the benefit of engaging with other disciplinary specialists to explain violence. An interdisciplinary teaching model would be appropriate. In addition to scholars of religion, scholars from other disciplines can contribute to the discussion. For example, sociology instructors could address the social impact of creating or reducing violence. Linguistics instructors could discuss how to analyze the language that is used and misused by all stakeholders, including the media.

Creating an interdisciplinary course requires that the instructors invest time and effort in preparation. Instructors should review the literature on team teaching. By reading what is published in the literature about the interdisciplinary teaching approach, and learning about the benefits and challenges, an instructor can be prepared for issues related to team teaching approaches. Instructors should also get to know other instructors who have participated in interdisciplinary classes. Talking with other colleagues who have experience in teaching interdisciplinary courses can help instructors to learn how to select a compatible colleague to teach with them. It can also help instructors think about how to overcome individual differences when they arise.

The main instructor needs to decide what subjects to include and who is going to co-instruct with him or her. The instructor will base these decisions on the purpose of the course. For example, team instructors can be invited to help students understand the role of violence in Muslim societies from psychological, sociological, or historical perspectives. The course also can include instructors who are experts in the issue of Islamic studies, the history of Islam, or violence generally. The instructor might want to invite media or film scholars to facilitate the discussion of movies, or in analyses of social media in promoting violence. Media images can be examined as both technologically sophisticated and representative of cultural beliefs.

The instructor needs to secure departmental agreement on several issues: the team teaching approach, the instructors who will partner in the course, the workload, and compensation. Instructors should also pay attention to how the course will be listed in order to make sure that students from multiple disciplines can participate. Course names should be carefully considered, and might include Islam and Violence; Islam, Violence and Media; Islam and Counter-terrorism; or Islam and Cyber Violence.

During the planning of the course, all team member instructors should meet regularly. The team members should discuss their goals and objectives and develop assignments that should meet the goals and objective of the course.[50] Instructors should plan for their individual responsibilities and how to divide class time. There are many ways of sharing teaching responsibilities, and multiple scenarios should be considered.[51]

It is important for team members to talk about how to deal with conflict that might develop during the teaching process based on different personalities or other factors. One thing that instructors can do is to have their disagreement discussions outside of the class to show they are working as a unified team and to reduce the chances that students will take advantage of disagreements. Instructors should share course policy and expectations with the students.[52]

Interdisciplinary teaching is not limited to engineering or science. Interdisciplinary courses are taught in anthropology, economics, languages, and other liberal arts field. Interdisciplinary courses are used more in the areas of humanities, business, law and economics, and women and gender.

Conclusion

The interdisciplinary, team teaching model is presented here as an example of how to tackle a complex issue like religious violence. Interdisciplinary teaching can help instructors to explain sensitive and controversial issues, to help students gain expertise in these areas, and to help participants (instructors and students) integrate the opinions of other fields. An interdisciplinary approach combines two or more disciplines and keeps all disciplines in focus. Its objectives include developing critical thinking skills using an integrated curriculum that is interesting and relevant to students and contemporary problems.[53] Interdisciplinary teaching has the potential for elevating students' motivation for learning and engagement because it involves an engaging collaboration among both professors and students, and it helps students see the value of what they are learning.[54] In practice, this form of education has involved interactive and collaborative problem-solving activities to solve an issue, an emphasis on critic thinking, and a fostering of cultural awareness. Students and instructors alike need to learn to make more informed decisions critical to their future in a way that meets the challenges of our interdisciplinary world. Not much research has been published addressing the issue of how instructors teach controversial issues like Islam and violence, what teaching methods can be used to help students engage in challenging discussions, and tools that can help students in the real world.[55] The most important questions instructors need to ask before they design their course is what do we want the students to know and what might be the best ways for them to learn it? I hope this study helps to invite more instructors to investigate this area of research.

Notes

1. Brian K. Pennington, ed., *Teaching Religion and Violence* (New York: Oxford University Press, 2012), 20–21.

2. Michael Dobkowski, "A Time for War and a Time for Peace: Teaching Religion and Violence in the Jewish Tradition," in Pennington, *Teaching Religion and Violence*, 47–48.

3. William Morrow, "Violence and Religion in the Christian Tradition," in Pennington, *Teaching Religion and Violence*, 94, 101.

4. Amir Hussain, "Confronting Misoislamia: Teaching Religion and Violence in Courses on Islam," in Pennington, *Teaching Religion and Violence*, 131, 134.

5. Randal Cummings, "Teaching Religion, Violence, and Pop Culture," in Pennington, *Teaching Religion and Violence*, 218–244.

6. Ken Derry, "Believing Is Seeing: Teaching Religion and Violence in Film," in Pennington, *Teaching Religion and Violence*, 185–186.

7. Catherine Caufield, "The Agency Paradigm: A Pedagogical Tool to Facilitate Nuanced Thinking on Sensitive Issues," *Teaching Theology & Religion* 20, no. 1 (2017): 90, 99.

8. Barbara E. Walvoord, *Teaching and Learning in College Introductory Religion Courses* (Malden, MA: Blackwell, 2008), 5.

9. Walvoord, *Teaching and Learning in College Introductory Religion Courses*, 2.

10. Allen F. Repko, *Interdisciplinary Research: Process and Theory* (Los Angeles: SAGE, 2008), xviii.

11. Julie Thompson Klein, *Interdisciplinarity: History, Theory, and Practice* (Detroit, MI: Wayne State University, 1990), 196.

12. Julie Thompson Klein, "Interdisciplinarity," in *Encyclopedia of Science, Technology, and Ethics*, ed. Carl Mitcham (Detroit, MI: Macmillan Reference USA, 2005), 1034, 1037.

13. See Joseph S. Johnston Jr. and Jane R. Spalding, "Internationalizing the Curriculum," in *Handbook of the Undergraduate Curriculum*, ed. Jerry G. Gaff and James L. Ratcliff (San Francisco: Jossey-Bass, 1997), 426.

14. Carter Victor Good, Dictionary of Education (New York: McGraw-Hill, 1973), 311.

15. Geoffrey Squires, "Interdisciplinarity in Higher Education in the United Kingdom," *European Journal of Education* 27, no. 3 (September 1992): 201.

16. Lizabeth B. Ballard and Ray Anderson, "Two for One: Integrating American History and English III." (1994), https://eric.ed.gov/?id=ED382506.

17. William H. Newell, "A Theory of Interdisciplinary Studies," *Issues in Integrative Studies* 19 (2001): 5, 22.

18. Klein, *Interdisciplinarity: History, Theory, and Practice*, 196.

19. James R. Davis, *Interdisciplinary Courses and Team Teaching: New Arrangements for Learning* (Phoenix: American Council on Education and the Oryx Press, 1995), 39.

20. Davis, *Interdisciplinary Courses and Team Teaching*, 51.

21. Foster Watson, *The Encyclopedia and Dictionary of Education* (London: Sir I. Pitman & Sons, 1921–22), 1662.

22. Marije van Amelsvoort, Carel van Wijk, and Hanny den Ouden, "Going Dutch or Joining Forces? Some Experiences with Team Teaching in the Netherlands," *Business Communication Quarterly* 73, no. 1 (2010): 99.

23. Charlotte Woods, "Researching and Developing Interdisciplinary Teaching: Towards a Conceptual Framework for Classroom Communication," *Higher Education* 54, no. 6 (2007): 855.

24. Bennis, *Beyond Bureaucracy: Essays on the Development and Evolution of Human Organization* (San Francisco: Jossey-Bass, 1993), 13.

25. Woods, "Researching and Developing Interdisciplinary Teaching," 852.

26. Sandra Mathison and Melissa Freeman, "The Logic of Interdisciplinary Studies," National Research Center on English Learning and Achievement, Report Series 2, no. 33 (Albany, NY: CELA, 1998), 11.

27. van Amelsvoort, van Wijk, and den Ouden, "Going Dutch or Joining Forces?," 99.

28. Thomas A. Angelo and K. Patricia Cross, *Classroom Assessment Techniques: A Handbook for College Teachers.* 2nd ed. (San Francisco: Jossey-Bass, 1993), 203–204.

29. Diana E. Hess, "Controversies about Controversial Issues in Democratic Education," *PS: Political Science & Politics* 37, no. 2 (2004): 260.

30. Hess, "Controversies about Controversial Issues in Democratic Education," 257.

31. Gershon Tenenbaum, Som Naidu, Olugbemiro Jegede, and Jon Austin, "Constructivist Pedagogy in Conventional On-Campus and Distance Learning Practice: An Exploratory Investigation," *Learning and Instruction* 11, no. 2 (2011): 89.

32. Barbara Leigh Smith, "Taking Structure Seriously: The Learning Community Model," *Liberal Education* 77, no. 2 (1991): 42.

33. Tim Hatcher and Barbara Hinton, "Graduate Student's Perception of University Team-Teaching," *College Students Journal* 30, no. 3 (1996): 367.

34. Kathryn M. Plank, "Team Teaching," IDEA Paper 55 (2013), 5.

35. Jorge Gaytan, "Instructional Strategies to Accommodate a Team-Teaching Approach," *Business Communication Quarterly* 73, no. 1 (2010): 82–87.

36. Wilson Ivins, "Team Teaching in the Southwestern Secondary School," *NASSP Bulletin* 48, no. 290 (1964): 25–30.

37. Pamela K. Morris, "Team Teaching of Creative Advertising and Public Relations Courses," *Journal of Advertising Education* 20, no. 1/2 (2016): 44–53.

38. van Amelsvoort, van Wijk, and den Ouden, "Going Dutch or Joining Forces?," 96–101.

39. Margaret R. Letterman and Kimberly B. Dugan, "Team Teaching a Cross-Disciplinary Honors Course: Preparation and Development," *College Teaching* 52, no. 2 (2004): 76–79.

40. Andrew H. Van de Ven and Paul E. Johnson, "Knowledge for Theory and Practice," *Academy of Management Review* 31, no. 4 (2006): 802–821.

41. Rebecca S. Anderson and Bruce W. Speck, "Oh What a Difference a Team Makes: Why Team Teaching Makes a Difference," *Teaching and Teacher Education* 14, no. 7 (1998): 671–686.

42. Davis, *Interdisciplinary Courses and Team Teaching*, 124, 127.

43. Anderson and Speck, "Oh What a Difference a Team Makes," 671–686.

44. Anuradha A. Gokhale, "Collaborative Learning Enhances Critical Thinking," *Journal of Technology Education* 7, no. 1 (1995): 22–30.

45. Linda Bakken, Frances L. Clark, and Johnnie Thompson, "Collaborative Teaching: Many Joys, Some Surprises, and a Few Worms," *College Teaching* 46, no. 4 (1998): 154–157.

46. Marica B. Cohen and Kate DeLois, "Training in Tandem: Co-Facilitation and Role Modeling in Group Course Work," *Social Work with Groups* 24, no. 1 (2001): 21–36.

47. Charles Henderson, Andrea Beach, and Michael Famiano, "Diffusion of Educational Innovations via Co-teaching," *AIP Conference Proceedings* 883, no. 1 (2007): 117–120.

48. Keilin Jahnke, Ann-Perry Witmer, Matthew Tan, and Grace Frances Witmer, "Bringing a Cross-Disciplinary, Contextual Approach to International Service Engineering Learning," paper presented at ASEEs 123rd Annual Conference & Exposition, New Orleans, LA, June 2016, Paper ID# 14756.

49. Jahnke et al., "Bringing a Cross-Disciplinary, Contextual Approach."

50. Edward C. Brewer and Terence L. Holmes, "Communication = Better Teams: A Communication Exercise to Improve Team Performance," *IEEE Transactions on Professional Communication* 59, no. 3 (2016): 288–298.

51. Wendy W. Murawski and Lisa Dieker, "50 Ways to Keep Your Co-Teacher," *Teaching Exceptional Children* 40, no. 4 (March 2008): 40–48.

52. Morris, "Team Teaching," 44–53.

53. Robert J. Marzano, "Fostering Thinking across the Curriculum through Knowledge Restructuring," *Journal of Reading* 34, no. 7 (1991): 518–525.

54. Leah Taylor and Jim Parsons, "Improving Student Engagement," *Current Issues in Education* 14, no. 1 (2011): 1–33.

55. Robert A. Waterson, "The Examination of Pedagogical Approaches to Teaching Controversial Public Issues: Explicitly Teaching the Holocaust and Comparative Genocide," *Social Science Research & Practice* 4, no. 2 (2009): 1–24.

LAILA HOUSSEIN MOUSTAFA is Assistant Professor and Middle Eastern and North African Studies Librarian at the University of Illinois at Urbana-Champaign.

chapter eight

THE IMMANENT IMMINENCE OF VIOLENCE
Comparing Legal Arguments in a Post-9/11 World

Nathan S. French

ON SEPTEMBER 12, 2001, LANCE MORROW penned a furious call to arms in the pages of *Time* magazine directed to a US audience reeling from the actions of Usama bin Ladin (1957–2011) and al-Qāʿida: "A day cannot live in infamy without the nourishment of rage. Let's have rage. What's needed is a unified, unifying, Pearl Harbor sort of purple American fury. A ruthless indignation that doesn't leak away . . . into a corruptly thoughtful relativism (as has happened in the recent past, when, for example, you might hear someone say, 'Terrible what he did, of course, but, you know, the Unabomber does have a point, doesn't he, about modern technology?'). Let America explore the rich reciprocal possibilities of the fatwa. A policy of focused brutality does not come easily."[1]

Morrow's call to his fellow citizens to act with a furious violence is saturated with national symbols and the visceral and raw emotions that swept across the United States in the days following the attacks. This should scream to the scholar of religions. One hears the ominous response to this call for "focused brutality," for example, in the words of Cofer Black, a former CIA official under George W. Bush, when he testified to Congress that "after 9/11, the gloves came off."[2]

A year after Morrow's essay, Usama bin Ladin responded to the application of this gloves-off "policy of focused brutality" with a report on the progress of the United States in its war against his movement. In his letter posted in October 2002 to the now-defunct *al-Qalaʿa* ("The Fortress") forum, bin Ladin chastised the United States for its hypocrisy:

> You have claimed to be the vanguards of Human Rights, and your Ministry of Foreign Affairs [i.e., the Department of State] issues annual reports containing statistics of those countries that violate any Human Rights. However, all these values vanished when the *mujahidin* ["those who struggle in

the cause of God"] hit you [on 9/11], and you then implemented the methods of the same documented governments that you used to curse. In America, you arrested thousands of Muslims and Arabs, took them into custody with no reason, court trial, nor did you disclose their names. You issued newer, harsher laws. What happens in Guantanamo is a historical embarrassment to America and its values, and it screams in your hypocritical faces: What is the value of your signature on any agreement or treaty?[3]

For Usama bin Ladin, the events of September 11, 2001, were intended to be a pedagogical lesson in jihadi-salafism exercised on a global scale.[4] Whether he killed 5,000 or 500,000, bin Ladin hoped that the United States would expose the global Muslim community (the *umma*) to what he considered the hypocrisy of the United States toward the application of human rights and the rule of law. Given that the United States financially and politically backed many of the governments in the region that bin Ladin considered un-Islamic, such as Egypt, Saudi Arabia, and Jordan, it was bin Ladin's hope that just as the *munafiqun* ("hypocrites") in Medina had revealed their betrayal of the Muslim community of Muhammad, so too would the global Muslim community, the *umma*, realize their betrayal at the hands of Arab and Muslim leaders backed by their disbelieving sponsors in the West.[5] Within this framework, the words of Morrow fit right into the expectations, if not the hopes, of bin Ladin. Yet, the lesson bin Ladin sought to teach the United States went, however arguably, unheard.

To imply that the national mood and sentiments of the United States were under the strategic influence of al-Qāʿida post-9/11 is scandalous. To push a comparison between US- and al-Qāʿida-endorsed responses to one another in the post-9/11 era reminds us of the challenge of comparison as an act of translation. As J. Z. Smith reminds the comparativist, "to venture to understand is not to approve or to advocate."[6] Understanding Morrow and Bin Ladin is to understand the drive by both to remove or prevent the causes of suffering within their societies. The calls for a struggle (jihad) and a war emerge from the identification by Morrow and bin Ladin of the causes of their suffering and the identification of the means of addressing those causes.[7] To realize that they share a common cause, one another, is scandalous.

It is the scandal that reminds us that those working and teaching within the academic study of religion are disciplined by the Enlightenment and therefore must be reminded, from time to time, that religion was transformed from "*pathos to ethos*."[8] Religion, Smith argues, was finally made intelligible, but what became intelligible were the ethical, relatable characteristics of human religiosity. Scholars forgot, Smith contends, that "religion is not nice; it has been responsible for more death and suffering than any other human activity."[9] Within the framework of comparative religious studies, the discourse of al-Qāʿida, and a product of its jihadi-salafi interlocutors, in comparison with that of the United States, a product of its citizens and government, reveals the challenge of studying how the desire to alleviate suffering establishes the principles by which violence of all forms and against all enemies may be justified.

In what follows, I argue that a comparative approach to religious studies, applied to a genealogy of the violence that erupted across the globe following September 11, 2001, is essential for evaluating the legal discourse of al-Qāʿida and the Bush and Obama administrations. In my "Introductory to the Study of Religion" classroom, which takes as its focus of study the events of September 11, 2001, I introduce students to a comparison of the legal logic underlying both the martyrdom operations (al-ʿamaliyyat al-istishhadiyya) called for by Usama bin Ladin's movement and the drone campaign of the Bush and Obama administrations in order for students to understand how the tactics of both, meant to prevent suffering and harm to the general population, reflect similar structures of ethical and logical reasoning. This similarity causes discomfort for students, but it also reveals to them the practical importance of empathy as a category for analysis: imagine if Morrow, for example, had understood that bin Ladin sought a "purple American fury" post-9/11?

INTRODUCING A COMPARATIVE APPROACH TO VIOLENCE POST-9/11

The lesson taught by Morrow's quote above originates in his mistranslation. Morrow fails to account for his rage as the intended response. The rejection of empathy, which Morrow dismisses as relativism, and also the call for exploring the usage of law as a means for reciprocal vengeance, are the reflexive responses sought by bin Ladin. The misuse and misunderstanding of the word "fatwa," whether intentional or otherwise, evokes the memories of the description of such nonbinding Islamic legal arguments as "death warrants" amid the issuance of a fatwa by Ayatollah Khomeini calling for the death of Salman Rushdie, author of the *Satanic Verses*. In reality, across Islamic legal history, a fatwa played a much more benign role: documents were issued granting advice on marriage, divorce, cigarettes, and, in the modern era, television and smart phones. Here, however, Morrow uses cultural appropriation as a cudgel: "Let's see how you like it, bin Ladin," he appears to say.

For Alain Badiou, those who would make such statements are those who would admit that "if our 'democracies' are attacked by terrorism, then, in view of their excellence, they have the right to avenge themselves. All that remains to be known is against whom these legitimate reprisals are to be carried out."[10] This call to rights to violence was echoed by George W. Bush in his famous "bullhorn speech" in Lower Manhattan: "I can hear you!... And the people who knocked these buildings down will hear all of us soon!"[11] These are, as Clifford Geertz would suggest in his 1973 definition of religion, "moods and motivations"—the mood of vengeance tied to the motivation of fighting against the enemy, Usama bin Ladin by all means available and any means necessary.[12] Whether unintentional or otherwise, the symbolic value of "Pearl Harbor," for Morrow, evokes not only the raid on Tokyo as the opening US rebuttal in the war of the Pacific but also the suspension of legal ethics realized within the opening of internment camps for Japanese Americans.

An identification of what underlies Morrow's fury, and an approach to his demand for an ethical suspension, must involve the approach to a suffering so insufferable that it demands a new world-affirming and world-constructing response. Equally, for bin Ladin, the world in which he argues for the setting aside of all classical Islamic legal restrictions on warfare, and the demand that unrestricted warfare is an individual duty, is a response to what he considers the origins of Muslim suffering across the globe: the hypocrisy of the United States and its alignment with oppressive governments. As he writes in the same message as the quote above: "It is commanded by our religion and intellect that the oppressed have a right to respond to aggression. Do not expect anything from us but *jihad*, resistance and revenge."[13] Both men are responding to a world with a disintegrating sociopolitical order, an anomie, as Peter Berger describes it, in which an individual's self-identity, which emerges through an ongoing conversation with beliefs, institutions, and cultural practices—in short a "world"—is lost.[14] The death of innocents becomes a reminder of the precariousness of existence and a demand upon the living to repair the sociopolitical order meant to secure life.

This is, as Badiou labels it, a political instrumentalization of religion.[15] Morrow's usage of "Pearl Harbor" and bin Ladin's usage of shared Islamic symbols of suffering and injustice like Palestine, motivate their audiences' specific modes of action. In his essay on Bush and bin Ladin's speeches written after September 11, Bruce Lincoln has a similar insight: "The speeches ... mirrored one another, offering narratives in which the speakers, as defenders of righteousness, rallied an aggrieved people to strike back at aggressors who had done them terrible wrongs."[16] Writing in defense of Geertz, against Asad's critique that comparative religious methods collapse within the weight of their Western genealogies, Lincoln argues that the comparative analysis of Bush and bin Ladin reveals that both men work within religious traditions that are "lacerated by political divisions" and vice versa.[17] Such divisions are products of attempts by various communities to have their politics reflect the explanatory frameworks for suffering offered by their religions, and therefore have their religions establish the justice of their political approaches. Yet, while what horrifies bin Ladin is the increasing powerlessness of Muslim communities to respond to the overwhelming global hegemony underwritten by the West, Arjun Appadurai suggests that the United States sees a world in which "terrorists blur the line between military and civilian space and create uncertainty about the very boundaries within which we take civil society to be sovereign."[18] Such an uncertainty is a parallel to Berger's anomie above—and it demands a restoration of the political order lost to alleviate the uncertainty of social boundary.

It is within this context that I introduce my students to an exercise in the intersection of religion and its political instrumentalization. This is a challenge. For many of these students, the idea of viewing Usama bin Ladin or Ayman al-Zawahiri as possessing any sort of logic is at the very least uncomfortable. To facilitate this conversation, I present my students with two redacted samples, both of which are discussed below. After the conclusion of the exercise, I stress to them the differences between an empathetic approach—the desire to confront and explain the world within the terms and concepts of another—and a sympathetic approach. All the symbolic discourse (e.g., "Americans," "jihad," "infidel," etc.) is removed from the texts in order to force the students to pay attention to the argument.[19] I divide the classroom into two groups, and subdivide these groups into smaller discussion circles. Following their reading of the sources, the students are asked to answer the following questions:

1. Who is writing? Describe the author. What is his or her education level?
2. To what is the text calling the reader? Why should one fight?
3. Whom should one fight and why?
4. What are the methods that may be used to fight?
5. Who is the intended audience of the passage?

In what follows below, I provide the context of these sources, which the students discuss after their analysis.

The First Source: The Holder Selection

By the time of US Attorney General Eric Holder's speech at the Northwestern University School of Law in March 2012, the deployment of unmanned aerial vehicles ("drones") in active combat roles spanned multiple continents and their usage was to kill high-ranking members of al-Qāʿida. While the Bush administration had inaugurated the feasibility of drones as a tactic in its "Global War on Terror," the Obama administration, in its pivot away from such terms, expanded the usage of drones with little public acknowledgment of their use. Circumstances, however, changed following mounting public demands for transparency and a demand for the administration to justify the tactic within international and domestic legal frameworks.

Holder's remarks must be read within this context. Prior to this policy offensive, Obama, in a quote from 2009 cited by Holder (see Appendix One, "Holder Sample," §2), argued that in this current conflict, "time and again, our values have been our best national security asset."[20] This tie of security policy, including both incarceration and lethal force, to the domestic and international law and to national values is meant to emphasize a restorative order—the claim that the US Constitution is able to account for the unlawful, external threat posed by the unconventional forces of al-Qāʿida. Much as in Morrow's quote, the belief in the values of the United States—which Holder identifies as securing the promises of "security, justice, and liberty"—must not mean a hesitance toward violence, but instead should be seen as a reassurance that the decision by the sovereign executive, the President, to take life, either American or otherwise, secures the promise of the US government toward protecting the lives and interests of its citizens.[21]

Almost two years prior to Holder's remarks, the then-State Department lead counsel Harold Koh, in an address to the Annual Meeting of the American Society of International Law, revealed a preliminary sketch of the Obama administration's legal architecture for targeted and extrajudicial killings of unlawful combatants including citizens. Following Koh and Holder, John O. Brennan and Jeh Johnson also addressed the legality of the drone campaign within both domestic and international law. In their remarks, all the administration officials made implicit reference to the ongoing attempts by the United States to locate and kill Anwar al-ʿAwlaqi (1971–2011), an American citizen whom the Obama administration considered an operational leader of al-Qāʿida in the Arabian Peninsula and whom it would later kill in a drone strike in Yemen.

Underlying the justification of the usage of targeted killings was the argument made by both the administrations of George W. Bush and Barack Obama that the United States was engaged in a defensive armed conflict against a nonstate actor. In the opening of his speech, Holder notes that the United States is a "nation at war" facing a "nimble and determined enemy" who is plotting to kill Americans at home and abroad.[22] Holder refers to this as an "inherent right of self-defense" (§4, established by the United Nations Charter, Chapter VII, Article 51).[23] The war, Holder claims, is unconventional (§4), as the various attacks against the United States and its interests originated from multiple countries. Holder maintains, however, that the United States must first seek the consent of any nation involved (§4) or, second, if the country either refuses or is unable to handle the threat, pursue the threat on its own terms—an always emerging principle of customary international law on extraterritorial self-defense.[24]

Much of Holder's detailed constitutional framework for authorizing the killing of an unnamed US citizen, itself a commentary on the Fifth Amendment of the Bill of Rights (the "due process" clause), is removed from the selection in order to outline the broader claim that US citizens are not immune from targeted killings. Here, Holder argues (§6) that the usage of lethal force against a US citizen becomes justified only if three conditions are met: (1) the US government determines that the individual poses an imminent threat of violent attack; (2) capture is not feasible; (3) the operation is consistent with law of war principles.[25] Imminence itself remains the responsibility of the calculative logic of the Executive Branch and, in particular the President, as both are authorized by the Constitution (§4).[26] Even without the context of the Fifth Amendment argument, two controversial concepts emerge: the temporality and spatiality of the threat.

For Holder, there must neither be time nor space within which to capture the target. The imminence of the threat is a theme repeated throughout the selection (§4, 5, 6), and it is repeated within the context of the unconventional, if not unprecedented, nature of the threat. Yet, as was discovered upon the release of the "White Paper" penned by Stuart Delery, a former Assistant Attorney General, the definition of imminence established by the US Department of Justice (DOJ) was fluid. Imminence, the DOJ argued, "does not require the United States to have clear evidence that a specific attack on U.S. persons and interests will take place in the immediate future."[27] Additionally, if the capture of the suspected militant was to prove too time-sensitive, too risky, too costly of American lives and material, or to be denied by the host country, then, Delery concludes, "capture would not be feasible."[28] Imminence collapses the justification, as Holder suggests (§6), when he notes that the concept of imminence weighs the relevant window of time to attack the target against the likelihood of harm to civilians, both American and otherwise.

Finally, in a culmination of his citation of international law throughout the selection, Holder establishes the application by the United States of lethal force within its armed conflict with al-Qāʿida within the framework of International Humanitarian Law (IHL). For Holder, the use of lethal force must comply with four principles: (1) principle of necessity;

(2) principle of distinction; (3) principle of proportionality; (4) principle of humanity (§7). The first three principles, established throughout the Geneva Conventions and their Additional Protocols, demands the minimization of civilian casualties and harm alongside the interest of the belligerent party. Yet, here, Holder brings into focus the underlying essence of the argument for targeted killings. Although exceptional, Holder argues, such a tactic is made necessary by an imminent threat and is authorized by an alignment with both international and national legal principles as well as the final decision of the President.

The Second Source: The al-Zawahiri Selection

On the morning of November 19, 1995, a pair of men armed with rifles and grenades approached the gate of the Egyptian Embassy in Islamabad, Pakistan, and opened fire. As the Pakistani and Egyptian security forces responded, a midsize vehicle carrying 250 lbs. of explosives careened through the firefight toward the ironclad embassy gates where it exploded, throwing them open. As the security forces reeled from this second strike, a second vehicle, a Jeep, drove through the exploded gates and detonated near the central building. By the end of the attack, 17 Egyptian and Pakistani security guards, civilians, and diplomats lay dead, 60 were wounded, a wing of the Egyptian embassy had collapsed, and wings of the Japanese and Indonesian embassies were also damaged.[29] While multiple groups had claimed the attacks, it was the Egyptian Islamic Jihad (EIJ) group under the guidance of Ayman al-Zawahiri (b. 1951), an Egyptian physician who had planned the attack shortly after uniting EIJ with Usama bin Ladin in 1994, that was responsible for the attack.

Much like the Bush and Obama administrations, which faced criticism from their own allies for their targeted killing campaign that would begin five years later, al-Zawahiri faced considerable criticism from his own movement for having ordered the bombing.[30] Although jurists and exegetes debate the applicability of qur'anic proscriptions against self-killing (in Arabic, *qatl al-nafs* or *intihar*), in the hadith literature of the prophetic Sunna, there is little question: suicide is forbidden.[31] Further, al-Zawahiri faced criticisms that he had killed innocent Muslim civilians, again, a decisively forbidden crime in Islamic jurisprudence.[32] To answer these criticisms, al-Zawahiri published "The Remedy for the Chests of the Believers (*Shifa'sudur al-mu'minin*)" in March 1996. The text, which he fashioned as a lengthy essay offering advice (*nasiha*) and nonbinding legal rulings (*fatawa*, sing. *fatwa*), sought to answer two main controversies related to the attacks in Islamabad: the legality of martyrdom operations (*al-'amaliyyat al-istishhadiyya*) and the permissibility of striking the disbelievers (*kuffar*) when Muslims or those whom it is not permitted to kill are mixed among them.[33]

The selection presented for comparison here is entitled "Jihad, Martyrdom, and the Killing of Innocents."[34] While the Arabic edition of this text seems lost, the arrangement of the passages and the specific language used suggest that the text is a blend of two separate discussions of martyrdom operations: the *al-Shifa'* text written by al-Zawahiri in 1996 and another text, penned by 'Abd al-Qadir bin 'Abd al-'Aziz (Sayyid Imam al-Sharif or Dr. Fadl, b. 1950) in 1988, "The Manual for Preparing the Essential Provisions toward Jihad in the Cause of God (*al-'Umda fi i'dad al-'udda li-l-jihad fi sabil Allah*)."[35] Dr. Fadl, who was at one time a contemporary of al-Zawahiri in the EIJ, argued for a minimization of the traditional authorities of theories of struggling in God's path (*jihad fi sabil Allah*) and emphasized the individual duty shared by all Muslims to fight against those unjust regimes, Muslim and otherwise, who oppressed Muslims and prevented them from the full realization of their faith.

The struggle (jihad) that al-Zawahiri describes here is one of self-defense (see Appendix Two, "al-Zawahiri Sample," §5). Those who have beset the Muslim community, he argues, are the tyrants (*taghut*), disbelievers (*kafirun*, or "infidels" who have rejected God and God's messenger and prophet, Muhammad), those Muslims who befriend Jews and Christians, and those Muslim rulers who govern by that which is contrary to al-Zawahiri's interpretation of the shari'a (§2, 3, and 5).[36] This is the general framework by which the lives of Muslims are declared anathema and licit for lethal force by jihadi-salafis—a process labeled *takfir*, the pronouncement of disbelief. Political identity, in this framework, is established not on the basis of citizenship and nation-states—two entities considered by al-Zawahiri to be unlawful violations of God's law—but rather on the basis of Islamic creed (*'aqida*) realized in applied action within the world (*minhaj*). Therefore, innocent civilians are in reality only those Muslims who are sympathetic to the creed of al-Zawahiri and his jihadi-salafi allies.

What makes the contemporary world so threatening to al-Zawahiri, and what made the lives of the Egyptian and Pakistani security forces, diplomats, and civilians licit for lethal force, is the incumbent duty upon every individual Muslim to repel the advance of foreign political ideologies and those oppressive forces that prevent Muslims from installing the jihadi-salafi vision of God's divine law. All Muslims, he writes, must resist this advance as a duty (§4). However, al-Zawahiri cautions that Muslim civilians must be warned to avoid centers, offices, and organizations of disbelieving governments (§10). With this warning in place, however, the attackers should take care to minimize civilian casualties—including women and children—although some civilians may be lost as collateral damage because disbelieving leaders shield themselves with thick armor and embed themselves within civilian populations (§8). Yet, implying that the loss of a minimized few may be justified for a greater good (§4), he argues that one "should never abandon this obligatory duty [for jihad] because some Muslims might be killed mistakenly, not intentionally" (§5).

Al-Zawahiri considers an overwhelming number of forms of attack licit. Noting that it is "next to impossible to confront them in open warfare (§7)," he argues for an asymmetrical attack founded upon deception (§1) and an avoidance of open warfare. The global reach (§3) and the brutality of his enemy, in particular their torturing of prisoners and desire to use force to impose disbelieving modes of government and life upon Muslims (§5), suggests for al-Zawahiri the imminent obligation upon Muslims to fight with all means available to them. As he mentions within his text, the deciding factor on the justice of the taking of innocent Muslim lives and the individual who takes his or her own life in the act of self-defense is the question of intentionality: Is the act a service to Islam or out of depression and despair?[37] For al-Zawahiri, the latter is a forbidden suicide, while the former is an expression of the highest ideals of the faith.

Concluding a Comparison: The Horror of the Partisan

Each time I present this comparison to students, they fail to identify correctly the piece from al-Zawahiri as being written by a partisan of al-Qāʿida. Students settle quickly on the authorship of the Holder speech, often describing the author as variously American or Western, and from some sort of governmental or military career. Yet, for the Zawahiri piece, the closest answer students provide is "an educated Muslim jurist." On numerous occasions, there is an audible gasp when the students see that it was al-Zawahiri who authored the second text—particularly when they have already outlined parallels between the Holder text and his.

At first, what draws their attention across the two texts is the demand by both authors to protect innocent civilian lives from unjust and oppressive rule. Both groups draw connections between the arguments that gesture toward combative action as forms of self-defense and as a rationally calculated use of force that balances the cost of life against success. As for the tactics of war, the students turn their attention toward the usage of lawful, if not humane, approaches to fighting that reduce civilian casualties and become necessary due to the inaccessibility of the target. Finally, students discuss the sense of urgency with which both authors demand action, which in the case of the Holder memo is framed through "imminence." Typically, even understanding these parallels, the students remain uncomfortable. One summed it up succinctly, "We just made Osama into Bush and Obama."

In his course on the "Introduction to Religion," J. Z. Smith reports that students often complain that his courses do not conclude on a "happy ending."[38] Such, he argues elsewhere, is the nature of an introductory course: "No course can do everything, no course can be complete."[39] Within this exercise, I have had students report the same: "I see the point, professor, but I do not understand what to do now. What should I do?" Faced with this ethical question, I often reformulate it, remaining mindful that the goal of the exercise is to help students to understand that out of comparison a new, broader insight might be gained. The pre- and post-9/11, the actions of the US government and al-Qāʿida were not undertaken in a vacuum, they were instead responsive to one another and, as I write this, their relationship continues into its fifteenth year following September 11, 2001.

Two texts, in particular, prove instructive for the students as we analyze the lessons to be learned from this exercise in comparison and translation. In his *Suicide Bombing*, Talal Asad writes that what is particularly horrifying about a completed act of self-weaponization and self-dissolution is the inability of society to inscribe punishment upon the body responsible for the act. Where once, as Durkheim observes, legal punishment was based upon "popular outrage and is therefore motivated by passionate vengeance," Asad suggests that the dissolution of the body makes it unpunishable and refuses any act of retributive vengeance upon it (the "purple American fury of Morrow"). Instead, such a death remains forever "unregulated by the nation-state."[40] Disapproving of this anomic challenge to its world, the state seeks a preventive response in order to protect its citizens and deny other bodies the same fate.

It is ultimately within this response that I direct my students' contemplation toward the possibility of the circularity of the discourse shared by Holder and al-Zawahiri as well as Morrow and Bin Ladin. In an effort to describe the intersectionality of a humanity shared by jihadi and Westerner alike, Feisal Devji offers a commentary on Carl Schmitt's *Theory of the Partisan*, where he notes that "the partisan or non-state fighter emerges alongside the nation-state's army as its particular product."[41] Such is the argument of Asad above—the response of bin Ladin, we might assume Devji and Asad would argue, is a response that exists within a long history of Western foreign policy and military expeditions. During such expeditions, Asad writes, the deaths of civilians were made legitimate by the proclamation of states of emergency meant to repel the partisan. Here, the partisan became that which threatened and the declaration of crisis acted as absolutions of the guilt of those nation-states that sought to "authorize the killing of human beings [i.e. the partisan, and demand] the ultimate sacrifice of its citizens when they are at war."[42] This move to combat imminent threat, toward the state of emergency, Devji writes, reveals that the "state and its regular army can combat the partisan by adopting his methods wholly or in part, which puts their integrity and very constitution at risk if the threat of irregular warfare is very great."[43] It is on this point—the declaration of the imminent threat posed by the Other, and the declaration of the use of extraordinary technology and tactics (the drone, the martyrdom operations)—that students begin to realize the fullness of the circle tying bin Ladin's cries of hypocrisy and injustice to Morrow's demands of furious, if not righteous, retribution. Such is an act of translating the politics of fear into actions that foster anomie, and the drive of those attacked to remake the world by force again, elsewhere.

APPENDIX ONE: HOLDER SAMPLE

(§1) I know that . . . there are people currently plotting to murder Americans, who reside in distant countries as well as within our own borders. Disrupting and preventing these plots—using every available and appropriate tool to keep the American people safe—has been, and will remain, this Administration's top priority.

(§2) We are a nation at war. And, in this war, we face a nimble and determined enemy that cannot be underestimated. . . . But just as surely as we are a nation at war, we also are a nation of laws and values. Even when under attack, our actions must always be grounded on the bedrock of the Constitution. . . . History has shown us that it is also the most effective approach we can take in combating those who seek to do us harm. . . . This is not just my view. My judgment is shared by senior national security officials across the government. . . . [As President Obama said,] "Time and again, our values have been our best national security asset."

(§3) We must also recognize that there are instances where our government has the clear authority—and I would argue the responsibility—to defend the United States through the appropriate use of lawful force.

(§4) Because the United States is in an armed conflict, we are authorized to take action against enemy belligerents under international law. The Constitution empowers the President to protect the nation from any imminent threat of violent attack. And international law recognizes the inherent right of self-defense. None of this is changed by the fact that we are not in a conventional war. . . . Al Qaeda and its associates have directed several attacks . . . against us from countries other than Afghanistan. . . . The use of force in foreign territory would be consistent with these international legal principles if conducted, for example, with the consent of the nation involved—or after a determination that the nation is unable or unwilling to deal effectively with a threat to the United States. Furthermore, it is entirely lawful—under both United States law and applicable law of war principles—to target specific senior operational leaders of al Qaeda and associated forces. This is not a novel concept.

(§5) Some have called such operations "assassinations." They are not, and the use of that loaded term is misplaced. Assassinations are unlawful killings. Here, for the reasons I have given, the US government's use of lethal force in self defense against a leader of al Qaeda or an associated force who presents an imminent threat of violent attack would not be unlawful. . . . Now, it is an unfortunate but undeniable fact that some of the threats we face come from a small number of United States citizens who have decided to commit violent attacks against their own country from abroad. . . . It's clear that ~~United States~~ citizenship alone does not make such individuals immune from being targeted. . . . Any decision to use lethal force against a ~~United States citizen~~—even one intent on murdering ~~Americans~~ and who has become an operational leader ~~of al-Qaeda~~ in a foreign land—is among the gravest that ~~government~~ leaders can face. The ~~American~~ people can be—and deserve to be—assured that actions taken in their defense are consistent with their values and their laws. ~~So, although I cannot discuss or confirm any particular program or operation,~~ I believe it is important to explain these legal principles publicly.

(§6) An operation using lethal force in a foreign country, targeted against ~~a U.S. citizen~~ who is a senior ~~operational~~ leader of ~~al-Qaeda~~ or associated forces, and who is actively engaged in planning to kill ~~Americans~~, would be lawful at least in the following circumstances: First, ~~the U.S. government~~ has determined, after a thorough and careful review, that the individual poses an imminent threat of violent attack ~~against the United States~~; second, capture is not feasible; and third, the operation would be conducted in a manner consistent with applicable law ~~of war~~ principles. The evaluation of whether an individual presents an "imminent threat" incorporates considerations of the relevant window of opportunity to act, the possible harm that missing the window would cause to civilians, and the likelihood of heading off future disastrous attacks ~~against the United States~~

(§7) Of course, any such use of lethal force ~~by the United States~~ will comply with the four fundamental law of ~~war~~ principles governing the use of force. The principle of necessity requires that the target have definite ~~military~~ value. The principle of distinction requires that only lawful targets—such as combatants, civilians directly participating in hostilities, and military objectives—may be targeted intentionally. Under the principle of proportionality, the anticipated collateral damage must not be excessive in relation to the anticipated ~~military~~ advantage. Finally, the principle of humanity requires us to use weapons that will not inflict unnecessary suffering.

Appendix Two: Zawahiri Sample

(§1) Deception in warfare requires that ~~the mujahid~~ bide his time and wait for an opportunity against his enemy, while avoiding confrontation at all possible costs. . . . Nonetheless, this deception needs to be gauged by the *shari'a's* prescriptions—for all advantages not regulated through the *shari'a* law are unworthy. Therefore engaging in that which is forbidden as a pretext for deception is inexcusable.

(§2) Among those needing to be fought at this day and age are those rulers who govern the people without ~~the *shari'a*~~—they who fight against the people ~~of Islam~~, who befriend the ~~infidels~~ from among the ~~Jews~~, ~~Christians~~, and ~~others~~ .... All *ulema* are agreed that leadership should never fall into the hands ~~of an infidel~~, or if ~~infidelity~~ should suddenly descend upon him, and he becomes an outcast not ruling in accordance to ~~the *sharia* of Allah~~, his authority diminishes and it becomes a duty to ~~revolt against him and eject him~~.

(§3) Today . . . the world is given over to the tyrants, thanks to the *fatwas* that command people to abandon ~~jihad~~. . . . Therefore, if the ~~believers~~ are weak, they are to ~~wage jihad~~ with their hearts and tongues; if they are able, they are to enjoin what is good and forbid what is evil, fight ~~the infidels~~, and spread ~~the call of tawhid~~. This is how to differentiate between the followers ~~of the messengers of tawhid~~ and the hypocrite ~~imams~~, who sell ~~the verses of Allah~~ for a paltry sum in service to the ~~apostates and~~ enemies ~~of Islam~~....

(§4) Often mixed among the ~~infidels~~, whom ~~the mujahidin~~ target in warfare, are those whom it is not permitted to kill—such as ~~Muslims~~, *dhimmis*, women and children, and so forth. So is ~~jihad~~, which is assigned to us, to be abandoned on account of their protected ~~blood~~, or is killing ones such as these—accidentally, not on purpose—~~forgiven~~ in the face of the highest goods that would be realized from waging *jihad* against the ~~infidels~~?

(§5) When ~~Muslims~~ are defending their religion and their sancties, and the ~~infidels~~ are surrounding them from every corner, [if] they are captured, [then] they torture and murder the ~~Muslims~~; or when the ~~infidels~~ settle in the lands ~~of Islam~~ trying to impose ~~infidelity~~ by the ~~power of the sword~~ [i.e., by the force of arms], making ~~Muslims~~ embrace their laws after first forfeiting the *shariʿa* ~~of God~~—in these situations it becomes a binding obligation on every ~~Muslim~~ to fight them anyway he can. He should never abandon this obligatory duty because some ~~Muslims~~ might be killed mistakenly, not intentionally.

(§6) [It is permissible] to bombard ~~the idolaters~~ even if ~~Muslims~~ and those whom [one is] ~~are~~ cautioned against killing are intermingled with them as long as there is a need or an obligation for ~~Muslims~~ to do so, or if not striking leads to a ~~delay of the *jihad*~~.

(§7) Bombarding the organizations of ~~the infidels and apostates~~ in this day and age has become an imperative of ~~*jihad*~~ in our war with the ~~idolatrous tyrants~~, where weakened *mujahidin* battle ~~massive and~~ vigilant armies ~~armed to the teeth~~: it has become next to impossible to confront them in open warfare.

(§8) The ~~tyrants and~~ leaders of ~~the infidels~~ shelter themselves in armored vehicles with lots and varied forms of intricate security measures, so that it has become exceedingly difficult to reach them without employing ~~explosives and rockets~~ and other missile weaponry. Therefore it is permissible to fire at them. The ~~tyrants and~~ enemies of ~~Allah~~ always see to it that their organizations and military escorts are set among the people and populace, making it extremely difficult to hunt them down in isolation. But if we hold off our ~~*jihad*~~ against them for this [reason], the ~~*jihad*~~ would be delayed.

(§9) These means of reaching them—explosives and missiles—have proven to be very effective in ~~Egypt~~, Algeria, ~~Palestine~~, and ~~Lebanon~~, wreaking havoc among the ~~ranks of the~~ enemies ~~of Allah Almighty~~.

(§10) The ~~*mujahidin*~~ should see to it that they repeatedly warn the ~~Muslims~~ who are intermixed with ~~the tyrants~~ and their aides to stay away from their centers, offices, and organizations—but this warning should be done in a general way.

Notes

1. Lance Morrow, "The Case for Rage and Retribution," *Time*, September 12, 2001.

2. Cofer Black, "Joint Investigation into September 11th: Fifth Public Hearing," Joint House/Senate Intelligence Committee Hearing, September 26, 2002.

3. Usama bin Ladin, "To the Americans," in *Messages to the World: The Statements of Osama bin Laden*, ed. Bruce Lawrence and trans. James Howarth (London: Verso Books, 2005), 170.

4. Jihadi-salafism has a multifaceted genealogy. In general, those who self-identify as jihadi-salafis argue that the most authentic expression of Islam was the practice of Muhammad (570–632 CE) and his earliest companions and followers (referred to collectively as the *salaf*). In the modern period, citing arguments ranging from the medieval period's Taqi al-Din Ibn Taymiyya (d. 1328) to the Egyptian Muslim Brother Sayyid Qutb (1906–1966), jihadi-salafis argue that the only means by which the Islam of the *salaf* may be practiced is by a violent struggle (jihad) to resist all forces in opposition. For further information, see Roel Meijer, ed., *Global Salafism: Islam's New Religious Movement* (New York: Columbia University Press, 2009).

5. For bin Ladin's discussions of hypocrisy, see Flagg Miller, "Dangers and Hopes (*Makhatir w-Amal*)," in *The Audacious Ascetic: What the Bin Laden Tapes Reveal about Al-Qaʿida* (New York: Oxford University Press, 2015), 153–177.

6. J. Z. Smith, *Imagining Religion: From Babylon to Jonestown* (Chicago: University of Chicago Press, 1982), 104.

7. For a history of jihad in Islamic thought, see Asma Afsaruddin, *Striving in the Path of God* (New York: Oxford University Press, 2015).

8. Smith, *Imagining Religion: From Babylon to Jonestown*, 104.

9. Smith, *Imagining Religion: From Babylon to Jonestown*, 110.

10. Alain Badiou, "September 11, 2001: Philosophy and the 'War against Terrorism,'" in *Polemics*, trans. Steve Corcoran (New York: Verso Books, 2006), 22.

11. Kenneth T. Walsh, "George W. Bush's 'Bullhorn' Moment," *U.S. News*, April 25, 2013.

12. The full definition reads, "A *religion* is (1) a system of symbols which acts to (2) establish powerful, pervasive, and long-lasting moods and motivations in men by (3) formulating conceptions of a general order of existence and (4) clothing these conceptions with such an aura of factuality that (5) the moods and motivations seem uniquely realistic," see Clifford Geertz, *The Interpretation of Cultures* (New York: Basic Books, 1973), 90.

13. bin Ladin, "To the Americans," 164.

14. Peter Berger, *The Sacred Canopy* (New York: Anchor Books, 1997), 21.

15. Badiou, "Philosophy and the 'War against Terrorism,'" 23.

16. Bruce Lincoln, *Holy Terrors* (Chicago: University of Chicago Press, 2003), 27.

17. Lincoln, *Holy Terrors*, 27.

18. Arjun Appadurai, *Fear of Small Numbers: An Essay on the Geography of Anger* (Durham, NC: Duke University Press, 2006), 92.

19. In the classroom, the full texts, included here as appendices, have large "black box" redactions, here, in the appendices, I have opted for a "strike-through" to provide context and to assist the reader with engaging in the exercise.

20. Eric Holder, "Speech at the Northwestern School of Law," US Department of Justice, March 5, 2012, https://www.justice.gov/opa/speech/attorney-general-eric-holder-speaks -northwestern-university-school-law.

21. Holder, "Speech at the Northwestern School of Law."

22. Holder, "Speech at the Northwestern School of Law."

23. Cf. United Nations, Charter of the United Nations, June 26, 1945, http://www.un.org/en /charter-united-nations/.

24. See, for example, Ashley S. Deeks, "'Unwilling or Unable': Toward a Normative Framework for Extraterritorial Self-Defense," *Virginia Journal of International Law* 52, no. 3 (2012): 485–550.

25. Holder, "Speech at the Northwestern School of Law."

26. Holder is likely referring to the framework of the Authorization of the Use of Military Force (2001) and its predecessor the War Powers Resolution (1973), both of which created an expansionary executive authority for war and the former of which established that the president is given the authorization to use "all necessary and appropriate force" by the Congress in lieu of a declaration of war (per Article II of the Constitution). See, respectively, Authorization for the Use of Military Force, Pub. L. No. 107-40, 115 Stat. 224-225 (2001) and War Powers Resolution, Pub. L. No. 93-148, 87 Stat. 555 (1973), codified at 33 U.S.C. §1541-1548 (1973). For a discussion of the Bush administration's development of jurisprudence around the AUMF, see Charlie Savage, *Takeover: The Return of the Imperial Presidency & Subversion of American Democracy* (New York: Little, Brown, 2007), and for the Obama administration's development, see Charlie Savage, *Power Wars: Inside Obama's Post-9/11 Presidency* (New York: Little, Brown, 2015).

27. Stuart Delery, "Lawfulness of a Lethal Operation Directed against a U.S. Citizen Who Is a Senior Operational Leader of al-Qaʿida or an Associated Force," Department of Justice White Paper, November 8, 2011, http://www.documentcloud.org/documents/602342-draft-white-paper.html.

28. Delery, "Lawfulness of a Lethal Operation."

29. See Associated Press, "Bombing at Egypt's Embassy in Pakistan Kills 15," *New York Times*, November 20, 1995; and Tim McGirk, "Bomb Kills 14 at Egypt's Embassy," *The Independent*, November 19, 1995, for further details.

30. For further on this debate, see Lawrence Wright, *The Looming Tower* (New York: Alfred A. Knopf, 2006), 217–219.

31. See, for example, Franz Rosenthal, "Suicide in Islam," *Journal of the American Oriental Society* 66, no. 3 (July-September 1946): 239–259.

32. See, for example, J. N. D. Anderson, "Homicide in Islamic Law," *Bulletin of the School of Oriental and African Studies* 13, no. 4 (1951): 811–828.

33. al-Zawahiri, *Shifāʾ sudur al-muʾminin,* Ilmway.com, http://www.ilmway.com/site/maqdis /MS_13066.html.

34. For the full text, see Ayman al-Zawahiri, "Jihad, Martyrdom, and the Killing of Innocents," in *The Al Qaeda Reader,* ed. Raymond Ibrahim (New York: Broadway Books, 2001), 141–171.

35. Cf. ʿAbd al-Qadir bin ʿAbd al-ʿAziz, *al-ʿUmda fī iʿdad al-ʿudda li-l-jihad fī sabil Allah,* Ilmway.com, accessed October 1, 2016, http://www.ilmway.com/site/maqdis/MS_636. Consider, for example, that several of the opening paragraphs of the Ibrahim text on "deceit" (*al-khudʿ*) is a word-for-word plagiarism of Sayyid Imam's *al-ʿUmda* (cf. Ibrahim, "Jihad," 142 and ʿAbd al-Qadir, *al-ʿUmda,* 338). Further, parts one ("The Shariʿa Perspective on Martyrdom Operations") and two ("The Permissibility of Bombarding Infidels When Muslims and Others Are Not Permitted to Be Killed Are Dispersed among Them") of the English text from Ibrahim almost exactly follow similar sections (down to the textual citations) from al-Zawahiri's *al-Shifāʾ* (cf. pp. 15, 50).

36. The concept of *taghut* is a term used in the Qurʾan (cf. 2:256 and 4:51), where it refers to idols or other forces of evil and oppression. For al-Zawahiri and other jihadi-salafi authors, the meaning of *taghut* seems to parallel the multidimensional definition of Muhammad ibn ʿAbd al-Wahhab (d. 1798), which includes the question of political or religious leadership that governs on the basis of other than that which God intended in God's divine law.

37. al-Zawahiri, "Jihad," 157.

38. J. Z. Smith, "Basic Problems in the Study of Religion," in *On Teaching Religion,* ed. Christopher I. Lehrich (New York: Oxford University Press, 2013), 27.

39. J. Z. Smith, "The Introductory Course: Less is Better," in Lehrich, *On Teaching Religion,* 13.

40. Talal Asad, *On Suicide Bombing* (New York: Columbia University Press, 2007), 90. The citation of Durkheim is Asad's.

41. Feisal Devji, *The Terrorist in Search of Humanity* (New York: Columbia University Press, 2008), 138.

42. Asad, *On Suicide Bombing,* 19.

43. Devji, *The Terrorist in Search of Humanity,* 139.

NATHAN S. FRENCH is Assistant Professor of Comparative Religion and an affiliate of Middle East and Islamic Studies at Miami University.

chapter nine

TEACHING ISLAMOPHOBIA IN THE AGE OF ISIS

Todd Green

THE CHALLENGE OF ADDRESSING MISINFORMATION and preju-
dices about Islam in an academic setting is unique neither to the post-9/11
era nor to the age of ISIS. Even so, college and university instructors teach
students who have come of age in a time when Muslims are increasingly
cast as public enemy number one. The very questions many students ask
about Islam, and the information they seek, reflect the clash of civilizations mindset that has dominated domestic and foreign policy as well as
mass media since 9/11. Non-Muslim students in particular often carry
with them deeply engrained assumptions about the incompatibility of Islam with Western values or about Islam's violent and misogynistic nature.
These assumptions have only intensified with the rise of ISIS.

How do we address these assumptions in the classroom? Should dispelling negative views of Islam and Muslims be one of the objectives in introductory courses on Islam? Should it be the primary objective? Or is it possible to teach Islam on its own terms, or at least to develop courses on Islam
that are not primarily driven by the need to tackle anti-Muslim stereotypes?

Many of the essays in this volume propose compelling ways to address
these questions in Islamic studies or Middle Eastern studies courses. I
want to tackle these issues from a different starting point. Instead of focusing on the objectives and challenges of teaching Islamic studies, I will
explore the significance of teaching about and against Islamophobia. I
will propose that a more effective way to address and deconstruct stereotypes, biases, and misinformation concerning Islam is through a course on
Islamophobia.

All of this may seem obvious. Yet the burden of addressing anti-Islam
stereotypes continues to fall heavily on Islamic studies courses, particularly
at the introductory level. Two explanations for this burden come to mind.
First, few college and university courses exist that focus primarily or exclusively on Islamophobia, despite the fact that Islamophobia studies is an

increasingly recognized discipline.[1] Second, the assumption that Islamophobia is largely driven by lack of information or knowledge of Islam is commonplace not only among students but even among some Islamic studies scholars. But as this edited volume demonstrates, using an Islamic studies course to dispel Islamophobia is no small feat, and a considerable amount of pedagogical creativity is needed to make this work given that ignorance of Islam does not fully account for the existence and persistence of Islamophobia.

Even if we acknowledge and address these problems, we must also wrestle with the fact that very little pedagogical literature exists to guide us in developing courses on Islamophobia, with a few exceptions. One is A. Kevin Reinhart's essay "On the 'Introduction to Islam'" in the seminal *Teaching Islam* (2003). Reinhart calls attention to challenges in introductory courses on Islam that I believe are pertinent to survey courses on Islamophobia as well, particularly the "pseudo-knowledge" of Islam that students bring with them into the classroom via the media and the essentializing of Islam that often exists in college and university curricula.[2] Another helpful resource is the edited volume *Teaching against Islamophobia* (2010), which provides useful perspectives on addressing Islamophobia in politics, popular culture, and the media.[3]

More recently, we are witnessing the development of resources for Islamophobia courses via social media and the internet, including the #IslamophobiaIsRacism syllabus generated in 2017 by a group of Muslim academics.[4] These efforts will undoubtedly produce fruitful discussions concerning how better to conceptualize and teach courses on Islamophobia, but much work still needs to be done when it comes to developing a sturdy pedagogical framework for these courses.

My modest goal in this chapter is to present and discuss the contours of an introductory course on Islamophobia. Drawing on my own experiences teaching such a course at a liberal arts college, I will propose topics that are promising in helping students identify, analyze, and deconstruct anti-Muslim narratives.[5] I will do this with an eye toward how such a course both reduces the burden that falls on Islamic studies courses to counter Islamophobia and helps students better understand the historical and political forces that give rise to Islamophobia.

WHAT THE STUDY OF ISLAMOPHOBIA IS (AND IS NOT)

In my experience of teaching an Islamophobia course, students often assume that the core of what we will be doing is learning Islamic teachings and practices that refute prevalent stereotypes. In other words, they expect some sort of introduction to Islam course, assuming the only difference will be that an Islamophobia course will address negative views of Islam more overtly than typical introductory courses on Islam.

It is important to be transparent about what the study of Islamophobia is and is not. The study of Islamophobia is not synonymous with the study of Islam. The study of Islam includes, among other things, an engagement with Islamic texts, teachings, and traditions that span many centuries and diverse cultures. It is the study of how Muslims, past and present, make sense of these resources in their daily lives and in the context of particular social, legal, and political systems.

The study of Islamophobia, by contrast, is focused on the anxieties and fears directed toward Islam and those who practice it. I frequently tell non-Muslim audiences that as a scholar of Islamophobia (and as someone who is not a Muslim), I primarily study "us," not "them." I want to understand "our" anxieties regarding Islam, the historical and political forces that have given rise to them, and their manifestations in the social and political orders of Western nations. To the extent that I study Muslims, I do so with an eye toward how Islamophobia affects their lives and livelihoods.

Some obvious overlap exists between the study of Islam and Islamophobia. When studying the latter, scholars and students inevitably piece together some understanding of Islam and its rich history. Analyzing stereotypes prompts one to seek out a more complete picture of that which is stereotyped. So yes, I do tell students that we will be learning about Islam as we study Islamophobia, but the manner in which such learning occurs is on an "as needed" basis, exploring Islamic texts and listening to Muslim voices that fill out the picture that is distorted by or missing from particular anti-Muslim narratives. But this piecing together is secondary to the course's primary focus on the causes and consequences of the non-Muslim majority's fears and anxieties.

The reason for spelling all of this out on day one (and repeating it frequently in the first several weeks) is that many students are unaccustomed to analyzing the complex forces that give rise to systemic prejudice. In the case of Islamophobia, most students assume that if they are equipped with objective facts about Islam they will have all they need to understand Islamophobia and to determine to what degree it can be rationalized or refuted. What students don't yet know at such an early stage is that absorbing "facts" about Islam does not lead to clarity on how Islamophobia arises and takes root. The reasons for this cannot be fully explained on the first day, but my job at this point is to complicate this picture and to point out the persistence of prejudice against maligned minority communities (religious, racial, or otherwise) even if majority populations have access to accurate information.

The related task that must be addressed early on is setting out the course objectives. I set out three objectives in my Islamophobia course, the first of which has already been noted above—identifying and deconstructing anti-Muslim prejudices and discrimination, with particular attention to the European and US contexts. An Islamophobia course need not be limited to the West. But to give the course focus, with an eye to the particular challenges Muslims face as minority communities, I design the course specifically to address Western Islamophobia.

A second objective is to separate legitimate questions and criticism of Muslims or Islam from anti-Muslim prejudice. Some critics worry that the term "Islamophobia" can stifle freedom of speech and inhibit a robust, open debate about Islam. Most scholars of Islamophobia take this concern seriously. Not every criticism of Islam is Islamophobic. It is possible to disagree with Muslims on a wide array of religious teachings or political matters without lapsing into prejudicial behavior. A question that runs throughout my Islamophobia course is how to determine when an individual, organization, or larger political entity has crossed the line from a plausible criticism or concern into Islamophobia territory. I lay out three criteria for making this determination. Criticism of Islam should: (1) be based on elements of the religion that many Muslims recognize as part of their faith and should avoid guilt by association or essentializing assumptions; (2) not take the form of hate speech or endanger the safety of Muslims; (3) not be translated into actions that undermine religious liberties for Muslims.

A final goal is to help students develop sensitivity to which individuals in a society have the privilege of telling the story of a religious tradition. It is important for students to grasp that Muslims are seldom in a position to shape the public narrative of Islam in Western contexts. It's often non-Muslims, including terrorism analysts, media pundits, politicians, and anti-Islam activists whose voices are heard and amplified and who often have the power to influence public attitudes. Attention to these dynamics better attunes students to the systemic and structural nature of anti-Muslim bias, not to mention the concerted effort by some people in positions of power to marginalize and mute Muslim voices in order to promote Islamophobia for personal or political gain.

WHAT IS ISLAMOPHOBIA?

After laying out course objectives, the first topic in my syllabus pertains to the larger academic debate over the very concept of "Islamophobia." Where did this word come from? How should we define it? What are the most common scholarly questions and criticisms raised about it? These questions, in turn, generate additional questions that complexify understandings of what sort of prejudice Islamophobia is and how it might differ from other prejudices.

The working definition we use in class comes from a study by the Runnymede Trust in the United Kingdom issued in 1997 called *Islamophobia: A Challenge for Us All*.[6] The study, often referred to as the Runnymede Report, was conducted in response to growing anti-Muslim sentiment in Britain in the years following the Iranian Revolution of 1979 and the Rushdie Affair of 1988-1989 as well as the ongoing Israeli-Palestinian conflict. The report defines Islamophobia as "dread or hatred of Islam" that translates into exclusionary and discriminatory practices aimed at Muslims.[7] The Runnymede Report proceeds to elaborate on a list of "closed" (biased) views of Islam that constitute Islamophobia, including the belief that Islam is monolithic, that Islam is inferior to the West, and that Islam is inherently hostile toward the West.

The advantage of using the Runnymede Report as a starting point is that I am able at an early stage to present scenarios to students—current events, controversial remarks made by public figures, and so on—and have them think through whether we are dealing with Islamophobia or plausible criticisms in light of the closed categories employed in the report. For example, I provide them with a quote from the prominent anti-Islam critic Ayaan Hirsi Ali, who argues that Islam "is incompatible with the principles of liberty that are at the heart of the Enlightenment legacy."[8] Has Hirsi Ali offered a legitimate criticism of Islam, irrespective of whether we agree with her? Or is she perpetuating a closed or prejudicial view of Islam that plays on stereotypes and is intended to malign an entire tradition? It's a challenging exercise for students, in part because many may not feel they know enough about Islam to evaluate the claim. But this opens the door to a larger conversation about whether knowing more about either the European Enlightenment or modern Islamic reforming movements would make a difference, and whether one can analyze assumptions embedded in the quote without any formal training in Islamic studies. It also prompts students to ask questions about Hirsi Ali's background and the context of the quote that might affect how the quote would be interpreted by a non-Muslim audience. In short, students are already thinking about one of the main course objectives—what distinguishes the study of Islamophobia from Islam—by reflecting on whether an in-depth knowledge of Islam is the key to understanding a particular criticism of Islam's presumed intellectual shortcomings.

While I address several other overarching questions in this section of the course, one that is worth pointing out here is whether Islamophobia is fundamentally fear of a religion or hostility toward a people. Is Islamophobia religious bigotry? Is it racism? These questions follow us throughout the course, but it's helpful to expose students at this point to the category of cultural racism.[9] Islamophobia is not racially blind, but it's also not a reproduction of older forms of racism based on biological inferiority. Cultural racism involves hatred or hostility based on religious beliefs, cultural traditions, and ethnic backgrounds. When animosity is expressed toward Muslims, it's often in the form of perceived cultural and racial inferiority. Muslims are not a race, as even the most ardent Islamophobes are willing to point out, but they are *racialized* by majority populations, and essentialist qualities are often projected onto them. The category of cultural racism helps students to consider how racism factors into the Islamophobia equation, and it provides a bridge to understanding how Islamophobia connects to other forms of bigotry in which religious communities are racialized—namely anti-Semitism.

A HISTORY OF ISLAMOPHOBIA

What is the connection between Islamophobia today and anxieties toward Islam that have persisted throughout much of Western history? The bulk of my Islamophobia course covers modern historical and political events, but I want students to recognize that anti-Muslim prejudice did not simply materialize after 9/11 or with the rise of ISIS. Western societies have inherited a prejudice that dates back to the earliest encounters between Muslims and European Christians. A survey of this history sheds much needed light on how long-standing political tensions drive much of the anti-Muslim sentiment we encounter even today. From the Crusades and *Reconquista* through battles with the Ottoman Empire, Europeans struggled with Muslims for territory and political power, viewing them as significant obstacles to creating and sustaining empires and nations. These struggles forged the lenses through which European Christians imagined and viewed Islam.

A helpful illustration of how political rivalry shaped European understandings of Islam is found in the writings of Martin Luther, the famed German Reformer. Luther had far more knowledge of Islam than most of his European contemporaries. He even spent time studying a Latin translation of the Qur'an. But his greater knowledge did not lead to a more benevolent interpretation of Islam, as evidenced in his treatise *On War against the Turk* (1529).[10] While Luther did put forth theological reasons for his hostility to Islam, notably his belief that, like Roman Catholicism, Islam trafficked in justification by works, he never deviated from classic medieval stereotypes, such as the belief that Islam was a violent, barbaric religion. Mostly, Luther sought to garner support for a war against the

Ottoman Empire in light of its military encroachment into Europe. His interpretations of Islam cannot be separated from this larger political context.

A survey of premodern understandings of Islam sheds light on how political tensions and rivalries consistently shaped the way European Christians viewed Muslims and vice versa. Even when more sympathetic portrayals of Islam were forthcoming, such as during the Enlightenment, fears of the Muslim "Other" as threats and obstacles to European political power did not fade. If anything, such fears only intensified in the context of nineteenth-century European colonialism.

Colonialism and Orientalism

From the Middle Ages onward, both Islamic empires and European Christian kingdoms vied with one another for political and military hegemony. Islamic empires had the upper hand for much of that history. This changed in the nineteenth century with the decline of the Ottoman Empire and European colonial expansion into the Middle East, Africa, and Asia. By the turn of the twentieth century, most Muslim-majority regions were subject to European imperial rule. Europe's investment in the colonial enterprise shaped the ways Europeans imagined and understood Muslims and Islam.

This introduction to European colonialism marks a crucial turning point in the course, both for historical and theoretical reasons. Historically, European colonialism sets the stage for many of the contemporary conflicts between the West and Muslim-majority countries, particularly those in the Middle East. Since college students in the United States often have a cursory knowledge of this history, it's important to provide them with this context. Theoretically, this is the section of the course in which I introduce students both to the rise of Orientalism and to Edward Said's postcolonial critique of Orientalism.

Students read and reflect on the images of Muslims and Islam as presented in nineteenth-century Orientalist literature and art. For example, a colleague of mine from the art history department gives a guest presentation on Muslim and Turkish women as depicted in French Orientalist art. Students examine paintings such as Jean August Dominique Ingres's *The Turkish Bath* (1862) and Jean-Leon Gerome's *The Slave Market* (1866) in order to consider how European artists imagined Muslim women. The women they encounter in these paintings are slaves, prostitutes, and members of harems. They are erotic yet domesticated, sexually available yet exploited. The point of this exercise is not to determine whether these paintings are accurate, "objective" representations. We focus on what the paintings might say about the painters or even about the intended audiences in

Europe. We also focus on the political context that gives rise to European interests in exotic feminine figures in the so-called Orient.

This exercise opens the door to the postcolonial critique of Orientalism and the work of Edward Said. I assign selections from Said's groundbreaking work *Orientalism* (1978).[11] Students struggle with Said, mostly due to the dense nature of his writing. But I have found that slowing down and spending time with Said pays off down the road. It is in wrestling with Said's critique of Orientalism that students really start to grasp the problems that arise with any claims in the West to an objective knowledge of Islam.

Drawing on Foucault, Said makes the important link between knowledge and power in the context of the academic study of Islam. Western knowledge of Islam, Said argues, is always the product of a particular discourse that is bound up with power. One excerpt from *Orientalism* comes to mind when we have this discussion in class: "I myself believe that Orientalism is more particularly valuable as a sign of European Atlantic power over the Orient than it is a veridic discourse about the Orient (which is what, in its academic and scholarly form, it claims to be). Nevertheless, what we must respect and try to grasp is the sheer knitted-together strength of Orientalist discourse, its very close ties to the enabling socio-economic and political institutions, and its redoubtable durability."[12] Said insists that Western discourse about the Orient reflects the drive for political domination over the Orient. Knowledge of Islam and Muslims is inextricably linked to power over Islam and Muslims. Orientalism as an academic discipline reinforces the European colonial project.

These are sophisticated arguments, but when students begin to grasp them, class discussions take on a new dimension. Students consider the possibility that Western interest in Islam, including in academic settings, has never been objective or neutral but has been connected to and influenced by particular political projects. This is often the point in the course when students begin to accept the premise introduced on the first day, that the academic study of Islam neither automatically nor necessarily eliminates prejudice against Islam. Equipped with this insight, students are better able to interpret and deconstruct neo-Orientalist clash of civilizations theories put forth by scholars such as Bernard Lewis or Samuel Huntington, theories that I present at the end of this section of the course.[13]

9/11 AND THE WAR ON TERROR

Now that the historical and theoretical framework has been established, students are ready to delve into Islamophobia in the post-9/11 context. It is important, however, to strengthen this framework, which is why I begin this section of the course with a discussion of US imperialism since World War II, with attention to how the United States' Cold War rivalry with the Soviet Union heightened the former's interest in the Middle East and other Muslim-majority regions. Students learn about the rise of political Islam, also known as Islamism, and important instances in which the United States supported more violent Islamist ideologies to further its own imperial interests, such as in the Soviet-Afghan War. They also learn about the United States' support for authoritarian regimes in the Middle East, its military presence in the region, and the challenges raised by its strong alliance with Israel. Again, students are drawn to concrete political circumstances that paved the way for how a Western nation has engaged Muslims.

This attention to US imperialism sets the stage for an analysis of the Islamophobic justifications behind the Bush administration's response to the 9/11 attacks. To galvanize support for the War on Terror and thereby further its larger imperial ambitions, the administration deployed three anti-Islam tropes to support the war: defending America against Muslim terrorists (because of Islam's violent nature), introducing democracy to Muslim countries (because Islam is anti-democratic), and liberating Muslim women (because Islam is misogynistic). Students study speeches, political ads, official statements at press conferences, and radio addresses that invoke these tropes.

This section of the course brings home the point that the Bush administration's case for the War on Terror, and the American public's initial support for the war, depended heavily on Islamophobic stereotypes. These stereotypes, in turn, diverted public attention away from the administration's desire to use the war to expand its military presence and to create regimes in the Middle East friendlier to US economic and political interests.

EUROPE AND THE MUSLIM "ENEMY WITHIN"

The United States was not alone in succumbing to fears of an "Islamic threat." Anti-Muslim panic began to sweep throughout Europe as well after 9/11. Some of this was due to the ongoing demographic changes in Europe that began with significant Muslim migration after World War II. Fears of "Eurabia" and the "Islamization" of Europe among Far Right elements, however, started to become more mainstream in the decade after 9/11. These fears were exacerbated by the new realities of violent extremism, including a series of events on European soil that generated concerns that Muslims posed a grave threat to security and to Western values.

Students survey some of these key events, including the Rushdie Affair (1988–1989), the murder of Theo Van Gogh (2004), the Madrid and London bombings (2004 and 2005), and the Danish cartoon controversy

(2005–2006). To this list, of course, can be added more recent episodes such as the *Charlie Hebdo* attacks (2015), the Paris attacks (2015), and the Manchester Arena bombing (2017). All of these events aggravated Islamophobia and contributed to a climate in which it became acceptable to question whether Islam and Muslims belong to the European political and social order.

The larger purpose in analyzing these events is to help students reflect on what preexisting tensions led to them, what larger issues of European/Western identity were raised by them, and how Muslim communities responded to or were otherwise affected by them. What emerges in most instances is the importance of political factors for understanding these events, particularly in episodes of violent extremism. A notable example comes from the videotaped confession of Mohammed Siddique Khan, the leader in the London bombings. To justify the violence he and his collaborators intended to commit, he stated: "Your democratically elected governments continuously perpetuate atrocities against my people all over the world. And your support of them makes you directly responsible . . . [U]ntil you stop the bombing, gassing, imprisonment and torture of my people we will not stop this fight."[14] Khan was not reacting to some decontextualized interpretation of the Qur'an but to a particular political context involving the military actions of the British government along with the British people's presumed support for them.

What also comes to the fore in this section is the double standards sometimes involved in reactions to these events. For example, editors at *Jyllands-Posten*, the Danish newspaper that published inflammatory cartoons of the Prophet Muhammad in 2005, insisted that Muslim leaders were too sensitive to criticism and incapable of embracing the freedom of expression that is crucial to all Western societies. And yet two years before, this same newspaper refused to publish cartoons that mocked the resurrection of Jesus for fear of the reaction it might generate. Moreover, several European countries had blasphemy laws well into the modern era, and many today have hate speech laws that prohibit public expressions that demonize and denigrate people based on race, ethnicity, religion, sexuality, and so forth. Muslims and non-Muslims alike express concerns over the parameters of freedom of speech, but as the cartoon controversy illustrates, it's usually Muslims who are painted as anti-Western and anti-modern in debates over this freedom.

PROFESSIONAL ISLAMOPHOBIA

After covering the significant events of the past two decades that fuel and frame much of the Islamophobia in the West, the course turns its attention to those individuals and institutions beyond prominent politicians who wield significant power in shaping the narrative of Islam. The first topic in this regard is what I call "Professional Islamophobia."[15] Professional Islamophobia refers to a cadre of right-wing politicians, anti-Islam activists and bloggers, and disgruntled Muslims or ex-Muslims who make a career out of demonizing Muslims. Those who participate in this network have powerful publishing and media platforms from which to stir up anxieties toward the Muslim "Other."

One effective means of introducing this topic is to reference several reports that highlight the funding that professional Islamophobes receive and the political impact they have. One report that works well is by the Council on American-Islamic Relations and is called *Confronting Fear: Islamophobia and Its Impact in the United States*. It reveals that anti-Muslim groups in the United States had access to over $205,000,000 in total revenue between 2008 and 2013.[16] Another report from the Southern Poverty Law Center documents campaigns by professional Islamophobes to introduce anti-shari'a bills in state legislatures, with fourteen states passing such laws between 2010 and 2017.[17] This kind of data helps students understand the motives of and impact from individuals and organizations who purposely stir up fears of Islam.

Gaining a bird's eye view of this anti-Islam industry, we transition to studying particular individuals and organizations that wield the most influence in professional Islamophobia both in the United States and Europe. Students read articles from Daniel Pipes's website Campus Watch that keep tabs on professors who might be sympathetic to Islam and/or critical of US interventionist policies in the Middle East. They track blog posts and tweets from Pamela Geller, the anti-Islam extremist who is largely responsible for inciting fear over the so-called Ground Zero Mosque, or as she called it, the "Monster Mosque," in 2010. They analyze anti-Islam billboards and pamphlets from organizations such as ACT! For America and the American Freedom Defense Initiative. They study speeches and Islamophobic campaign gimmicks from right-wing populists in Europe such as Geert Wilders and Marine Le Pen. And they keep track of the web of relationships between the professional Islamophobia network and mainstream politicians, including key advisors and officials in the Trump administration.

Without a doubt, the most compelling component in this section of the course is the phenomenon of the native informant—the Muslim or ex-Muslim "insider" who draws on personal knowledge and experience of Islam to promote the belief that Islam is opposed to Western values and to assure Western audiences that their fear of Islam is justified. The figure I focus on for this purpose is Ayaan Hirsi Ali. Born in Somalia, Hirsi

Ali sought asylum in the Netherlands as a young woman. She eventually abandoned Islam, made her way into politics, and got elected to the Dutch parliament. Her political career depended heavily on her outspoken criticism of Islam, particularly Islam's treatment of women. She eventually moved to the United States, where she now works for the neoconservative American Enterprise Institute and serves as a fellow at Harvard's Kennedy School of Government and Stanford's Hoover Institution.

The benefit of reading Hirsi Ali's autobiographical writings and watching her provocative movie *Submission* (2004) is that students wrestle with how a public figure who claims "insider status" is in a unique position to stir up fears toward Islam.[18] Hirsi Ali's success and notoriety depends almost solely on her willingness to cast Muslims as incapable of critical thinking and embracing Western values of tolerance and freedom. She also gives Western audiences permission to ignore the role that Western colonialism and racism have played in shaping our negative perceptions of Muslims. She is our "Muslim friend" who tells us we have good reason to be afraid of Muslims.

By this point, students have ample experience identifying common Islamophobic stereotypes, but Hirsi Ali's background and status as a former Muslim gives them pause. I find that students are far more hesitant to criticize Hirsi Ali, at least initially, than they are other professional Islamophobes such as Daniel Pipes or Robert Spencer. This makes for a great discussion on what makes Hirsi Ali different from other public figures who criticize Muslims as well as which Muslims (or in this case ex-Muslims) are acceptable to Western audiences when it comes to telling "truths" about Islam.

The questions raised in this portion of the course are crucial in furthering the course's objectives: Who gets to tell the story of Islam? What story do they tell, and why? Who/what do they include/exclude from the story? For what purposes? Which stories and storytellers do Western audiences gravitate toward, and why? Wrestling with these questions in the context of professional Islamophobia enables students better to appreciate the degree to which Islamophobia arises not from ignorance alone but due to a concerted effort by individuals and organizations who have much to gain professionally and politically from marginalizing Muslim voices in discussions of Islam.

MUSLIMS IN THE MEDIA

We would know little about figures such as Ayaan Hirsi Ali or other professional Islamophobes if not for the media. In fact, any effort to respond to the questions in the previous paragraph must consider the media's pivotal role in framing the narrative of Islam. Most of what "we" know about Islam, or think we know, depends on how the media packages and presents Islam to Western audiences.

The first time I taught my Islamophobia course, I ran into considerable difficulties at this point. Students were willing to engage complex theories and to deconstruct political speeches to uncover anti-Muslim bias. But here I was asking them to apply their analytical tools to news stories, television programs, and movies. I met resistance, and sometimes, I still do. Students are quick to give CNN or the BBC the benefit of the doubt if their stories about Muslims focus mostly on violent extremism. As for *American Sniper*, well, sure there are lots of angry, nameless Muslims in the film, but the movie isn't really about them, right?

I have plenty of theories that try to make sense of this resistance to media analysis, including the possibility that many of my students, most of whom are between 20 and 22 years old, simply want to turn on the TV or go to the movies without having to ask critical questions about the content they encounter. The media is for entertainment and that applies even to news media.

My pedagogical response is to introduce students, even if briefly, to the field of critical media studies. We spend an entire class session learning the basic tools and theories that constitute critical media studies. I usually have a colleague from the communication studies department help me on this day, and we focus our initial discussions on topics other than Islamophobia, such as how the media frames race, ethnicity, gender, and sexuality.

In the following class session, we transition from this bird's eye view of critical media studies to media framing of Islam. I have students watch Jack Shaheen's documentary, *Reel Bad Arabs*, which we then discuss in conjunction with selections from Edward Said's *Covering Islam*.[19] This discussion gives them the opportunity to take some of the theories and questions from critical media studies and apply them specifically to Islam, though still maintaining a broad perspective. Finally, students apply these theories and insights to particular assignments, ranging from watching news clips from CNN or Fox on terrorist attacks to "binge watching" season one of *Homeland* to analyzing Orientalism and Islamophobia in *Argo*.[20]

I have generally experienced success with this approach, though one sticking point that persists in our class discussions is the issue of intent. If journalists or filmmakers are not intending to reproduce negative stereotypes or encourage Islamophobia, is it fair to describe news stories and films that perpetuate these stereotypes as Islamophobic? If Clint Eastwood is not purposely trying to portray Muslims as angry hoards in *American Sniper*, does he get a pass on Islamophobia? The issue of intent is a great one to wrestle with, particularly since it raises larger questions about how people who do not see themselves as prejudiced might still be complicit in the persistence and spread of Islamophobia. As students quickly realize, this is not simply a question about Clint Eastwood but about the rest of us.

THE CONSEQUENCES OF ISLAMOPHOBIA

The bulk of the course focuses on the historical and political forces that give rise to Islamophobia. Along the way, we address the effect of Islamophobia on Muslims, such as casualties in the War on Terror. But it is important to spell out more fully Islamophobia's impact on Muslim communities, which is why as we move toward the end of the course, we concentrate on the discrimination, exclusion, and violence Muslims living in Europe and the United States experience.

This section begins with a survey of the securitization of Muslims and the sweeping counterterrorism initiatives on both sides of the Atlantic within the context of the War on Terror. Students learn about the National Security Entry-Exit Registration System (NSEERS), Countering Violent Extremism initiatives, FBI and NYPD surveillance programs, detentions and deportations, extraordinary renditions, and torture. Students then consider legislation, particularly in Europe, that has placed significant restrictions on freedom of religion for Muslims, including bans in various countries on hijabs, full-face veils, and minarets. We finally consider hate crimes and the sharp rise in violence toward Muslims and Muslim "look-alikes" (Sikhs, non-Muslim Arabs, etc.) since 9/11.

In many ways, this is the most straightforward portion of the course. But it does have its challenges. It is all too easy to inundate students with hate crime statistics or lists of surveillance programs. The larger purpose, however, is not to drown students in information but to encourage them to explore how such widespread discrimination is able to persist in nations ostensibly devoted to democracy and human rights. To this end, I assign students group presentations on some of the topics mentioned above. This helps them delve more deeply into the particular political and historical conditions that contribute to violence and/or systemic discrimination in particular countries. It also helps students understand how these conditions lead to different challenges for Muslims living in France versus Britain or the United States.

CHALLENGING ISLAMOPHOBIA

The first time I taught the course, I concluded with the section on the consequences of Islamophobia. On my course evaluations, students' most common complaint was the dire note on which the course ended. They appreciated the exploration of the historical and political causes of Islamophobia. They found the widespread discrimination experienced by Muslims both eye-opening and appalling. But how do we respond to Islamophobia? What can we do to combat Islamophobia? The pilot version of the course did a great job of deconstructing anti-Muslim prejudice, but it left much to be desired when it came to exploring constructive ways forward.

I have remedied this shortcoming by devoting a concluding section to combating Islamophobia. The starting point for our discussions is a series of interviews I conducted with eight prominent individuals who are prominent advocates for Muslim-minority communities and who fight Islamophobia from different occupational perspectives.[21] Among the interviewees are: Ingrid Mattson, a prominent Muslim scholar and the first woman to serve as president of the Islamic Society of North America; Keith Ellison, the first Muslim ever elected to the US Congress; and Tariq Ramadan, one of Europe's most prominent Muslim intellectuals. Students read the responses of these and other individuals to a series of questions that include: What is the one thing you wish more people in the West knew about Islam? What is the best way to address the media's negative portrayal of Islam? What can Muslims and non-Muslims respectively do to combat Islamophobia?

These interviews feed into a terrific discussion on what we can do to combat Islamophobia and how our journey through the course equips us in this endeavor. In this regard, we come full circle as we address how the study of Islamophobia, and not of Islam itself, offers an important perspective on the causes of anti-Muslim prejudice and the means to counter this prejudice.

It's too much to expect that Islamic studies courses will be completely rid of the pressure to address anti-Muslim prejudice, even in academic contexts where students have the opportunity to take a course on Islamophobia. At the very least, an Islamophobia course affords a resource and a recourse to students whose primary interest is the desire to understand anti-Muslim stereotypes and discrimination as opposed to Islam itself. It also helps students focus more clearly on the complex historical and political forces that give rise to Islamophobia and to move away from problematic assumptions that learning more facts about Islamic teachings and traditions necessarily reduces anti-Muslim bigotry. Finally, it provides Islamic studies professors with some pedagogical breathing room in their introductory courses, allowing them to develop syllabi that are not overwhelmingly burdened by the need to address Islamophobia or to defend Islam's reputation in the age of ISIS.

1. The emergence of Islamophobia studies as a distinct discipline in the United States is evidenced by the creation of the *Islamophobia Studies Journal* in 2012 and the Islamophobia Research and Documentation Project (IRDP), an initiative of the Center for Race & Gender at the University of California, Berkeley. The study of Islamophobia, however, is far reaching and consists of scholars throughout the world from fields as diverse as sociology, anthropology, history, political science, critical media studies, and religious studies.

2. A. Kevin Reinhart, "On the 'Introduction to Islam,'" in *Teaching Islam*, ed. Brannon Wheeler (New York: Oxford University Press, 2003), 22–45.

3. Joe. L. Kincheloe, Shirley R. Steinberg, and Christopher Darius Stonebanks, eds., *Teaching against Islamophobia* (New York: Peter Lang, 2010).

4. See "Islamophobia Is Racism: Resources for Teaching & Learning about Anti-Muslim Racism in the United States," available online at https://islamophobiaisracism.wordpress.com/.

5. For a fuller discussion of relevant assignments and readings for a course on Islamophobia, see the sample syllabus on my website: http://www.thefearofislam.com/sample-syllabus/.

6. Commission on British Muslims and Islamophobia, *Islamophobia: A Challenge for Us All* (London: Runnymede Trust, 1997).

7. Commission on British Muslims and Islamophobia, *Islamophobia*, 1.

8. Ayaan Hirsi Ali, *Nomad: From Islam to America: A Personal Journey through the Clash of Civilizations* (New York: Free Press, 2010), 214.

9. See Liz Fekete, *A Suitable Enemy: Racism, Migration and Islamophobia in Europe* (New York: Pluto, 2009), 194; Mehdi Semati, "Islamophobia, Culture and Race in the Age of Empire," *Cultural Studies* 24 (2012): 256–275; Nasa Meer and Tariq Modood, "Refutations of Racism in the 'Muslim Question,'" *Patterns of Prejudice* 43 (2009): 335–354.

10. Martin Luther, *On War against the Turk*, in *Luther's Works*, ed. Robert C. Schultz (Philadelphia: Fortress Press, 1967), 46:155–205.

11. Edward W. Said, *Orientalism* (New York: Vintage Books, 1978).

12. Said, *Orientalism*, 6.

13. Bernard Lewis, "The Roots of Muslim Rage," *Atlantic* (September 1990): 47–60; Samuel Huntington, "The Clash of Civilizations?," *Foreign Affairs* 72 (1993): 22–49.

14. Quoted in "London Bomber: Text in Full," BBC News (UK), September 1, 2005, http://news.bbc.co.uk/2/hi/uk/4206800.stm.

15. Nathan Lean refers to this phenomenon as "the Islamophobia industry," while the Center for American Progress refers to it as "the Islamophobia network." See Nathan Lean, *The Islamophobia Industry: How the Right Manufactures Fear of Muslims* (London: Pluto, 2017); Ali Wajahat et al., *Fear, Inc.: The Roots of the Islamophobia Network in America* (Washington, DC: Center for American Progress, 2011).

16. The Council on American-Islamic Relations and the Center for Race and Gender at the University of California, Berkeley, *Confronting Fear: Islamophobia and Its Impact in the U.S. 2013–2015.*

17. "Anti-Sharia Law Bills in the United States," Southern Poverty Law Center, February 5, 2018, https://www.splcenter.org/hatewatch/2018/02/05/anti-sharia-law-bills-united-states.

18. See Ayaan Hirsi Ali, *The Caged Virgin: An Emancipation Proclamation for Women and Islam* (New York: Free Press, 2008); Ayaan Hirsi Ali, *Infidel* (New York: Free Press, 2008); Ayaan Hirsi Ali, *Heretic: Why Islam Needs a Reformation Now* (New York: Harper, 2015).

19. Sut Jhally, Jeremy Earp, and Jack Shaheen, *Reel Bad Arabs: How Hollywood Vilifies a People* (Media Education Foundation, 2006); Edward W. Said, *Covering Islam: How the Media and the Experts Determine How We See the Rest of the World* (New York: Vintage Books, 1997).

20. I also assign students a few examples of television programs or movies that refute Muslim stereotypes or otherwise portray Muslims in complex and more nuanced ways. Examples of television programs include Germany's *Türkisch für Anfänger* (2006–2009) and Canada's *Little*

Mosque on the Prairie (2007–2012). Examples of movies include *Babel* (2006) and *Mooz-Lum* (2010).

21. For a full discussion and analysis of these interviews, see Todd H. Green, *The Fear of Islam: An Introduction to Islamophobia in the West* (Minneapolis, MN: Fortress Press, 2015), 311–335.

TODD GREEN is Associate Professor of Religion at Luther College and a former US State Department advisor on Islamophobia in Europe. He is the author of *The Fear of Islam: An Introduction to Islamophobia in the West.*

PART III
APPLICATIONS

chapter ten

FROM MEDINA TO THE MEDIA
Engaging the Present in Historically Oriented Undergraduate Courses on Islam

Sabahat F. Adil

THESE DAYS, THOSE OF US who teach courses in the United States on some aspect of Islam likely do not have to worry about students' lack of curiosity about the subject matter. Given their constant media exposure to topics about Islam, the Middle East, and Muslims, students tend to enroll in our courses with a ready interest to learn more, sometimes in order to affirm what they already know and at other times to study these topics from different perspectives. Yet the popularity of such courses does not ease the pressures stemming from designing and teaching them in this day and age, but rather fosters an urgent need to face the unique pedagogical challenges and opportunities that they pose. One of the ways to squarely address these challenges and opportunities is through active engagement with discussions on pedagogy. Any such discussion should frequently engage with conversations preceding it and try to anticipate those that may follow. In a similar vein, pedagogical discussions ought to occur alongside our primary research areas, given that encounters in the classroom likely intersect with our scholarly concerns in very real ways.

This chapter will consider what it means to teach historically oriented courses on Islam in the contemporary undergraduate American classroom in a charged sociopolitical climate by exploring the following questions: (1) How do students encounter Islam, the Middle East, and Muslims *before* they enter our classrooms? (2) Should we address their encounters and conceptions in a course that is historically oriented, particularly toward the premodern past? (3) If so, how do we harness students' preexisting conceptions to create a productive space for learning, given the vast diversity of students in our classrooms? By addressing these questions, this chapter will explore how we can facilitate opportunities for students to grapple with the premodern past while addressing their present and future needs. In turn, these opportunities can nurture productive learning spaces and help us as professors to sharpen our engagement with the texts and pasts with which we are most familiar.

Through concrete examples of introductory and advanced undergraduate courses such as "Introduction to Arab and Islamic Civilizations," "The World of Classical Arabic Literature," "Islamic Culture and the Iberian Peninsula," "In the Footsteps of Travelers: Travel Writing in Arabic Literature," and "Art in Islamic Cultures," this chapter will explore how we can think about teaching the premodern past in light of the present through an intentional juxtaposition of assigned readings, alongside accompanying key questions, assignments, and predetermined course goals. Including, for example, material on Thomas Jefferson's copy of the Qur'an in the same session as verses from the scriptural tradition itself when covering topics such as women and inheritance facilitates a space through which we can stress to our students (1) how to examine a topic critically and from multiple angles; (2) how texts are informed by the circumstances of their production; and (3) how we are inclined to view the past is very much informed by the present. Ultimately, these guiding principles will equip us to engage most productively with students in our ever-diverse classrooms, lead them to become critical thinkers at home and abroad, and produce classroom settings that foster active engagement with both the past and present.

More broadly, we must pay attention to contemporary events and/or attitudes and consider them throughout a given term. Such an approach pays heed to how the worlds that our students are living in actively shape their understandings of the past. Yet we must also avoid thinking about our courses as *exclusively* a means to counter prevailing attitudes toward Islam, the Middle East, and Muslims in the United States and the world today, especially if it entails leaving out or including certain texts or historical moments. In other words, through learning goals that we establish we ought to focus on the foundational knowledge that we would like students to gain at the end of a given course—and whether this foundational knowledge is a particular historical perspective, rhetorical skill set, or content knowledge ought to also be considered—all while remaining mindful of the particular circumstances in which this information is being conveyed.

Literature Review

Scholarship on this topic is both limited and extensive, and it continues to inform my approach to teaching specific courses, which I detail below.

When it comes to scholarship on pedagogy specifically related to Islam, the Middle East, and Muslims in the American classroom, much of the material has been produced after 9/11 and responds to this context, thus confined to just over the last fifteen years. One of the most significant of such works is the *Teaching Islam* volume to be discussed subsequently. To address why pedagogical studies on Islam may be so limited, one has to recognize the specific trajectory of the study and teaching of Islam in European and North American contexts, the second of which can be considered in a relatively younger phase of development, which has been considered in a volume edited by Mumtaz Ahmad, Zahid Bukhari, and Sulayman Nyang.[1] Meanwhile, material on pedagogical practice, particularly in light of topics that carry wider domestic and/or global resonance, is far more robust. Without attempting comprehensively to review all available literature on the topic, this chapter encompasses these overlapping bodies of scholarship in its consideration, and in this section provides an overview of some of the notable works in this regard.

An important work on pedagogy related to Islam is titled *Teaching Islam* (2003).[2] Its chapters focus on a variety of topics, ranging from the teaching of Islamic law to teaching Islam through contemporary literature. The scholars who have authored the articles come from an impressive array of institutions, and many of them are senior scholars with extensive teaching experience. This work was published as part of the Teaching Religious Studies Series by the American Academy of Religion. It focuses minimally on matters related to the digital world and its impact on pedagogy in the college classroom, given limited scholarship and research into the subject matter at the time of publication. One important exception is a chapter titled "Incorporating Information Technology into Courses on Islamic Civilization" by Corinne Blake. Other works in the Teaching Religious Studies Series may also be consulted, many of which do not focus particularly on Islam, Muslims, or the Middle East. For example, the volume *Teaching Religion and Violence* (2012) includes chapters on the interrelations between these two realms, but without a particular focus on a specific tradition.[3]

Professional academic organizations such as the American Academy of Religion (AAR) and the American Historical Association (AHA) also publish materials related to the topic in a journal format. In terms of the latter, the *Journal of the American Academy of Religion* is an important source to consider. Likewise, AHA publishes *Perspectives on History*, which includes essays. One example is an issue linked by the theme "Controversy in the Classroom." Articles in this issue touch on a similar set of topics, but ones that are not exclusively limited to teaching about Islam (i.e., Richard

Shaefer's "Let's Talk about Religion").[4] What would be important is for more works on teaching Islam specifically to emerge in such publications.

Online, the Wabash Center for Teaching and Learning in Theology and Religion offers an array of resources that are organized by topic, including "Teaching Religion" and "Teaching Diverse Students." The Wabash Center also publishes the peer-reviewed academic journal *Teaching Theology and Religion*. Finally, this web resource additionally features links to other resources on pedagogy that are internet-based. These resources are significant to mention because they point to the centrality of the internet medium for ongoing conversations on pedagogy.[5]

Additionally, scholarship on college students in the twenty-first century, often characterized as "millennials," offers a useful set of texts to consider. This literature is particularly helpful because it provides a way to consider pedagogy while keeping notable characteristics and traits in mind. These characteristics do not, of course, need to pertain to the study of religion alone, but they provide an angle through which to consider how various topics might be received or ought to be conveyed to this set of students. A notable work in this regard is by Neil Howe and William Strauss (2000) called *Millennials Rising: The Next Great Generation*. Although some scholars consider the empirical evidence supporting the ideas in the work to be limited, it is nonetheless an important textual foundation that offers a perspective on the type of students who may be in our classrooms today. Notably, the authors describe this generation based on a series of core traits that they possess.[6]

These are just a few relevant sources that ought to be considered when it comes to pedagogy on Islam, Muslims, and related topics. My own teaching experiences coupled with such preexisting scholarship by others continue to be in constant conversation and provide an opportunity to make sure that what I do in the classroom is informed by tried-and-true methods and ideas, which themselves are frequently changing. This can make what I do in the classroom current and provide a means for students to finish the semester with a sense that they have both acquired concrete "data" on the topics at hand but can also confidently approach other areas of study and their lives through the underlying methods of critical inquiry that inform the class.

THE LANDSCAPES

Sociopolitical

Students in our undergraduate classrooms today are living their lives at a time when they have ready access to rhetoric about Islam, Muslims, and the Islamic world. Much of this is heightened because the 2016 presidential election cycle included constant rhetoric about the aforementioned topics, both at home and abroad, as a result of constant yet unpredictable terrorist activity, refugee crises, and so on. Generally speaking, this has created a certain kind of hostile environment in which students learn about these topics through a negative engagement with them from the outset. Indeed, these attitudes extend throughout the United States; in a 2014 Pew Research Center study asking participants to rate religious groups on a scale of 0 to 100, Americans gave Muslims the remarkably low rating of 40, the lowest of any religious group. The study was conducted on the basis of a "feeling thermometer" and random phone surveys.[7]

Beyond the recent years in which ISIS or ISIS-inspired attacks were constantly at the helm of world events, the horrific events of September 11, 2001, also loom large in sociopolitical memory. Yet students coming into our undergraduate classrooms likely have little to no memory of that day, even though much of what they see taking place at home and abroad today continues to stem from reactions and responses to it. September 11th, like other defining moments in global and US history such as the Vietnam War and the Oklahoma City bombing, may be considered "a major resonant event," which has had immeasurable impacts on the world.[8] While Robin Murphy's work elucidates changes in literacy depending on the time period (e.g., time periods following World War II, the Vietnam War, the Oklahoma City bombing, and 9/11), it is compelling to think about changes in other areas of academic inquiry in such periods, including the current period of ISIS activity or ISIS-inspired attacks and a post-9/11 context more broadly.

It is worth considering how teaching differs in today's age compared to teaching those who were undergraduate students at the time of 9/11. At that time, books such as María Rosa Menocal's *The Ornament of the World: How Muslims, Jews, and Christians Created a Culture of Tolerance in Medieval Spain* (2003) were published that included authors' remarks about 9/11 as a resounding and singularly resonant event and its impact on the author and the content of the book.[9] Yet nowadays students are not growing up in a time where a singular event has occurred in their memory. There are multiple such events occurring regularly and frequently, and they are not confined to certain parts of the world. Rather, international events have been "brought home" with immediate repercussions in their lives. One must ask: How does teaching these students differ from those who were being taught when a singular horrific event occurred? Given that global terror seems to be a "new normal," this shift seems to have given people the green light to publicly say anything about and do anything to anyone, no matter how harmful. How we teach in this context is an important question to ask and consider. Reflecting on these issues could help us determine whether particular methods of teaching may need to be changed, for example, how we navigate questions of political correctness.

Finally, another challenge facing students today, given the volatility in various countries, is that they are often discouraged from traveling to one or another place in North Africa or the Middle East as a part of their studies, with the notable exception of certain countries. Since students may have travel constraints due to events in the recent past and also because they do not have to travel far to see a climate in which the Middle East, Islam, and Muslims are constantly in the spotlight, we must think about how to harness this reality for learning, which is a particular challenge in classes on the premodern world.

Technological

The sociopolitical landscape is not the only arena that has seen rapid transformation in the last two decades. Students enrolling in colleges and universities today have grown up with ready access to the internet and in an overall mass-mediated age. They have not necessarily known a time in their lives without access to the internet and immediate access to information. As a part of the Pew Internet Project surveys conducted in 2010, the study revealed that 98 percent of American college students are internet users. The only group that ranked higher was that of graduate students, which ranked at 99 percent.[10] In this light, it is important to develop an understanding of what students know, how they came to know it (i.e., how did they acquire the information), and their means of accessing—and therefore processing—information more broadly because it is often different than in an age where ready access to information and the internet did not exist. Furthermore, the internet is more than a means of acquiring information for people today; it is a venue for social interchange, which, too, has invariably had an impact on how students conduct in-person communication versus interaction in the virtual realm.

Academic

The final area that is important to consider is what the American higher education landscape looks like today. What is the demographic makeup of our undergraduate student bodies? How have they changed (or stayed the same) in recent decades? The group of individuals entering our classrooms today, often labeled "millennials," is understood as a diverse generation that shares certain core qualities, which are outlined in the work by Howe and Strauss discussed above. While much attention has begun to be paid to this generation in scholarship, it suffices to note here that this is an important factor to keep in mind when discussing pedagogical approaches in the classroom in light of the current sociopolitical and technological climate.

Undergraduate Courses

Some of us may teach courses in religious studies or divinity schools where theological concerns are at the forefront of many discussions. Yet others of us teach subjects related to religion, specifically Islam in this case, but through historical, sociocultural, and/or literary angles. In my case, the teaching of subjects related to Islam and Islamic societies partly occurs in the Department of Asian Languages and Civilizations; it is neither in a department of religion nor history. The situatedness of my courses in such a department speaks to the nature of the concerns highlighted here. In the latter classrooms, to what extent do we engage with students' concerns about Islam and Muslims, many of involve theological debate? In teaching a course on Islamic visual culture, for example, when a student asks about "the difference between Sunnis and Shias," is this the space to engage such a question?

To examine the questions raised above and others, several courses will be considered. Introductory undergraduate courses titled "Introduction to Arab and Islamic Civilizations," which is currently taught as a one-semester course, and "The World of Classical Arabic Literature" provide ample fodder for such a discussion, along with several advanced undergraduate courses, including "Islamic Culture and the Iberian Peninsula," "Travel Writing in Arabic Literature," and "Art in Islamic Cultures." Given the range of topics considered in these courses, the myriad pedagogical approaches taken in them, and the diverse range of students enrolled in the courses, they function as excellent examples to consider the questions highlighted in the introduction.

"Introduction to Arab and Islamic Civilizations" is intended to introduce students with little to no background in the academic study of Arab and Islamic civilizations to relevant content. The course is organized chronologically, beginning in Late Antiquity and ending in the modern day. Clearly this is a great deal of material to cover in a single semester, so naturally decisions have been made by each professor teaching the course to expose students to a range of issues in this broad chronology. This iteration of the course starts by situating students in the pre-Islamic Near

East, and it emphasizes ideas about the complexity of religious identity and practice, which is exemplified through quotes such as these, which we discuss in great detail during the first few weeks of the course: "The Near East inherited by the Muslim Arabs was more than anything else a mosaic of religious identities, the pieces of which were colored by distinct traditions."[11] This course ends with a nod toward the present day, but as someone whose own work focuses on the premodern world, it almost always seems like too few hours of class time have been devoted to the modern period.

"The World of Classical Arabic Literature," another introductory course for undergraduates, relies on Arabic literary texts in translation starting from the pre-Islamic Arabic literary tradition and spanning the seventeenth century. This course proceeds chronologically through time, and students discuss a lively array of texts in translation. Eventually, they memorize lines of classical Arabic poetry in translation for a class-wide competition.

The second set of courses under consideration is geared toward advanced undergraduates and may include graduate students from time to time. These include "Islamic Culture and the Iberian Peninsula," "In the Footsteps of Travelers: Travel Writing in Arabic Literature," and "Art in Islamic Cultures." All these courses are organized chronologically, even though they address diverse themes and topics. In the first, students are exposed to the history and cultures of Islam and Muslim peoples in the Iberian Peninsula starting in the eighth century and moving through the seventeenth century with the final expulsion of *Morisco* (Muslims and their descendants who had to convert to Catholicism in the Iberian Peninsula) populations. The Visigothic period of Iberian history and post-seventeenth century history are periods that are also covered in order to show students the broader context in which this history and culture is situated, but relatively little by way of class time is spent on these areas.

In the "In the Footsteps of Travelers: Travel Writing in Arabic Literature" course, even though we progress chronologically through time, there is more of a topical focus. Students read works on a range of themes related to travel and travel literature, including accounts of travel by Arabs in the Volga region, Muslim female travelers going on the Hajj, and so on. Finally, in the "Art in Islamic Cultures" course, students are exposed to the artistic and visual cultures of Islamic societies in historical context. This course, too, proceeds chronologically, starting with the visual cultures of the Byzantine and Sasanian empires and ending with a consideration of modern Arab artistic production in the twentieth century. From time to time, guest lecturers have been invited to speak with students in these courses, which has elicited positive responses from students. Future iterations of this course may depart from a chronological method of organization, given the rich potential to address these issues in a more heavily thematic fashion.

Overall students in these courses vary greatly in terms of their background and level of expertise. Some students have no background on the topics, while others do, either in the form of previous classroom study or through a variety of personal experiences. Their experiences vary so much and, often, if not for our classrooms, their paths may have never crossed. Such a complex cross-section of identities creates potential pedagogical challenges but also many opportunities.

Historical Periodization

The questions being posed in this essay and in this volume more broadly are particularly salient because they also suggest concerns that are important even outside of historically specific events such as terrorist activity or enflamed rhetoric stemming from presidential election cycles. In particular, they provide an opportunity to help us revisit questions pertaining to historical periodization, not necessarily in terms of how we use it in our research, but in terms of how it impacts our teaching.[12] For example, do assumptions that we make about where Islamic history "begins" and "ends" prevent us from making potentially more compelling connections between the past and present to a greater degree of effectiveness in the classroom? Furthermore, we must also consider revisiting how to talk about transitions between periods. Are we making clear enough in our classrooms what it is about the Middle Periods, for example, that distinguishes this moment from others? In what material ways can we see the transition actually taking place? In our classrooms, we may be quick to tell our students to be wary of drawing connections between a historical religious injunction about figural depiction and the modern controversies around the Charlie Hebdo cartoons, for example, but there is something to be said about helping students tackle the very questions of the space between the crystallization of such an injunction and contemporary reactions. In other words, we can encourage students to be mindful of historical space that separates two points in time, but we can also aim to create a space for a productive discussion that encourages students to think of this space as flexible and malleable and potentially changeable depending on the topics under discussion.

Let us return to the earlier stated example of the civilizations course. Some might argue that a chronological approach to the past, one that begins in the pre-Islamic Sasanian and Byzantine landscapes and ends at some future point in a linearly constructed path is an ideal way to introduce students to the history of Arab and Islamic civilizations. But the reality is that students are inevitably coming to the classroom shaped by ideas about the past based on their present engagement with the subject. Perhaps it would be ideal to recognize that this is the case rather than set it aside for the duration of the semester, only to approach it (and maybe not even then!) at the end of a given semester. They have been processing what we have been teaching in the term through their particulate lenses anyway, so it would be worth mobilizing their vantage points in the classrooms. One way to do this would be to address these various viewpoints more squarely and actually devote time to discussing how they might be informing their engagement with the material.

Engaging the Present in the Historically Oriented Classroom

The courses that have been introduced above are generally focused on the premodern period, which in these courses ranges from the years between the rise of Islam until Napoleon's conquest of Egypt in 1798. Yet students taking these courses know about the topics at hand largely through particular lenses, either through mass-mediated means or through personal experiences of some kind. For example, if they see the terms "shari'a" or "caliphate" in their readings, students might be inclined to think about recent rhetoric in the media that defines these words, albeit for particular rhetorical purposes. The same might happen with students who have been raised in households where they came to know terms such as these through particular definitions. Through the examples that follow, this chapter explores different ways through which to bring together material related to the premodern past with students' preexisting understandings of the material.

The first example one can consider is the course on classical Arabic literature. There is little about the topic that overtly screams contemporary events or contemporary Islam, but much can be done to bridge the two, especially in the beginning of the semester when students are still deciding how a given course fits best with their interests and/or academic goals. One way that was effective in the classical Arabic literature course was to spend the first week of the semester discussing contemporary uses of classical Arabic poetry, particularly when it has been used for political ends. There have been videos, notably one included on *The New Yorker*'s website, which featured the very public recitation of poetry by ISIS members.[13] While this class spends little time delving into political history during the course of the semester or discussing modern Arabic literature, the use of this video and building a discussion around it was an effective way to dive into a class that might seem like it has little relevance to students today. In the second week of the semester, we dove into pre-Islamic Arabic literature from the Arabian Peninsula, and I could refer back to ideas that we discussed such as the importance of an oral tradition and the sociable nature of poetic recitation while also highlighting important differences in context.

During the first week, we watched the aforementioned short video together a few times. I provided little to no context about the video at first. In order to collectively develop an understanding of what we were watching and why we were watching it, I asked students a series of questions to direct the conversation. These questions included: (1) What do you think this is a video of? (2) What leads you to think that this is a video of X? (3) If you had to express an initial reaction to the video, what would it be? (4) What do you think its relevance is to a class on classical Arabic literature? (5) What do you think is the relationship between the classical texts that we will be reading in this course and the present day?

Students were intrigued with this video and the overall exercise, and it seemed like it created a certain level of increased investment in the course where there may not have initially been as much. (Many students take the courses to fulfill various general education requirements, given that they have been approved for this purpose.) For one, they expressed interest in seeing how classical Arabic literature had continued resonance with the present and were happy to see connections being forged. A number of students also expressed surprise to see this "side" of a given group of demonized people. Some expressed discomfort at this apparent humanization of people through their recitation of poetry, a craft that the students seemed to associate with "high" culture and the arts. Overall, it turned out to be a constructive activity because we were able to then in subsequent weeks step back into the pre-Islamic period and start to look at Arabic literature, especially poetry, from the pre-Islamic context. It helped the material become more immediate to them, and it also made apparent the links between the materials with the past.

The example above stems from attempts to forge connections between upcoming course materials with students' contemporary contexts. Yet the same kinds of connections must be made at other points in a given term as well; just the beginning is not enough. As such, there might be an appropriate time or moment in the duration of a course to remind students that what they are learning about has repercussions and relevance to the present day. In this vein, another day in the travel course I invited a speaker to visit who had spent a great deal of time as a photojournalist documenting manuscripts and Muslim scholarly cultures in West Africa. This turned out to be a great day for the students to make historical and modern connections because the course tended to focus on medieval and early modern travel in Islamic societies with topics such as pilgrimage, knowledge, and exile. We had spoken so regularly in that course about topics such as the age-old Arabic notion of "travel in search of knowledge," but this was one of the first times that students were able to speak firsthand with someone who was invested in a project documenting such a long-standing tradition in recent times and also possessed an awareness of the changes that had been brought upon it in recent times.

With this speaker coming in and showing photographs she had taken in West Africa, we were able to engage in conversations on multiple levels. For one, it allowed us to look at images of a tradition of scholarship and learning that has maintained continuities since the premodern period. Yet it also allowed us to discuss recent destruction of these objects and historical sites. These photographs served as a link between the historical and the modern in the course. It allowed us to talk about how travel routes and activity are very much dependent on political and other types of circumstances. This also allowed them to complicate the paradigm of travel as being something difficult in the past, but it being easy in the present. While modes of movement have certainly sped up travel, our speaker made clear that current circumstances in the region have prevented her from traveling there more recently. This helped to complicate students' understanding of historical time.

In the art course, we have looked at contemporary renditions of historically resonant visual phenomena intermittently throughout the course, and students have continuously asked for more examples. Thus far, this course has seemed to provide some of the greatest opportunities to bring the past and present together, ranging from examples of American Muslim paintings that interpret "classical" visual vocabulary to museum exhibits on modern Arab art.

An approach to bringing different perspectives into conversation with one another that extends beyond the resources of a given course are dialogues programs that exist on various campuses.[14] These classroom dialogues allow for a facilitated conversation around particular topics and are geared toward learning objectives that an instructor may bring to a given course. While I have not yet engaged with this program in my courses, I plan to do so going forward, even though my courses focus on the premodern past.

Engaging Technology in the Historically Oriented Classroom

The internet and mass-mediated technologies are very important in this whole discussion. We must be asking ourselves the following questions, some of which have been mentioned above: (1) What materials do students have access to online? (2) What materials are students relying upon to provide them with information? (3) Has this changed in the last few decades? (4) How does this impact our teaching? (5) How does instantaneous access to information impact our teaching? (6) How do we harness the internet? (7) How do we use it to teach? (8) How do we teach students to distinguish between the varieties of sources that they may come across online?

One example from my courses, both introductory and advanced, is using Wikispaces to help students learn both content and also how the use of technology may impact our interaction with such content. What I have done is to ask students to list terms that they think are important for the course on the Wikispaces site. Once they listed these and I double-checked them, they were asked to define the terms using the assigned texts. They were also asked to define the terms through the key questions I posed on the syllabi to guide their readings. Part of the purpose of this exercise was to create a working glossary that students themselves created and could go back to at any point in the semester, especially to study for exams. Another part of the exercise, which allowed for a great deal of discussion in the classroom, stemmed out of complaints I received from students that their answers had been edited, deleted, or somehow modified. This allowed us to talk about knowledge production and competing narratives. One of the course goals for this class is for students to be able to analyze texts critically, and their own involvement in textual production provided a space to discuss how narratives are produced in the texts that we read. Furthermore, this permitted us to look at primary texts and collectively see how processes of editing, deletion, and authorship have impacted the content that we are now reading. They were involved firsthand in that process, which seemed to help shape their understandings of both what we were reading and also what they might end up accessing in their own time.

There are other areas in which the internet impacts us that are not just on the level of ideology. This is in how students write and read and what they think are acceptable methods of writing and reading. An important question, then, is how do we teach students to access websites that are scholarly, especially in an age where polemical or otherwise unreliable online sources are not just abundant, but have multiplied and continued to crop up, as well as what role do they play in our courses? To help convey this, I ask students to submit annotated bibliographies for their final papers in my advanced courses where they discuss the reliability of a given source that they have found online and also those that they have found in print.

This is a good space to discuss what arguments might be made *against* integrating the present into one's courses on the premodern past. Some might argue that students must first have a good grasp of past circumstances in order to analyze the present. Others might argue that incorporating too much material from the present day or allowing the present to "seep" too much into our courses might mean that we are constantly adjusting our courses for relevance in the present day. Still others might argue that such an approach is overly concerned with "giving" students what they "want" (seeing them too much as consumers, in other words) and the negative implications of this on our own teaching.

These are all valid arguments, and ones that ought to be taken into account and taken seriously when deciding how to structure our courses and syllabi. It is important to address each of them here. It is true that a classroom space that focuses on the premodern past may ask students to set aside their notions of Islam and Islam-related topics informed by the present while they move through such a course. However, if students are coming into the classroom fully situated in the present, denying them a chance to engage with some of these ideas may provoke a great deal of confusion and create some sense of distraction among students. Also, it is plausible to consider whether there are ways to adjust a given course at certain levels, yet allow it to remain the same on other levels. For example, if we have courses that incorporate lectures, discussions, and assignments, perhaps discussions and maybe even assignments would be good places to extend ourselves into "updating" our courses or addressing various student concerns. This way if there is a particular historical narrative we want to maintain, then we can do so in our lectures and preserve them without making many changes to that component.

Another place to think about making potential adjustments would be in the readings assigned. Even though we can make the bulk of the readings stay consistent from one iteration of a course to another, we could change a subset of them in order to accommodate or even at the very least acknowledge student interests and concerns. This might seem problematic because it might sound like we have to "give" students what they want, which makes them seem like consumers and we as professors as some kind of providers. Yet that is not necessarily what we are doing here. We are acknowledging large-scale and rapid changes happening in society, which is not necessarily something that is only important to students, but indeed potentially very important and relevant to us as well. In other words, even though these are courses on historical texts, we can use these spaces as a way to convey that how we interpret and write history is not set in stone, a point that is significant in both research and pedagogy.

Conclusion

Through the approaches outlined above, we may help students become more adept at thinking about course texts and materials in relation to the present. Certainly how this affects students depends on the types of students we have, the types of courses we are teaching, and the types of institutions in which we teach. Students from across the university take many of the courses discussed above. They are majoring in a variety of subject areas and may be taking a given course on Islam in order to supplement their major or for their own interest. To facilitate students' interest in these courses, particularly when they focus on the premodern period, it is of the utmost imperative to find ways to link what interests the students with premodern topics.

More broadly, during particular historical periods, educators have long had to tackle the challenge of teaching about a given topic in a moment when the political climate has been polarized and negatively charged against that topic. A future follow-up study could take a comparative approach to the themes engaged in this chapter and in this volume more broadly in order to examine how others have dealt with the challenges described here. In this vein, it does not appear that this discussion is exclusively about ISIS or some other entity or historical event. This is a discussion about how we teach something in a time of volatility, a time in which students have strong ideas and preconceived notions of what a topic is all about, and the nature of this volatility is constantly evolving. As an example, this chapter was being written during the 2016 US presidential election cycle, and it underwent some revision in 2017. Even in the life cycle of this single chapter and discussions on pedagogy contained therein, notable changes occurred. Historically resonant events will come and go, but this is a time which we can use as an opportunity to (re)learn how to teach a topic in a time of volatility and change. For these reasons and others, it is incredibly important for us to start and continue these discussions with one another.

Notes

1. Mumtaz Ahmad, Zahid Bukhari, and Sulayman Nyang, eds., *Observing the Observer: The State of Islamic Studies in American Universities* (London: IIIT, 2012).

2. Brannon Wheeler, ed., *Teaching Islam* (New York: Oxford University Press, 2003).

3. Brian K. Pennington, ed., *Teaching Religion and Violence* (New York: Oxford University Press, 2012).

4. Richard Shaefer, "Let's Talk about Religion," *Perspectives on History*, May 2010.

5. Wabash Center for Teaching and Learning in Theology and Religion, accessed April 15, 2017, http://www.wabashcenter.wabash.edu/.

6. Neil Howe and William Strauss, *Millennials Rising: The Next Great Generation* (New York: Vintage Books, 2000).

7. Michael Lipka, "Muslims and Islam: Key Findings in the U.S. and around the World," Pew Research Center, 2017.

8. Robin M. Murphy, *How Social Trauma Affects How We Write: Post 9/11 Rhetorical Theory and Composition Pedagogy* (Lewiston, NY: Edwin Mellen Press, 2010), 54.

9. María Rosa Menocal, *The Ornament of the World: How Muslims, Jews, and Christians Created a Culture of Tolerance in Medieval Spain* (New York: Back Bay Books, 2003).

10. Aaron Smith, Lee Rainie, and Kathryn Zickuhr, "College Students and Technology," Pew Research Center, July 19, 2011.

11. Jonathan Berkey, *The Formation of Islam: Religion and Society in the Near East, 600–1800* (Cambridge: Cambridge University Press, 2003), 52.

12. Marshall G. S. Hodgson, *Rethinking World History: Essays on Europe, Islam and World History*, Studies in Comparative World History (Cambridge: Cambridge University Press, 1993); Fred Donner, "Periodization as a Tool of the Historian with Special Reference to Islamic History," *Der Islam: Journal of the History and Culture of the Middle East* 91, no. 1 (2014): 20–36. Konrad Hirschler and Sarah Bowen Savant, "Introduction: What Is in a Period? Arabic Historiography and Periodization," *Der Islam: Journal of the History and Culture of the Middle East* 91, no. 1 (2014): 6–10.

13. Nate Lavey, "Commentary—The Poetry of Jihad," *The New Yorker* Videos, 2015, http://video .newyorker.com/watch/commentary-the-poetry-of-jihad.

14. "Classroom Dialogues," CU Dialogues Program, University of Colorado-Boulder, accessed September 1, 2016, http://www.colorado.edu/cudialogues/classroom-dialogues.

SABAHAT F. ADIL is Assistant Professor of Pre-Modern Arabic Literature and Culture in the Department of Asian Languages and Civilizations at the University of Colorado at Boulder.

chapter eleven

MUSLIMS ARE PEOPLE; ISLAM IS COMPLICATED

Kecia Ali

UNDERGRADUATES ARRIVE IN COLLEGE AND university classrooms across America already knowing a great deal about Islam and Muslims. Much of what they know is wrong; some of it is technically correct yet fragmentary and misleading. Myriad challenges confront us as we attempt to correct outright errors in their knowledge and provide useful frameworks to think about Islam and Muslims using the tools of religious studies specifically as well as the humanities more broadly. Although my topics and strategies vary depending on the course, my main goal is always the same. By the end of the semester, students should understand that Muslims are people and that Islam is complicated.

MUSLIMS ARE PEOPLE

Carl Ernst makes a version of this point in his *Following Muhammad,* an essayistic overview which I've used with undergraduates since it was published in 2003. At a 1992 workshop on teaching Islam in America, he and his colleagues chose an "absurdly simple" goal: "to convince Americans that Muslims are human beings."[1] Twenty-five years later, with well-funded and carefully orchestrated bigotry paving the way for a major upsurge in hateful speech, violent attacks on Muslims, vandalism and arson at mosques, and election-year calls to do everything from banning shari'a to blocking Muslims from entering the country—even detaining Muslims in special camps—getting students to understand that Muslims are people is not as straightforward as it sounds.

Even apart from rejecting insinuations that all Muslims secretly support terrorism or cannot be loyal Americans, insisting on the humanity of Muslims means having students really understand that for good or ill—and sometimes it's one, sometime the other—Muslims are like other people. Some are profoundly ethical; others are not. Some scrupulously observe religious rules for devotion; others ignore them entirely. Many more occupy the fuzzy middle ground. It's relatively simple to get students to accept the notion that, like all human beings, Muslims are varied and imperfect in the ways they live their lives.

Because they are used to hearing Muslims discussed as one uniform group, it's trickier for them to grasp that one can seldom generalize accurately about Muslims' beliefs and worldviews. A time-tested technique is invaluable here: comparison. A student who asks "Do Muslims believe in evolution?" does not need (though he may get) a lengthy excursus on truth versus fact in scripture, modern Muslim scientism, and the reception of Darwin in the Arab world. It's likely to be more effective if I respond by asking: "Do Christians believe in evolution?" Oh, he subsides. Yeah. I see what you mean. (This technique would be still more effective if I could arch one eyebrow but, surprisingly, that is not one of the pedagogical strategies for which a workshop is offered on my campus.)

ISLAM IS COMPLICATED

It may take some time for students to get out of the habit of assuming that Islam explains everything about Muslims' lives or beliefs, but convincing them that Islam is complicated is harder still. What do I mean by this? I want them to grasp that there is rarely if ever a simple, adequate answer to the question "What does Islam say about X?"

Students ask this question in part because, unless they are religion majors, they generally assume that religions are bounded, clearly defined entities rather than complex, contested, continually negotiated set of contentions and practices that we have come to classify, label, and study as "Islam" and "Christianity." The assumption that one may easily refer to "what religion X says" about a given topic is not unique to Islam, but it is pervasive there. For non-Muslim students, this may owe to its unfamiliarity; Christian and Jewish students are typically more aware of diversity within their own traditions and less aware of it in other traditions. Muslim students, some of whom are foreign, may have been raised and educated to think that there is a single, simple, straightforward answer to questions of Islamic doctrine and practice. Both Muslim and non-Muslim students are affected by widespread tendencies in mass media, popular culture, and even from religious authorities and Muslim organizations to speak and act as though there were a single "true" Islam—though Islamophobes and Muslim extremists, on the one side, and apologists, on the other, disagree profoundly about the content of that singular Islam. In other words, there's a fair amount of unlearning that must happen as learning proceeds. Thinking of Islam as a unified whole is a hard habit to break.

At the end of a semester, students still sometimes ask "But what does Islam say about X?" The difference is, by that point they sometimes catch themselves—perhaps aided by a significant look from me.[2] If one doesn't catch on, another may point it out.

Teaching about Islamic Law at Boston University

Islamic law is a very effective way to teach both that Muslims are people and that Islam is complicated. In dealing with the full range of human behaviors and by assuming that people sometimes violate rules, law implicitly demonstrates Muslims' humanity. More important, showing how what is popularly taken for granted as Islam shapes and is shaped by law illustrates the complexity of the Muslim tradition. As Jonathan Brockopp argued in his contribution to *Teaching Islam*, the jurisprudential tradition is absolutely essential if one wishes to understand diverse Muslim histories and complex contemporary societies.[3] Of course, and as he also warns, despite its central place in Muslim intellectual life, one must not lapse into the error of treating law as the defining feature of Muslim religiosity. I remind students that many Muslims largely ignore both its ritual and its social dimensions in their daily lives, centering other elements of religion. I also show that even among those who follow it and consider it central, there are extensive and far-ranging debates about when, how, and why to apply it. Still, I find it a useful and essential way of teaching about Islam and Muslims.

I have been teaching at Boston University since 2006. I teach an undergraduates-only introduction to Islam and mixed graduate/undergraduate upper-level courses on "The Qur'an," "Islamic Law," and "Islam and the West." I also teach a seminar on "Women, Gender, and Islam." These latter courses attract a mix of undergraduates, masters' students in a variety of disciplines including (Christian) theology, and doctoral students, mostly in religion. Islamic law has a place in all my courses. This essay focuses on my Islamic law course. I discuss the major topics, main readings, and some of the exercises I use to good effect in the classroom. I explore how I have dealt with current events when appropriate.

My Islamic law class tends to enroll between fifteen and twenty students, half to two-thirds undergrads. Most of these are international relations or political science majors. Some are "heritage learners" majoring in the sciences. A few are religion majors. My spring 2015 syllabus expresses the overall goals of my class:

> Islamic law is both very important and very poorly understood. This course will cover its development, concepts, and methods as well as its implementation in diverse societies over more than a millennium, also addressing its

place in the world today. We will begin discussing notions of law—what law is and how Islamic law compares to other legal systems. We will discuss the early development of Islamic law, its sources and methods, its division into legal schools, and its application in a variety of places and times including the central Arab lands during the Abbasid caliphate, the Ottoman empire, and the Middle East and North Africa under European colonial rule. We will see that far from being monolithic, Islamic law is diverse in both theory and practice. As we look at doctrines and implementation of Islamic law, we will focus on purity rules, "forbidding wrong," jihad, and family law in the classical, medieval, Ottoman, and modern eras, up to the present day.

I thread several through lines through the lectures, readings, discussions, and small-group exercises. Topically, I highlight gendered rules, especially but not only those governing marriage and sex. Diversity is an ongoing theme: doctrinal diversity within and across legal schools and divergences in practical implementation, especially where practice deviates from doctrine. These are not the only possible through lines: one could use the same texts to focus on the changing and complicated role of the ruler/state in Islamic legal thought and practice, to explore various manifestations of violence, or to emphasize rules governing property rather than gender.

The Course: Readings, Topics, and Assignments

My Islamic law course meets three times a week for fifty minutes. I usually teach in my department seminar room, with a big table, ample space, and extra chairs around the edges of the room. This setup facilitates seminar-style conversation, while the room allows students to move around for breakout and small-group work.

I assign six books, with a seventh (supplementary) for graduate students, and a number of book chapters and articles, not all of which I mention here. The books are:

- Wael B. Hallaq, *An Introduction to Islamic Law* (Cambridge: Cambridge University Press, 2009)
- Graduate students should, and others may, consult Hallaq's more in-depth survey: *Islamic Law: Theory, Practice, Transformations* (Cambridge: Cambridge University Press, 2009)
- Nuh Ha Mim Keller, editor and translator, *Nawawi's Maqasid*, rev. ed. (Beltsville, MD: Amana Publications, 2002)
- John Kelsay, *Arguing the Just War in Islam* (Cambridge, MA: Harvard University Press, 2007).
- Ron Shaham, *The Expert Witness in Islamic Courts: Medicine and Crafts in the Service of Law* (Chicago: University of Chicago Press, 2010)

- Michael Cook, *Forbidding Wrong in Islam* (Cambridge: Cambridge University Press, 2003)
- Judith Tucker, *In the House of the Law: Gender and Islamic Law in Ottoman Syria and Palestine* (Berkeley: University of California Press, 1998)

I find textbooks a mixed blessing at best and avoid them in most of my courses. For this course, though, I use Wael Hallaq's short survey *An Introduction to Islamic Law* to give a basic chronological orientation to the subject matter. For a few years, I assigned his weightier *Shari'a: Theory, Practice, Transformations*, but it proved too daunting for most undergraduates. One year, I assigned *Shari'a* to the graduate students and *Islamic Law* to the undergrads but found that the chapters did not correspond quite neatly enough. I now assign chapters from *Shari'a* as required graduate (and optional undergraduate) reading for some weeks. This compromise, too, has its flaws. An increasing number of graduate students in my courses are MA students in International Relations or Christian MDiv (divinity) or MTS (theology) students from Boston University's School of Theology preparing for ministry, interfaith work, or comparative theology careers. They are not necessarily more prepared, and indeed are sometimes less prepared, than advanced undergraduates for detailed technical discussions of Islamic law. It seems increasingly unreasonable to have them share the same assignments and expectations as religious studies or Islamic studies doctoral students.

The basic primary text for the course is Nuh Keller's translation of Nawawi's *Maqasid*. Originally composed in the thirteenth century by a Syrian Shafi'i jurist as a memorizable primer for low-level jurists, who would then be taught elaborations upon its key points, the text has now been translated by an American Muslim intellectual trained in the legal-jurisprudential tradition and strongly committed to its ongoing relevance and authority. The *Maqasid*'s advantages include a low price, readable English, and a focus on purity and ritual that disrupts what many students, particularly those from Protestant backgrounds, think they know about prayer, law, and religion.[4] One disadvantage is that the translation near-seamlessly incorporates material from more advanced legal texts, thereby masking some of the *Maqasid*'s strangeness. It's incumbent on me to demonstrate for students how the text has been manipulated, reformulated, and framed in a way that takes it from being part of a scholarly tradition keeping authority in the hands of a juristic class to being a resource for D-I-Y Muslim laypeople who have little access to the sources of traditional authority the translator/editor lauds.[5] It's vitally important to do this work because otherwise the *Maqasid* appears as an "authentic" medieval text—and part of my objective is to show students change over time in Muslim understandings of law.

Nawawi's text is an integral component in one of my key assignments. It treats legal method through a discussion of ablution. Here's how I describe the exercise in my foreword to a translation of the earliest extant work of Muslim legal theory:

> We devote one session to an in-class exercise on ablution, the ritual washing before prayer. Together, we read the Qur'an's two brief passages on the topic which, they quickly conclude, provide insufficient guidance on exactly how to wash. I then distribute an eight-page handout with selected hadith-reports of the Prophet Muḥammad's practice. These relate how Muḥammad washed before prayer and also the advice he gave to others about washing. I divide the students into small groups and charge each with answering a specific question: for instance, how many times does one wash one's face? There are so many reports, some of them contradictory, that students decide that they now have too much information. Last, we turn to a medieval legal manual that explains in precise detail how to perform ablution. It tells how many face-washings are required and how many are optional. The students are always a bit baffled: how did this scholar get from the Qur'an's vague commands and the many competing accounts in the hadith-reports to specific rules? How, from a profusion of possibilities, did he arrive at categories like obligatory and recommended? The answer, it turns out, is legal theory.[6]

This in-class assignment introduces our study of legal theory. I assign chapters from my biography of Imam Shafi'i, the eighth-century jurist and legal theorist known as "the mother and father" of Islamic jurisprudence.[7] Using this understanding of Shafi'i's legal approach and its effects on the other Sunni legal schools as a base, we do another in-class exercise. We discuss consent to marriage, using translated snippets from primary texts from all four Sunni legal schools. (In a future iteration, I will translate a relevant Shi'i excerpt.) This assignment explores matters of legal diversity and its relationship to legal-methodological differences, and demonstrates shared presumptions about women and girls as well as men and boys. Issues around gender and sex continue to resonate through the semester, eventually raising crucial questions about shifting assumptions about law, ethics, and authority in modernity. (In a 2001 paper presented at the American Academy of Religion, and available online since, I made the case for the reverse: not that women and gender were useful ways of learning about the law but that Islamic law was a useful way to teach about women and gender.[8] Both remain true.)

These latter concerns are also central to two books that have relatively little to say about gender: Michael Cook's *Forbidding Wrong in Islam* and John Kelsay's *Arguing the Just War in Islam*. Cook's study, a thematic abridgment of a much larger work, explores the way Muslim scholars have discussed "commanding right and forbidding wrong," or, roughly, the duty of one Muslim to intervene when another is acting badly. This book gets students talking about concepts of personhood, liberty, and privacy. What is a victimless crime? Who has the right to correct whom? What sorts of hierarchies must be respected? What sorts of debates over those hierarchies took place? Cook includes a chapter on women's involvement in forbidding wrong. By the time we get to it, students can usually recognize the inherent tensions between premodern presumptions of gendered hierarchy in family and society, on the one hand, and, on the other, the recognition of women's full moral and legal personhood.

Like Cook's treatment of forbidding wrong, Kelsay's discussion of jihad gets mileage from the contrast between widely shared Muslim assumptions about the significance of certain moral matters and intra-Muslim diversity of opinion. *Arguing the Just War* centers less on doctrines around the permissibility or proper conduct of war and more on what he terms "sharia reasoning," the basic norms and practices governing how one makes claims to authority within traditional structures of Islamic legal thought. Kelsay discusses the formative period of Muslim legal thought, emphasizing the now-familiar Shafi'i; provides an overview of classical and medieval doctrines governing jihad; and then explores three twentieth-century thinkers who not only deviated from the substance of classical rules but also, he argues, violated the basic precepts of shari'a reasoning. Among the authors we read, Kelsay has the least to say about gender, beyond brief discussions of women as combatants and noncombatants. However, his study does provide two crucial elements that help focus students thinking on the larger points I'm trying to make with the course.

First, Kelsay's book helps students realize that the diverse, diffuse, decentralized nature of Islamic has positive and negative ramifications. In other words, the legitimacy of particular guidance to individuals needn't come from government legislation, but can come from individuals perceived as authoritative. This allows for progressive interpretations but also (*pace* Keller, in the supplementary material in the *Maqasid*) removes possible constraints on idiosyncratic or troubling interpretations. Our discussion of the role of muftis (jurisconsults) and fatwas (nonbinding but authoritative legal opinions) benefits from this exploration. Second, class discussions of Kelsay, along with Hallaq and others, critically analyze their rosy portraits of the nuanced, pluralistic premodern jurisprudence. This, they contrast to the less-sophisticated, blunt "emergency" reasoning used by Osama Bin Laden and other jihadi thinkers, discussed by Kelsay, or the simplified post-Ottoman national legal codification projects in the Middle East, discussed by Hallaq.

I confess to sharing this predilection for revealing the oversimplification of contemporary fatwa literature on some topics in my assignment on muftis and fatwas. My students read the introduction to a coedited volume, *Islamic Legal Interpretation: Muftis and Their Fatwas*, from which I've used case studies in other semesters.[9] Then we revisit, together, one to three fatwas on a topic that I have chosen from online sites such as Islamicity.com or IslamQandA.com. The big student projects are fatwa presentations. I allow them to either write their own fatwa (a) or analyze a cluster of fatwas (b). They give a five-minute report and submit the question, fatwa, and a list of their sources (a) or a write up of the analysis and copies of the fatwas discussed (b). I grade primarily based on the presentation; the reports are so I can check evidence and sources. Here's how I describe the assignment:

Option 1: Write your own fatwa
Select a question—it can be your invention or one that has already been discussed in class or something you have read online—and have it approved by me. If it is a topic we have covered or one you have seen addressed, you'll need to approach the topic differently). Write and deliver a fatwa of approximately two pages, supported by relevant sources and notes. Your objective is not to mimic some of the more poorly supported fatwas available but rather to construct the strongest argument possible in favor of the position you take. You should marshal your evidence from Qur'an and sunnah, make reference to relevant legal principles or analogous cases, and anticipate and provide defenses against the strongest counterarguments, whether counter-texts from within Qur'an and sunnah or established positions of legal schools, etc.

Option 2: Analyze a cluster of fatwas
Select a topic on which there is a range of fatwas available. Have the topic *and* fatwas approved by me. These should present different answers and/ or different arguments in support of the same answer. Your job will be to discuss the range of answers, explain how muftis reached them (explaining both legal-methodological choices and other assumptions that may have guided them), and analyze their relative strengths and weaknesses. You may use both premodern and modern fatwas, online or in books. Your presentation here should again be no longer than five minutes, but your report may be somewhat longer if necessary.

We devote a couple of class sessions to student presentations, leaving time for brief question and answer sessions afterward. The exercise is typically a class favorite and discussions at the end of a session can be very lively. Students affirm that it teaches them both how easy it would be to write a bad legal opinion and how difficult it can be to write a good one, marshalling available evidence from Qur'an, hadith, and local practice, and justifying themselves methodologically. Most semesters, nearly all undergraduates write their own fatwas while most graduate students opt for analysis. In spring 2015, however, all the female students chose analysis, and the (fewer) male students opted for drafting their own opinions. I am unsure why this happened. Perhaps it was mere chance; perhaps the day that I went over the assignment in class I somehow signaled the need for a type of expertise that female students took as discouragement. (Attending to gendered assumptions and dynamics in the classroom is important.) In any case, the split was noticeable. A student pointed it out at the end of the presentations. Her comment led to a spirited discussion about not only the gendering of authority in medieval Muslim texts but also the way that women's authority is circumscribed in contemporary American contexts, including but not limited to scholarship and the classroom.[10]

The interplay between gender dynamics and authority comes to the fore again in our treatment of Judith Tucker's excellent, accessible monograph *In the House of the Law*. Tucker builds on our early discussions of marriage and our exploration of the relationship between fatwa-giving and verdict rendering. It also touches on the relationship between court practice and everyday life. Tucker, a historian rather than a legal scholar, presents a case study of seventeenth- and eighteenth-century Syrian and Palestinian debates and practice on matters of marriage, divorce, sexuality, and child custody. Drawing on Ottoman court archives as well as published collections of legal opinions, Tucker makes a strong case for the presence and persistence of patriarchal norms and assumptions as well as the role of judges and jurists in restraining men's capricious exercise of their authority. The book, read alongside historical material from Hallaq about the pluralist Ottoman legal system, allows for a more sophisticated understanding of multiple legal domains and the way that similar cases could predictably result in certain outcomes by drawing on widely known pragmatic courtroom strategies.

Tucker's book simultaneously engages and unsettles students with its anecdotes and analysis. Some of its material is wildly unfamiliar and generates student discomfort, such as the chapter on consummation of marriages with minors; class discussions address underlying assumptions about childhood, male and female sexuality, and the role of the individual versus the family in making "personal" decisions. In teaching Tucker, I return briefly to our class exercise on marriage, reminding students that a few points that Tucker takes for granted (the ability of adult women to contract their own marriages, for instance) are not universal; I highlight the range of other ways that diversity emerges, as she shows how Hanafi judges appoint deputies from other legal schools to grant divorces their doctrine prohibits them from granting. Eventually, we will compare and contrast the ways judges worked to circumvent obviously unjust outcomes with the strategies adopted in the twentieth century to formulate new legal codes governing divorce by explicit adoption of doctrines from another legal school.

Issues around patriarchy and protection, as well as the shift to codified national law, also arise in Ron Shaham's book *The Expert Witness*. Shaham's study spans the medieval era, through the Ottoman period, into contemporary Egypt. Shaham's focus on procedure—the ways in which scattered scriptural references and prophetic precedents are formalized and incorporated into legal decision-making—allows students to glimpse the many things that Islamic Law can mean in practice. Students have been deeply engaged by his chapter on women's witnessing. Shaham's chapter title, "Agents of Patriarchy in the Secluded World of Women," gives the flavor of his approach. Like Tucker, he acknowledges women's agency without naively celebrating their autonomy. Women, like men but more so, operate within patriarchal constraints. Although women can and do intervene in a variety of ways, they also may uphold male-centric standards of female propriety.

Tucker and Shaham's studies bring into sharp relief the complicated, local, historical, contingent factors that affect the application of Islamic law. Read alongside Hallaq's account of successive Ottoman legal reforms followed by national codification projects, these texts illuminate the impacts of colonialism and nationalism, and illustrate the symbolic role that "family law" has come to play in shaping modern debates over Islamic law.

These books put fatwas, court practice and decisions, and people's lived realities into conversation, spanning the modern and premodern. Following our discussion of Tucker, we explore contemporary discussions about gender. There are crucial questions about the assumption that the modern era is always good for women and that there is a straightforward narrative of progress toward women's "equality" and "equal rights." One perpetual problem in teaching women, gender, and religion is that students frequently compare their twenty-first-century assumptions about what is proper, fitting, and ideal to other traditions' medieval or early modern ideas and realities. Here, strategies to combat historical ignorance or selective amnesia are vital. Occasional comparative examples help. I have been known to bring up Greek, Roman, and rabbinic marriage rules—and data on when precisely marital rape became criminalized in the United States. When discussing Muslim women's general capacity to own and transact property regardless of marital status, I might mention medieval European rules on married women's property ownership—or the discussion of when married American women could get credit in their own name. I also offer periodic reminders not to compare ideals in one case with worst-case-scenario realities in another.

I often leave the last week of the semester open, or schedule a self-contained topic that can be changed without difficulty. I like having the flexibility to address in more depth a topic that emerged during the semester as a focus of student interest, perhaps something in American or global news. For spring 2015, I had tentatively planned to offer a discussion of American legislative initiatives to ban shari'a. That March, Graeme Wood's much-discussed *Atlantic* article ("What ISIS Really Wants") appeared and, in its wake, a whirlwind of writings on the Islamic state and its laws.[11] Our topic was clear. We read selections from the 2014 "Open Letter to Baghdadi." We focused on the way it deploys scriptural and other sources, discusses legal qualifications, and appeals to authority.[12] Then, in one class session we worked our way through Sohaira Siddiqui's essay "Beyond Authenticity," written partially in response to Wood. Siddiqui's essay argues Islamic State jurists' claim to authority and legal acumen is invalid.[13]

I brought printouts of the article to class, so that everyone was working with a hard copy of the text with the same pagination; this reduces time fumbling to find passages. I divided the class into four groups and charged each with focusing on a particular element of the article, building on our discussions of the Open Letter. For instance, one group looked at how scriptural/prophetic sources appeared and how they were used. Another tracked how jurisprudential qualifications and authority were described, asserted, and invoked. The small groups worked for about twenty minutes. We reconvened as a unit and each group spent four or five minutes presenting their findings. We spent the rest of the period relating the groups' findings to earlier readings and ongoing themes. Since we were out of time, at the start of the next class, I asked students to reflect on what they took away from the previous session. Repeatedly, students noted the salience of intra-Muslim disputes over the legitimate methods and scope of Islamic legal authority, and the ways those debates were intertwined with thinkers' subject positions. This reminder of humanity and complexity was a good note on which to have the semester end.

NOTES

1. Carl W. Ernst, *Following Muhammad: Rethinking Islam in the Contemporary World* (Chapel Hill: University of North Carolina Press, 2003), x. For a helpful reflection on using Ernst to teach about the academic study of religion, see SherAli Tareen, "Genealogically Attuned Teaching in an Introductory Course on Islam," http://wabashcenter.typepad.com /teaching_islam/2016/10/genealogically-attuned-teaching-in-an-introductory-course-on -islam.html.

2. It would definitely be better if I could raise just one eyebrow to accompany this look.

3. Jonathan Brockopp, "The Essential Sharia: Teaching Islamic Law in the Religious Studies Classroom," in *Teaching Islam*, ed. Brannon Wheeler (New York: Oxford, 2002), 77-93.

4. A number of other major Muslim legal texts have been translated into English—sometimes with parallel Arabic—in recent years, mostly by pious Muslims who present the translations as material for study and application by non-Arabic-speaking Muslims. So far, these texts are too pricey to assign. I use handouts from them for specific exercises—for instance, the comparison of the four major Sunni schools on women's consent to marriage, mentioned below. I also allow students to consult them during my office hours if useful for their assignments.

5. I assigned Nawawi's *Maqasid* in my intro to Islam class for several years. We spent time discussing the ways in which Keller constructs authority and how he connects the legal tradition with Sufism. The very existence of the appendices discussing "Why Muslims follow Madhhabs [legal schools]" and the importance of a shaykh (Sufi guide) testify to the contemporary intellectual climate among Muslims and the need to defend once largely taken-for-granted elements of the Sunni intellectual tradition. Thus, in an intro to Islam, Keller's text provides both an intro to ritual practice and Islamic law and a springboard for discussions of modern Muslim contestations of scholarly authority.

6. Kecia Ali, foreword to *Al-Shāfi'ī's Epistle*, trans. Joseph Lowry (New York: Library of Arabic Literature/New York University Press, 2015), xi–xii.

7. Kecia Ali, *Imam Shafi'i: Scholar and Saint* (Oxford, UK: Oneworld Publications, 2010), 115.

8. Kecia Ali, "Teaching about Women, Gender, and Islamic Law: Resources and Strategies," Paper presented at the American Academy of Religion Annual Meeting, 2001, 1–12.

9. Muhammad Khalid Masud, Brinkley Messick, and David S. Powers, eds., *Islamic Legal Interpretation: Muftis and Their Fatwas* (Cambridge, MA: Harvard University Press, 1996), 3–32.

10. As to gender and authority: at this point, only one of six (or seven) required course books is written by a woman, though the gender balance is substantially better when one includes articles and chapters in the tally. However, I aim to have a better balance of authors in future iterations of the course.

11. Graeme Wood, "What ISIS Really Wants," *The Atlantic Monthly*, March 2015.

12. The full text of the letter is available at www.lettertobaghdadi.com. I discuss the letter and Wood's article, in Kecia Ali, "Redeeming Slavery: The 'Islamic State' and the Quest for Islamic Morality," *Mizan: Journal for the Study of Muslim Societies and Civilizations* 1, no. 1 (September 2016): 1–19.

13. Sohaira Siddiqui, "Beyond Authenticity: ISIS and the Islamic Legal Tradition," Jadaliyya .com, February 24, 2015, http://www.jadaliyya.com/pages/index/20944/beyond-authenticity _isis-and-the-islamic-legal-tra.

KECIA ALI is Professor of Religion at Boston University. Her books include *Sexual Ethics and Islam: Feminist Reflections on Qur'an, Hadith, and Jurisprudence* and *The Lives of Muhammad*.

chapter twelve

THE FIVE QUESTIONS ABOUT ISLAM YOUR STUDENTS DIDN'T KNOW THEY HAD
Teaching Islamic Studies to an American Audience

Phil Dorroll

THE "TIGHTROPE"

Teaching courses in Islamic studies in the present American political and cultural environment is marked by a particular type of tension: the need to combat prejudice against Islam, on the one hand, and the need to maintain a critical academic stance toward real problems in the Muslim world that have religious bases, on the other. Due to the prevailing suspicion of Islam as a religion, teachers in Islamic studies constantly have to weigh the relative pedagogical importance of these two goals based on the particular audience of their courses. Mark Berkson calls this tension the "tightrope" that all teachers in Islamic studies must walk.[1]

At the same time, the intellectual impulse that animates sincere interest in Islam and the Muslim world is often related to curiosity about the threat of terrorism, the roots of misogyny, and a general anxiety about Islam's "role" in complex human events and social structures (such as war, poverty, patriarchy, and ideology). In other words, what draws people into courses on Islam is often the very thing that must be questioned and broken down in order for genuine learning about Islam to take place. Berkson refers to the students in his courses "who signed up in droves to study Islam in order to understand terrorism or geopolitics."[2]

The contemporary Islamic studies classroom demands that instructors both take seriously the politicized tension that infuses students' interest in their subjects and, at the same time, try to redirect that tension into productive discussions about the complexities of Islam in history and the real world. Every instructor has a unique, and uniquely successful, model for trying to balance these interests. This chapter will discuss one such method that I have found successful in navigating the highly politicized environment of an Islamic studies classroom. I argue that one productive way to engage with this politicization is to directly engage certain "frames" or ways of thinking about Islam that are endemic in media and popular discourse. J. Z. Smith, among many others, has argued that the guiding rule of choosing course content is to choose content that addresses specific concepts and ideas that the instructor wishes to prioritize in their course.[3]

I suggest that one way of doing this is to choose readings and discussion questions that address the most common "frames" in media discourse through which most Americans attempt to understand Islam. I do not argue that addressing these media frames must be the *primary* goal of all Islamic Studies courses; but rather that my utilization of them in my Introduction to Islam courses has helped accomplish the primary learning goals of the course (to introduce students to the most common discourses and practices of Islamic religious traditions throughout history) by engaging students within the framing of the most urgent questions that brought them into the course in the first place.

ISLAMOPHOBIA AND MEDIA DISCOURSES IN THE UNITED STATES

Islamophobia is by no means a new feature of American culture. As Thomas Kidd demonstrates, since the earliest days of American history many American Protestants have associated Islam with lust, deception, and tyranny.[4] In the American colonies, Islam was construed as the natural antithesis to liberal enlightened thinking, civilizational progress, and political and human freedom. Because of these associations, comparisons to Islam were often used to discredit political opponents.[5] Furthermore, many Protestant religious discourses in the colonial period described how the defeat of Islam or conversions of Muslims by Christian powers would figure as a key component of the Apocalypse.[6]

These descriptions of Islam also played a major role in the American branch of nineteenth-century dispensational theology, or the theological premise that history is divided into a series of discrete and decisive divine interventions into world history, effectively dividing human history into a series of "dispensations" that marked out "distinct eras" in the history of human salvation.[7] The depictions of Islam as inherently "other" and antagonistic to Christian civilization was woven tightly into these theological discourses and remains a key element of Islamophobic discourse in certain strains of American Protestantism.

Building on this theological history, many Protestant groups in the twentieth century began to elaborate an even more active role for Islam in

End Times prophecy due to a shift in American foreign policy focus toward the Middle East after the Iranian Revolution in 1979.[8] Because dispensational theology endeavors to interpret contemporary geopolitical events in light of biblical prophecy, once American entanglement in conflicts in the Middle East became an urgent concern to American citizens, numerous strains of American Protestantism began to view the Muslim world as the site of the emergence of the Antichrist in the impending apocalyptic drama described in the Book of Revelation. A new genre of prophecy literature has emerged in the past decade or so that warns of the impending emergence of an "Islamic Antichrist" that will rise in our lifetimes to challenge the forces of good in the world. In this worldview, Islam is described as essentially a worldwide multi-century demonic conspiracy; in this conception, Islam's role in the drama of human salvation has been to serve as a fount of demonic influence everywhere that it exists.[9]

Parallel to these religious developments, American politics has often nurtured what Richard Hofstadter has famously called "The Paranoid Style." The paranoid style in American politics often detects a massive conspiracy at work within the United States that is supposedly "directed against a nation, a culture, a way of life."[10] Contemporary anti-Muslim sentiment closely mirrors the kind of prejudices that Hofstadter describes in his discussion of the paranoid style.[11] There is a particularly strong parallel with anti-Catholic prejudice: in certain nineteenth-century political discourses (and in American colonial religious discourse as well), Catholicism was described as a civilizational threat to American democracy and the American way of life because Catholicism was represented as a form of tyranny.[12] Many Americans were intensely afraid of the growth of Catholic immigration because it was believed that immigrant Catholics would collude with foreign governments to undermine the American way of life.[13]

Islamophobic discourse has mirrored American anti-Catholic prejudice in curiously specific ways. Appealing to historical instances of Catholic governments' persecution of religious minorities, nineteenth-century American anti-Catholic discourses often stoked fear of "an impending Catholic war of mutilation and extermination" and argued that Catholicism rejected secular governance in favor of the union of church and state.[14] These specific forms of anti-Catholic hate speech invite obvious comparisons with the politicization of history engaged in by Islamophobic discourses that stoke widespread fear of jihadist slaughter and attempt to prove that Muslims are inherently incapable of supporting certain forms of governance (such as American democracy). What unites all these forms of paranoia and prejudice is a common fear of a religious or political enemy that threatens the essence of what it means to be an American, urging that the patriotic few among us are "always manning the barricades of civilization."[15]

With such deep roots in American culture, Islamophobia was set to thrive after the national trauma inflicted upon the American psyche on 9/11. In his seminal text *The Fear of Islam*, Todd Green isolates a number of distinctive elements to post-9/11 American Islamophobia that have a particularly strong grounding in American media discourse. These include the depiction of Islam as inherently violent, Islam as inherently anti-democratic, and Islam as inherently misogynist.[16] These characterizations played a major role in media discourse that urged support for the American Global War on Terror (GWOT), which was often supported by favorable references to Samuel Huntington's widely critiqued assertion that Islam and Christianity constitute entirely distinct world civilizations that are destined to violently collide until one forcibly subdues the other.[17]

These contemporary American Islamophobic discourses exhibit anxieties about the defense of American civilization found in earlier historical discourses discussed above. Islam is cast as the eternal antithesis to all that America is and must be: subduing the forces of Islam epitomizes the American struggle against tyranny, and the status of Islam as a religious tradition entitled to robust American legal and constitutional protections is correspondingly diminished or outright denied. The 2016 American election cycle and the rise of Donald Trump's political movement have seen perhaps the most direct public attacks on Islam as a religion in modern American history. Such attacks (most notably Trump's famous proposal to ban Muslims from entering the United States) have become so commonplace as to be too numerous to name; but one opinion piece published on March 30, 2016, in the *Wyoming Tribune Eagle* vividly echoes the tenor of current Islamophobic discourse in the United States: "Say what you will, but Islam is evil like no other group of any kind, except maybe the Nazis. . . . Islam, no matter who is practicing it, does not fit into American culture and beliefs, or any other relatively free nation's."[18]

Current opinion polls bear out the widespread influence of these Islamophobic discourses in contemporary American society. According to a study conducted by the Brookings Institution in the summer of 2016, only 44 percent of Americans reported having a favorable attitude toward the religion of Islam (in November 2015, this number was even lower, at 37 percent).[19] The same study revealed that terrorism—namely, the fight against ISIS—remained among the top "global priorities" for Americans, meaning that concern about Islam and violence remains at the top of the American cultural and media agenda. Findings from the Public Religion Research Institute (PRRI) 2015 American Values Survey revealed similar anxieties.

According to this study, 56 percent of Americans agreed with the statement that "the values of Islam are at odds with American values and way of life"; 47 percent of Americans agreed with the same statement in 2011.[20]

Finally, it must be emphasized that in the contemporary United States, internet and broadcast media are the primary avenues of exposure to Islamophobic discourse. As Todd Green notes, "the media determines who tells the story of Islam, which elements and perspectives are included or excluded, and how the story is packaged and presented. Without a doubt, the media functions as the most powerful conveyor of 'knowledge' about Islam."[21] A. Kevin Reinhart insightfully refers to the problematic ways in which American media frame Islam as the problem of "pseudo-knowledge."[22] Reinhart points out that many Americans are exposed to a series of oversimplifications, distortions, and biases presented in the media as common-sense "facts" and "cultural truisms" about Islam.[23] This relatively stable set of preconceptions that includes associations of Islam with violence, tyranny, and misogyny (as Green demonstrates) manifest as a series of specific "frames" that I attempt to deconstruct in my Introduction to Islam course. I argue that deconstructing these frames advances general learning objectives in my introductory course—namely, to introduce students to the most common discourses and practices of Islamic religious traditions throughout history: because students' (and anyone else's) knowledge of the world is mediated through their own cultural context, steering my course content through these problematic media frames helps clear the path for more genuine learning about Islamic religious traditions to take place.

THE FIVE FRAMES

Based on the scholarship discussed above and my own experience[24] teaching an Introduction to Islam course (with no prerequisites), I argue that there are, at this historical moment, at least five major frames through which students approach the topic of Islam:

1. Religion and violence
2. Religion and politics
3. Religion and patriarchy
4. Religion and foreign policy
5. Religion and national identity

I define a "frame" as a question or conceptual issue through which someone views a topic. I also think of these frames as a set of questions about a topic that may unconsciously condition the kinds of inquiries a person makes into a particular topic: in other words, questions that someone might not know they have, whose very "common-sensical" nature may ensure that their pervasive influence remains uninterrogated. These frames may also be thought of as examples of basic questions within the discipline of religious studies that can effectively be addressed through engagement with specific examples from Islamic religious traditions.[25]

In my experience, these five frames constitute the primary set of questions and issues that students seek, consciously or unconsciously, to address through their study of Islam. In other words, I argue that just as no one comes to a topic without a preexisting interpretive framework through which they seek to understand that topic, students in my introductory level Islam course often seek to interpret the religion of Islam with reference to these much larger and more urgent conceptual questions. Moreover, these broad questions manifest in very specific ways relative to prevailing media discourses.

Each of these frames manifests as a question very specific to the way American media discusses matters related to Islam and the Muslim world. Being able to answer the deeper questions implied by these five frames means first addressing the specific questions that students usually pose:

1. For religion and violence: Is Islam violent?
2. For religion and politics: Does Islam want to dominate non-Muslim societies or politics?
3. For religion and patriarchy: Does Islam oppress women?
4. For religion and foreign policy: Who are the terrorists (such as ISIS) and where do they come from?
5. For religion and national identity: Is Islam a threat to the United States?

These questions are not here posed in the way that I seek to answer them. Rather, these questions represent my best attempt to simply reproduce the most urgent questions students bring to my course, and to classify them based on the broader frame issues that students are seeking to grapple with by asking these specific inquiries.

To summarize what I am proposing: students often enter my Introduction to Islam course with the specific anxious and urgent questions that I have reproduced above, and that are derived from media framing of events in the Muslim world. I argue that these questions reflect deeper issues—what I am calling "the five frames"—that students are seeking to address by engaging with the topic of Islam. Finally, I argue that in order to best serve the learning objectives of the course (to introduce students to the most common discourses and practices of Islamic religious traditions), I must provide answers to these questions that both satisfy students' sense of urgency and also point their attention to useful ways to conceptualize the larger issues implied by their questions (the five frames). In addressing the specific elements of the interpretive framework that many of my students bring into class, I seek to enable them to engage with Islam in ways that are more productive and insightful than the limited horizon of anxiety that our present media and cultural environment has placed in front of them.

Frame I: Religion and Violence, or "Is Islam violent?"

Given the anxieties of post-9/11 America, this is probably the most urgent question brought into the classroom. In order to answer it by directing attention toward the complex relationship between religion and violence, I use this issue as an opportunity to introduce one of the consciously stated cardinal methodological lessons of the entire course: the importance of listening to the voices of Muslims themselves. While emphasizing the well-known religious studies dictum that religions don't speak, only their followers can, I emphasize the importance of listening to how Muslims themselves address this issue. What follows are some suggestions for how to open this discussion that have worked for me in my classroom.

One effective content medium through which to get at this question is the body of Quranic interpretation that deals with controversial Quranic verses that discuss violence (most famously 9:5). I often use my broader discussion of Quranic interpretation as a way to approach this specific scriptural debate. To begin, I assign Ingrid Mattson's extraordinary essay "How to Read the Qur'an," included in *The Study Qur'an*.[26] Mattson's essay vividly describes not only the inestimable ritual and personal significance that the Qur'an holds for Muslims but also very effectively drives home the complexity involved in Muslim interpretation of the Qur'an: "'Muslims believe the Quran is the verbatim Word of God.' This is true. At the same time, this does not mean that the Quran is supposed to be read literally, if that means denying the historical meaning of terms and expressions, ignoring the social context of particular rulings, or neglecting its symbolic and inner meanings."[27] Mattson's discussion not only reinforces the absolute necessity of paying attention first and foremost to how Muslims themselves read the text (as Mattson is herself not only academically expert in the text but also a devout Muslim who engages deeply with the text on a devotional level); it also reveals to students the subtlety with which the text is read and interpreted.

This makes reductive statements about "Islam and violence" seem less plausible once the point is made that such a question, even in the Qur'an, is treated with great subtlety and attention to historical context (as it is, of course, in Christian and Jewish scripture as well). Further discussion on this hermeneutical point could involve discussion of the medieval *tafsir* debates about verses such as 9:5, 8:61, and 60:8. Asma Afsaruddin summarizes these debates very effectively in chapter 5 of her *Contemporary Issues in Islam*, entitled "War and Peacemaking in the Islamic Tradition."[28] Afsaruddin's discussion elaborates in detail how even within the medieval commentary tradition (to say nothing of the modern mainstream Muslim consensus on the defensive nature of jihad) there was a lively debate on the meaning of these Quranic discussions of violence. Some commentators argued that the Qur'an supported the imperial ambitions of medieval Muslim rulers, while others (such as the eminent tenth-century scholar al-Tabari) argued instead that the Qur'an verses that reference peacemaking with non-Muslims have normative significance (and those referring to making war on nonbelievers were restricted in their application to situations that the Prophet faced in his lifetime).[29]

Pointing out this complexity in the medieval tradition often helps address the common false assertion that the entirety of Muslim tradition is in agreement on the eternal necessity to commit violence against non-Muslims (an assertion usually based on a tendentious discussion of the concept of abrogation and a general neglect of important distinctions made in traditional Quranic interpretation, such as that between general and specific applicability; and the specific contexts of Quranic revelation itself). Afsaruddin aptly summarizes the larger conceptual issues at stake in a sensitive discussion of the relationship between religion and violence: "It is abundantly evident that the specific sociopolitical circumstances of [Muslim] exegetes were frequently decisive in shaping their views, an awareness of which fact allows us to appreciate the highly contingent— and contested—nature of these discourses."[30]

Frame 2: Religion and Politics, or "Does Islam want to dominate non-Muslim societies or politics?"

I have often found that the anxiety behind this question is driven by apprehension of shari'a, which is almost always presented in American media as a totalizing political project. I point out to my students that American media discourse on shari'a is perhaps the most egregious example of pseudo-knowledge about Islam in current circulation: American media commentators and politicians have, in essence, accepted the most radical of political Islamists' definition of "shari'a" and held the rest of the Muslim world to account for it. Rather than discuss the shari'a as most Muslims understand it (as a system of ritual duties and social ethics that not only prioritizes individual ritual devotions but also does not include a set formula for politics or state law), many American political commentators insist on describing shari'a as a project of global Islamic domination of which every Muslim is either consciously or unconsciously a part.[31]

Therefore, introducing in my class discussions a nuanced discussion of the term "shari'a" has effectively addressed this particular frame by giving students a better sense of the enormous complexity of what this term means to Muslims and, by extension, the enormous complexity of the relationship between Islam (or any religious tradition) and the immensely variable practices of human politics and governance. I have found two short writings in particular to be very effective in beginning this discussion: Kecia Ali's "Whose Sharia Is It?"[32] and Jerusha T. Lamptey's "Boko Haram: Not My Sharia."[33] Written by two of the most important scholars of Islam writing in America today, these short and accessible pieces (both written for a wide reading audience) shed much light on the many conceptual dimensions of the term "shari'a" and in doing so invite the reader to think more deeply about the complicated relationship between religion and social practice.

As Ali writes, "Claims like that of the Sultan [of Brunei] or Boko Haram that 'Islam' demands implementation of 'sharia' ignore the complex reality in which there is not now nor has there ever been a uniform set of identifiable rules that Muslim scholars have agreed on much less that governments in Muslim majority countries have implemented over the centuries."[34] Ali goes on to call attention to the fact that modern forms of patriarchy are often the most influential factors in shaping current interpretations of what God's law should look like in practice and that the variability built into the concept of shari'a itself is crucial to understanding just how big a role local social conditions play in interpretations of shari'a. Lamptey provides a particularly illuminating summary of what the term "shari'a" actually signifies: "Shariah *is* part of Islam, and shariah *is* important to Muslims. But shariah is *not* a codified, static or agreed upon collection of laws. Shariah is better understood as guiding principles according to which Muslims attempt to live their lives. A good analogy here is the founding ideals of our nation. These ideals, especially as expressed by the founding fathers, continue to inspire us today. Our laws, however, sometimes fall short, and when they do they require change. It is similar with shariah and Islamic law."[35]

Lamptey's discussion brings out the conceptual nuance of shari'a, a key dimension of the term that is entirely ignored in the vast majority of American media discussions of shari'a. Simply beginning to better understand what this term means can often go a long way in resolving students' anxieties and questions about the relationship between Islam and politics. Finally, I would also suggest that instructors consider making use of the work of Mohammad Hashim Kamali, whose widely available and very accessible texts in English provide excellent discussions of key theoretical and practical features of shari'a.[36] Khaled Abou El Fadl's recent scholarship is also an indispensable part of contemporary discussions on the nature of shari'a.[37]

Frame 3: Religion and Patriarchy, or "Does Islam oppress women?"

Such a question is often based on the presumption that Muslim societies (and by extension Islam itself) feature an exceptionally high degree of patriarchy and degrading treatment of women.[38] This frame offers the opportunity to reinforce with students the point made above: the need to listen to Muslim voices, particularly the voices of Muslim women. Following the work of Lila Abu-Lughod, a classroom discussion of this frame can lead students to discussing the importance of analytically prioritizing the experiences of Muslim women themselves and their own descriptions of these experiences.[39] Ethnographic accounts such as Abu-Lughod's work can serve a crucial pedagogical function when addressing this question by shifting attention away from the artifice of media discourse about Muslim women and toward the specific types of discourses and practices actively employed by people in their own circumstances. As Abu-Lughod puts it, this kind of analysis is a form of "writing against culture": a way to resist conceiving of Muslim women's experiences in terms of oversimplified and essentialized tropes about "Muslim culture."[40] Rather than attempting to abstractly define or discuss supposedly essential features of "Muslim culture" as it relates to women, this analysis can be used to encourage students to begin to think about this important question by listening to the voices of Muslim women themselves.

Engagement with this frame also offers the opportunity to reinforce the point made above about the complexities of Islamic scriptural hermeneutics. As Zayn Kassam points out, pedagogical engagement with such texts should focus on how constructions of gender and gendered norms are made through a reading of Islamic sacred and classical texts, and how Muslim women themselves read these texts.[41] I also personally have found it useful to bring Hans Gadamer into this discussion by referring to his famous description of an interpretive challenge (such as the challenge of interpreting difficult gendered language in a sacred text) as "the experience of being pulled up short by the text."[42] In fact, in order to demonstrate the need to approach such hermeneutical questions with extraordinary sensitivity, I sometimes simulate in class this experience of "being pulled up short by the text" by having an impromptu class discussion of difficult biblical verses. One example I have used is 1 Timothy 2:12: "I permit no woman to teach or to have authority over a man; she is to keep silent."[43] After presenting this quote to the class, I first ask simply how it makes them feel to read this text. In other words, what experience do they have when they read it? If they read this quote in another context, would they agree with it? How should we understand it? I do not attempt in any way to criticize the text or quote itself: rather, I invite them to deal with it however they feel most comfortable doing so.

While watching this interpretive process take place, I have noticed that many students begin to quite spontaneously articulate very sincere ways in which the text can be contextualized or theologically understood in a way that maintains a due sense of reverence for the biblical text and at the same time does not injure the ethical requirement of equality and fair treatment. I then simply point out that this is precisely how *any* believer approaches her sacred text, including Muslims: in such a way that maintains both the sanctity of the text and our own deeply held sense of human rights and social values. Fortunately, numerous powerful examples of Quranic hermeneutics with respect to gender and sexuality are now widely available to use in these discussions, including the works of Jerusha T. Lamptey, Kecia Ali, Aysha A. Hidayatullah, Asma Barlas, and Amina Wadud, to name only a very few.[44]

Frame 4: Religion and Foreign Policy, or "Who are the terrorists (such as ISIS) and where do they come from?"

I acknowledge immediately that inclusion of this topic in an Introduction to Islam course is very controversial, and rightfully so. As I emphasize to my students, my approach in this course is to introduce to students what I informally call "the historical average" of Muslim religious discourses and practices: an extraordinarily variable mix of topics to say the least, but I do attempt to demarcate some of the most important basic elements of Islamic religious tradition across time and space. These basic elements, of course, are entirely unrelated to such marginal and recent phenomena as international jihadist terrorism. Including a brief discussion of jihadist terrorism at the end of the course has, however, served two crucial pedagogical functions. First, it addresses a question that my students find extremely urgent. Moreover, many of my students may never again be exposed to highly informed academic discussions of this topic, leaving them, to use a phrase, potentially at the mercy of deeply problematic media discussions on this topic. Second, it actually has the potential to demonstrate how complex human motivations can be by using jihadist terrorism as a test case to demonstrate the profound *inability* of traditional Muslim discourses to explain the existence of jihadist extremism.

In the past few semesters, I have dedicated one to two class periods at the end of each semester to discuss the rise of ISIS. This provides an opportunity to discuss the disastrous US invasion of Iraq in 2003, a worthy pedagogical goal in itself as I have found that most of my students know little to nothing about this crucially important event in the contemporary Middle East. To introduce this topic, I assign students to read a short article entitled "U.S. Blunders in Iraq: De-Baathification and Disbanding the Army," by James Pfiffner, a distinguished professor of public policy at George Mason University.[45] Discussing these two specific foreign policy decisions made during the Iraq War has been very effective in opening students' eyes to the crucial role that very specific geopolitical conditions have played in the rise of ISIS. This discussion allows our conversation about ISIS to revolve around concrete questions of ISIS' political and social origins, rather than enter into a discussion of ISIS' supposed level of "Islamic-ness"—a discussion that leaves students totally unsatisfied about how to begin to grapple with the constant bombardment of media soundbites and analytical dead-ends regarding the question of jihadist violence. Discussion about the war in Iraq and its relationship with the growth of jihadist movements such as ISIS therefore has the potential to demonstrate one key point about religious studies and the study of Islam that is beautifully phrased by Carl Ernst: "To assume that Muslims, and Muslims alone, are driven to act exclusively by religion, apart from any of the other factors that shape our lives, is more than absurd. It dehumanizes Muslims and makes them into frightening monsters who are not only alien but also hostile."[46]

Frame 5: Religion and National Identity, or
"Is Islam a threat to the United States?"

As demonstrated above, this particular form of Islamophobic cultural anxiety is thriving in the contemporary United States. I use engagement with this frame as an opportunity to discuss the responsibilities of citizenship in American democracy, which includes engagement with crucial questions of religious freedom and the definition of national identity. One piece of literature that I find particularly useful in this discussion is the recent survey report produced by the Institute for Social Policy and Understanding, "American Muslim Poll: Participation, Priorities, and Facing Prejudice in the 2016 Elections."[47] This report highlights the close connection American Muslims feel between their civic and religious identities, and the close connection between mosque participation and civic engagement (rather than with "radicalization"). Discussion of these connections with students helps to create productive conversations about the complexities of contemporary American civic and religious identity, further highlighting the theoretical point made regarding Frame 4: that Muslim political identity is, as with any other religious community, highly specific to prevailing cultural and social conditions and must be analyzed within those frameworks (rather than with reference to a supposedly universal "Islamic" ideal form of politics that has never actually existed).

Concluding Remarks

This essay has argued that intentionally engaging with media frames that consciously or unconsciously structure many students' approach to understanding Islam enhances the overall learning goals of introductory level Islamic studies courses. The brief, but hopefully illustrative, examples outlined above constitute my own suggestions, based on my own experience, as to how this engagement might be conducted. I wish to reiterate again that I make no claim that these suggestions can or should be universally applicable to all, or even most, Islamic studies courses. Rather, I offer them as examples of how I have successfully engaged with some urgent questions that a great many of my students have brought to my Introduction to Islam course, semester after semester.

At the end of my Introduction to Islam course, I ask my students to reflect on the fact that as a democracy, the American voters have control over American politics; and since the United States possesses one of the most powerful militaries the world has ever seen, American voters make decisions that do not just affect the United States but also the lives of billions of people for many generations to come. Ultimately, I view my teaching as being rooted in the liberal arts ethical imperative to empower students to be better citizens and neighbors. At the beginning of this fall semester of 2016, one student made a point to tell me after class that they had signed up for Introduction to Islam in order to make themselves "a better voter." Put another way: "Every kingdom divided against itself is laid waste, and no city or house divided against itself will stand."[48] And, "work not corruption upon the earth after it has been set aright, but call upon Him in fear and in hope. Surely the Mercy of God is ever nigh unto the virtuous."[49]

Notes

1. Mark Berkson, "A Non-Muslim Teaching Islam: Pedagogical and Ethical Challenges," *Teaching Theology and Religion* 8, no. 2 (2005): 88.

2. Berkson, "A Non-Muslim Teaching Islam," 86.

3. J. Z. Smith, *On Teaching Religion*, ed. Christopher I. Lehrich (Oxford: Oxford University Press, 2013), 13.

4. Thomas Kidd, *American Christians and Islam: Evangelical Culture and Muslims from the Colonial Period to the Age of Terrorism* (Princeton, NJ: Princeton University Press, 2009), 9.

5. Kidd, *American Christians and Islam*, 1.

6. Kidd, *American Christians and Islam*, 18, 26–27.

7. Kidd, *American Christians and Islam*, 84.

8. Kidd, *American Christians and Islam*, 136.

9. One of the most popular examples of this genre is Joel Richardson's work, especially his New York Times bestseller, *The Islamic Antichrist* (Los Angeles: WND Press, 2015).

10. Richard Hofstadter, *The Paranoid Style in American Politics* (1964; repr., New York: Vintage Books, 2008), 4.

11. Nathan Lean, *The Islamophobia Industry: How the Right Manufactures Fear of Muslims* (New York: Pluto Press, 2012), 23. Lawrence Davidson ("Islamophobia, the Israel Lobby and American Paranoia: Letter from America," *Holy Land Studies: A Multidisciplinary Journal* 10, no. 1 [May 2011]: 87–95) has also compared Hofstadter's concept of "the paranoid style" with American Islamophobia.

12. Kidd, *American Christians and Islam*, 8, 36.

13. Hofstadter, *The Paranoid Style*, 19-20.

14. Hofstadter, *The Paranoid Style*, 23, 8.

15. Hofstadter, *The Paranoid Style*, 30.

16. Todd Green, *The Fear of Islam: An Introduction to Islamophobia in the West* (Minneapolis, MN: Fortress Press, 2015), 103.

17. Green, *The Fear of Islam*, 113.

18. Robert Shaffer, "Open Your Eyes: Followers of Islam are Real Threat," *Wyoming Tribune Eagle*, March 30, 2016.

19. Shelbi Telhami, "American Attitudes toward the Middle East," *The Brookings Institution*, July 11, 2016.

20. Robert P. Jones, Daniel Cox, Betsy Cooper, and Rachel Lienesch, "Anxiety, Nostalgia, and Mistrust: Findings from the 2015 American Values Survey," *Public Religion Research Institute*, November 17, 2015, 4.

21. Green, *The Fear of Islam*, 223.

22. A. Kevin Reinhart, "On the 'Introduction to Islam,'" in *Teaching Islam*, ed. Brannon Wheeler (New York: Oxford University Press, 2003), 23.

23. Reinhart, "On the 'Introduction to Islam,'" 22–23.

24. I have drawn these conclusions from a variety of in-depth interactions I've had with students and other community members. These include daily readings reflections required of each student, questions I've received from community members beyond campus during public speaking events about Islam and the Muslim world, course feedback, and the many in-class discussions each semester that revolve around students' desired learning goals for the course and the preconceptions they have brought with them to the course (primarily Introduction to Islam courses but also other introductory level religion courses).

25. See note 3 above, and also Brannon Wheeler, "What Can't Be Left Out: The Essentials of Teaching Islam as a Religion," in Wheeler, *Teaching Islam*, 3–21.

26. Ingrid Mattson, "How to Read the Qur'an," in *The Study Quran: A New Translation and Commentary*, ed. and trans. Seyyed Hossein Nasr, Caner K. Dagli, Maria Marissa Dakake, Joseph B. Lumbard, and Mohammed Rustom (New York: HarperOne, 2015), 1587–1600.

27. Mattson, "How to Read the Qur'an," 1588.

28. Asma Afsaruddin, *Contemporary Issues in Islam* (Edinburgh: Edinburgh University Press, 2015), 115–140.

29. Afsaruddin, *Contemporary Issues in Islam*, 124.

30. Afsaruddin, *Contemporary Issues in Islam*, 119.

31. Examples of this kind of distortion are legion. Some notable ones that have had a particularly strong impact on contemporary American politics include literature published by the Center for Security Policy and the writings of Andrew McCarthy.

32. Kecia Ali, "Whose Sharia Is It?," *Huffington Post*, May 29, 2014.

33. Jerusha T. Lamptey, "Boko Haram: Not My Sharia," *Time*, May 8, 2014.

34. Ali, "Whose Sharia Is It?."

35. Lamptey, "Boko Haram: Not My Sharia."

36. I have found that selections from Mohammad Hashim Kamali's *Shari'ah Law: An Introduction* (Oxford, UK: Oneworld, 2008) are particularly useful in undergraduate contexts.

37. See especially Khaled Abou El Fadl, *Reasoning with God: Reclaiming Shari'ah in the Modern Age* (Lanham, MD: Rowman & Littlefield, 2014).

38. See also in Zayn Kassam, "Engendering and Experience: Teaching a Course on Women in Islam," in Wheeler, *Teaching Islam*, 125.

39. Lila Abu-Lughod, *Do Muslim Women Need Saving?* (Cambridge, MA: Harvard University Press, 2013), 26.

40. Abu-Lughod, *Do Muslim Women Need Saving?*, 6.

41. Kassam, "Engendering and Experience," 124.

42. Hans Georg Gadamer, *Truth and Method*, trans. Joel Weinsheimer and Donald G. Marshall (London: Continuum, 2004), 270.

43. From the New Revised Standard Version (NRSV).

44. See the bibliography for their main works.

45. James P. Pfiffner, "US Blunders in Iraq: De-Baathification and Disbanding the Army," *Intelligence and National Security* 25, no. 1 (February 2010): 76–85.

46. Carl W. Ernst, *Following Muhammad: Rethinking Islam in the Contemporary World* (Chapel Hill: University of North Carolina Press, 2003), 28.

47. Dalia Mogahed and Fouad Pervez, "American Muslim Poll: Participation, Priorities, and Facing Prejudice in the 2016 Elections," *Institute for Social Policy and Understanding*, March 2016.

48. Matthew 12:25, NRSV.

49. *The Study Qur'an*, Surat al-A'raf 56.

PHIL DORROLL is Assistant Professor of Religion at Wofford College.

chapter thirteen

REFLECTIVE PRACTICE IN ONLINE COURSES
Making Islamic Studies Interactive and Approachable

Lyndall Herman

INTRODUCTION

In the field of teacher training and teacher effectiveness, "reflection" is a current buzzword. Yet, by and large, this mechanism has not made the leap from teacher training into mainstream use in either the physical or the virtual classroom. Katelyn Barney and Elizabeth Mackinlay's course is one of the exceptions. [1] Some research also exists on shorter, ad hoc reflective practices, such as muddiest point papers,[2] which are used for specific lesson-focused reflection. This essay focuses on the practice of reflection in fully online classes and its role in enhancing student learning, by arguing that guided reflection practices enhance the student learning experience and depth of knowledge acquired.[3]

In an adaptation from Barney and Mackinlay's approach to studying Aboriginal music, reflective practice is applied to another area of non-Western study: Islamic and Middle Eastern studies, in the current political context of ISIS and Islamophobia. In an evolution of the above reflective journaling approach, instead of utilizing a daily or weekly hard-copy journal, this guided reflective practice asks students to respond to broad prompts on an online class forum. Students then return to reflect on these public posts through "diary entries" that are private and shared only with the instructor. These "diary entries," in conjunction with the forum posts, start a virtual conversation between the instructor and student. Discussion of such engagement techniques in fully online, asynchronous courses is important, as this is a growing area of instruction and learning.

This case study addresses the use and effectiveness of guided reflection practice in four courses of Middle Eastern Humanities taught at the University of Arizona and Cochise College. By using the practice in these courses, student participation in the virtual classroom and interactivity with their peers and the instructor increased, which led to valuable student-led learning scenarios. This essay presents a brief summary of the relevant literature on teaching Islamic studies online and reflective practice in teacher training and its place in student-centered teaching. It then discusses the necessary adaptations for using reflective practice in an online, asynchronous course and the specific pedagogic approach and methods used in teaching the courses involved in this case study. After outlining the approach and methods, the essay presents and discusses examples of student formative and summative reflections that show the compelling student growth that can take place when using guided reflective practice. Such student engagement and growth is particularly important when teaching courses on Islam and the Middle East in this current climate of fear.

LITERATURE REVIEW

The literature about using educational technologies in teaching Islamic studies is quite slim. In part this is because of the very rapid and recent development of educational technologies. One of the most respected volumes regarding the teaching of Islamic studies, *Teaching Islam* edited by Brannon Wheeler, includes one chapter on the use of "information technology" in the classroom.[4] While at the time of publication, 2003, the curated use of internet sources in the classroom yielded substantial benefit to students, this material is less helpful in 2017. A more recent 2016 edited volume on the use of digital humanities in teaching Islamic and Middle Eastern studies also focuses on the use of information technologies in the form of digital archives and the manner in which such technologies have changed students' access and ability to interact with previously inaccessible material.[5] While these are valuable contributions detailing the use of online resources, neither of these volumes addresses effective practices in teaching Islamic studies online.

There are also a small number of publications that address specific educational technologies that can be used to enhance student learning in Islamic studies courses. These publications tend to focus on using educational technologies to enhance the learning process and student knowledge, such as Ayla Göl's work on e-Portfolios. These e-Portfolios, hosted through the university's learning management system, proved to be useful formative assessment mechanisms that allowed for more timely and substantive feedback to students.[6] However, the focus remains on specific technologies rather than addressing best practices in teaching Islamic studies in a fully online, asynchronous learning environment. This essay makes an original contribution by addressing pedagogic concerns and practices when teaching Islamic studies in a fully online setting. It does so through connecting this limited literature with the literature on reflective practice, a prominent pedagogic tool used predominantly in teacher training programs.

The literature on the role and effectiveness of reflective practices in the classroom can be broken into three broad categories: the role of reflection in teacher training settings, the place of reflection in discipline-specific scenarios (in particular the medical field), and the use of reflection with students in face-to-face classroom settings. The largest amount of research and literature is found in the first category: the role of reflection in teacher training. By and large, this literature lauds the role of reflection in teacher training programs.[7] Much of this research focuses on developing critical reflective skills in student teachers and teacher trainees to create awareness among this population of the need to constantly revisit the question of what works in the classroom.[8] The aim of such critical reflection is to revise classroom activities to enhance the knowledge acquisition of students.[9] Another area of prominence in this research is the role of reflection in teacher professional development.[10] This suggests that all instructors can benefit from using reflective practice throughout their careers. Some pieces also assert that reflective practice is more effective for student teachers when enacted through different media, such as poetry.[11]

The second body of literature focuses on reflective practices in specific disciplines. Interestingly, the majority of this literature is focused on reflective practices in medical fields.[12] In particular, there are a substantial number of pieces that address the beneficial role of reflective journaling in the field of nursing. There is some focus on how reflective journaling practices empower nursing students[13] and assist in developing their critical thinking skills.[14] Similar literature addresses reflective practice in dental student training. The literature on dental students also looks to link reflective practices to academic achievement[15] and assessment outcomes, including peer- and self-assessments.[16] There is also some work on the use of reflection in social work training. This is one of the few examples of work on reflective practices in a partially online setting.[17] Lynn Bye et al. find that, when comparing online discussion forums with hard-copy reflective journaling, student satisfaction with learning outcomes is linked to participation in the online discussion forum rather than personal journaling.[18] This is particularly interesting as the methodology below combines an online discussion forum with personal journaling activities. Bye et al. do postulate that student age is significant to their findings in this particular study.[19]

The final category to address is the use of reflective practices in a face-to-face course with students not enrolled in teacher training courses. This literature finds that reflective practices in such settings tend to enhance student learning.[20] Including a compelling finding from work by Rebecca O'Rourke that "writing about new information or ideas, enables students to better understand and remember them, and that articulating connections between new information or ideas and existing knowledge secures and extends learning."[21] It is also particularly important to acknowledge the place of emotion in the learning process.[22] Too often we as instructors do not acknowledge the prior experience and perceptions that students bring to the classroom. When studying such politicized topics as the religion of Islam, particularly in this age of ISIS and rampant Islamophobia, it is essential to acknowledge these emotions. Preconceptions must be addressed and unpacked before significant learning can take place.

Barney and Mackinlay focus on reflective journaling practices in a face-to-face classroom setting. However, their focus on non-Western subject matter, here a course on Aboriginal music in the field of Indigenous Australian studies, and the way in which reflective practices can deconstruct the mainstream biases perpetuated about such subject matter is key to this study.[23] Their focus is on examining "how reflection can assist students and teachers in exploring their assumptions, expectations and positionings in relation to Indigenous Australian music."[24] While the focus in the course addressed here is the religion of Islam and the cultures and traditions of the Middle East, this is simply a geographic shift in focus while the intentions of introducing, acknowledging, and confronting these biases remain the same. Likewise, when describing the appropriateness of reflective journaling for their course, Barney and Mackinlay note that the sensitive nature of much of the material and its relationship to colonialism, racism, and continued oppression can challenge students.[25] Similar material and histories are encountered when studying Islam and the Middle East in the Western collegiate setting. For this reason, guided reflective practice can have an important role in encouraging students to discuss material that challenges their preconceptions and replace these by constructing new understandings in a nonjudgmental space.[26]

METHODOLOGY

This essay focuses on the application of guided reflective practice in four Middle Eastern Humanities courses taught at the University of Arizona and at Cochise College. The two University of Arizona courses occurred during the condensed three-week winter session in 2013/14 and the five-week summer session in 2016, and the two Cochise College courses took place during the traditional sixteen-week spring semesters in 2015 and 2016. All courses were taught in a fully online, asynchronous environment. Due to the differences in the length and pace of the course, two different models of guided reflective practices were employed. Both models borrow heavily from the journal approach used and discussed by Barney and Mackinlay.

The course in this case study, Middle Eastern Humanities, is a tier-one general education course that meets the general education requirements for the "Traditions and Cultures" track. All undergraduate students attending the University of Arizona must take two courses that meet this tier-one Traditions and Cultures designation. Middle Eastern Humanities is one of the options and provides an overview of many important aspects of Middle Eastern studies, including the study of stereotypes of Islam and the Middle East, the history of Islam in the Middle East, the five pillars of Islam, the sectarian divide in Islam, traditions of private and public space, the place of women in Islam and Middle Eastern society, music and literature, Arab nationalism, political Islam, and the Arab Spring. Students tend to take their tier-one general education course requirements either as freshmen or as second-semester seniors. The same course content is taught at Cochise College, where the course also meets the humanities general education requirement.

Similar core elements exist between the two models, as both models focus on using the online discussion forum and the private assignment options of the online learning management system.[27] Participation in the discussion forum was linked to points earned. In order to receive full participation credit for their posts, students were required to post an initial response to a question posed by the instructor and then to make two unique and engaging comments to two separate peers' initial posts.[28] These public interactions were followed up with personal reflection assignments ("diary entries"), submitted directly to the instructor. These "diary entries" were one- to two-page journal-like responses regarding the content on the discussion boards during a given period of time. The frequency of these assignments depended on the course length and so was different in each of the models. The final assignment for each course was a reflective essay, in which students addressed two key points. Students were first asked to reflect on their public discussion forum posts and address any changes in their perspectives. The second portion of the paper asked students to reflect on how the material learned in the course would be relevant in their future professional lives. Importantly, these reflective practice activities did not replace exam-based assessment. Rather, the reflection activities were a separate assessment technique that focused on critical thinking faculties. Students were still required to complete unit exams (usually covering four or five book chapters) and a final exam, providing content-focused formative and summative assessments.

Much of the burden for these guided reflective practices falls on the instructor who must be present in the online environment and offer guidance and mediation as necessary. Similarly, discussion forum questions need to encourage interaction and discussion among the course participants. These questions should be open-ended and require students to critically engage with the new material and any of their own biases on the topic. Finally, the discussion forum must be a safe space for students to ask questions they might feel are "dumb" and to seek feedback from both their peers and the instructor. Supplementary materials, particularly videos, can be very important in providing depth for and context to the course readings. These videos can be recordings of lectures or educational videos produced for use in the classroom.

A few of the discussion prompts that have provoked the most thoughtful responses and high levels of interaction[29] include:

1. Now that you have watched *Reel Bad Arabs*,[30] how do you feel about stereotypes of the Middle East? Do you believe that stereotypes can ever be completely harmless or serve a purpose?
2. After watching *Islam: Empire of Faith*,[31] did you learn something new about the religion of Islam? Did the movie challenge any of your preconceptions about the religion?
3. Please write a short paragraph about which of the five pillars you believe is the best example of *twahid* and why.
4. What do you think about headscarf bans? Would you support one? Where, when, and why?

When the course participants have a particularly strong reaction to a given discussion question, that question becomes the focus of the next individual reflection activity ("diary entry"). As stated earlier, this approach requires constant monitoring and updating of the course site and assignments.

The Condensed Three- or Five-Week Model

In order to more thoroughly explain reflection activities, the models for both course lengths are presented in detail, and several specific student reflections are discussed. In the three- or five-week model, students are required to author two original discussion posts each week, in response to two separate teacher-provided prompts. In addition, students must provide two pairs of original and engaging comments (for a total of four comments) on a peer's post. Initial posts are due by Tuesday and Thursday at midnight, and all four comments must be posted by Friday at midnight. This allows the instructor time to incorporate the comments into the weekly reflection activities, which are due the following Wednesday. These reflection activities are akin to journal entries to a question posed by the instructor and are private assignments submitted directly to the instructor. Only the student sees the instructor's feedback. Importantly, these assignments are graded based on completion and response to the prompt. They do not replace content-based assessments; those weekly assignments are due each Saturday, once all new content for the week has been covered. Rather, these reflections provide a nonjudgmental space for students to voice thoughts, concerns, and questions that they may not be comfortable writing in the public discussion forum. These four reflections are then used as reference material for each student's final reflective essay on the place of the course material in their future career. The final essay asks students to review their earlier discussion forum posts and discuss how their perspectives have been challenged, reinforced, and altered and how they believe the material learned in the course will impact their future professional lives.

The strength of this model comes from these student reflections and so, with their permission, select examples from the five-week summer 2016 course follow. The first comes from the week one public discussion forum from the summer of 2016. The response, posted by a Middle Eastern student, is in response to prompt one, listed above in the methodologies section,[32] regarding stereotypes:

> The feeling that I had when I come [sic] to the United States is "scared." Because if someone asks me about my country which is Kuwait many of them do not know where that is so at first they do not react, however, eventually they know that I am from the Middle East and that scares me because I do not know what idea they have in mind about Arabs. Is it what on the media or they met Arabian person before and they are fine with it.[33]

This is a powerful statement on the real and very personal implications of stereotypes both about and held by the students in this course. This initial post received the highest number of comments in the entire course; most of these comments thanked the student for contributing such a personal and revealing perspective on the issue. In fact, the impact of this one post resonated throughout the five weeks of the course and was referenced in other students' final reflective responses. Another student commented that "as I leave this class, all I can think about are the past, present, and future stereotypes that reside all around me, that I wouldn't have noticed before," adding that "this class has taught me that if I choose the person that looks and speaks just like me versus one who doesn't, then I am engaging a stereo-type. It is one of those subtle stereotypes that I wouldn't have thought of before; just because it isn't obvious, doesn't mean it doesn't exist."[34] It is important to note that this is representative of only one course and that the personal nature of the reflection was beyond the control of the course instructor. However, similar interactions and learning opportunities have occurred in the other courses as well, indicating that this approach pro-vides a starting point that allows and encourages students to capitalize on personal reflections when they are posted to these discussion forums.

Another example, this time from the winter 2013/14 course, is equally compelling. The students in this course were 90 percent juniors and se-niors. These students were taking a final, mandatory general education course in order to graduate. Two students submitted particularly striking final reflection papers. The first student, who was graduating with a nurs-ing degree, stated that "I will take the information I learned about the 5 pillars of Islam with me into the field of nursing and that will allow me to better relate to Muslim patients."[35] The student went on to note the im-portance of understanding Ramadan fasting traditions and standards of modesty when working with Muslim patients. A second student wrote "I am currently training with Air Force ROTC and took this course to help with mental preparedness. Learning about Islamism and its differences from Islam has helped me to understand the conflict in the Middle East."[36] For both of these students, this final reflective paper bridged the gap be-tween proficiency in the course content and realizing a tangible use of the material in their future careers.

The Sixteen-Week Semester Model

The sixteen-week semester model has all the same goals of the more con-densed and intensive three- and five-week models, however, the additional time in this model allows for more student-guided reflection. In the six-teen-week semester-long model, students make weekly public discussion forum posts each Tuesday, and then they contribute a minimum of two comments total to peers' initial posts. This model allows for a total of fif-teen initial discussion forum posts.[37] This is significantly more than the six or ten discussion forum posts from the condensed format courses. Addi-tional reflection activities, spread over a greater period of time, encourage students to engage more deeply with the material. These public discussion forums also serve the purpose of creating a community in the online en-vironment. While it is always important to create a communal environ-ment in the classroom, it is even more relevant in the online environment when students never meet face-to-face. In the sixteen-week session, it is particularly important because if students do not feel engaged with their peers then they will not feel present in the classroom. Student disengagement from the online classroom is detrimental to learning in the online environment. By establishing early in the course a schedule for these discussion and comment posts, students come to understand the importance of their responses to their own and their peers' learning.

The construction of this communal learning environment is further reinforced through the "diary entry" reflections. In the instructions for these assignments, students are told that a portion of each diary entry must reflect on their earlier discussion forum responses, encouraging them to return to and reflect on both their posts and the comments of their peers. There are four diary entries due throughout the course, one for each unit, and they are due in quarterly increments, every four weeks. The slower pace of the graded reflection activities encourages students to more deeply engage with the material in each of their entries. Students are once again graded on completion and responding to the given prompt. The prompt specifically tells students to review their forum discussion posts for the last quarter and reflect on these posts, noting any changes in or reinforcement of their opinions. Students are also asked to link these changes and reinforcing of opinions to specific resources, activities and interactions in the online environment. These forum activities and the subsequent reflections on them are important tools for guiding students through the learning process in the online environment.

In a face-to-face classroom, students are constantly engaged in reflective practices as the material covered cycles back into the discussion throughout the semester. Even in face-to-face classroom settings, guided reflection through responses to prompts and graded assignments can be very beneficial to students. However, in an online course environment such practices become essential to keep students engaged in the material, even as they move through the units at their own pace. Students in the sixteen-week semester model also submit a final essay, linking their new knowledge gained through the course to their future careers. Again, this reflection is important in guiding students to review their earlier perceptions of and views on the course material. This encourages students to address and acknowledge their growth throughout the semester. This final reflective essay does not replace a final exam, which assesses the students' content-based knowledge.

In the two courses that I have taught based on this model, I have found the diary entries to be the points of greatest growth. Through these guided reflections students are forced to revisit their previous discussion posts for each unit and reflect on how their positions and viewpoints have been challenged or reinforced. The diary entries, which are private and submitted directly to the instructor for grading through the assignment function in Moodle, are one and a half to two pages in length and ask the student to make reference to particular activities, readings, and supplemental material that have impacted their thoughts and opinions on the course material.

Included here are a few examples from these diary entries, where students address the changes in their opinions and understanding of Islam and the Middle East through course activities. The first example comes from the 2016 spring semester course and is taken from the second diary entry reflecting on the religion of Islam unit. The student is responding to the portion of the prompt that asks students to reflect on how their opinions on Islam have been impacted by the course material, stating:

> this unit was the one I was most interested in, I wanted to study Islam rather than just read what is on the internet. After watching *Empire of Faith* I now think that Islam in its infancy was ahead of its time. I am intrigued by Islam's focus on community and providing aid to your fellow man. My favorite pillar of Islam is Zakat because I like the idea of everyone giving a little to better their surroundings and help one another.[38]

By asking students to revise earlier course material and reflect on their major takeaway points, the students must interact once again with the material. This interaction asks them to contemplate the material in relation to their daily lives and is more likely to be relevant to them in the future than material memorized for a test.

The second example comes from the 2015 spring semester and is also in response to the second diary entry, which addresses the unit on the religion of Islam. This student writes:

> *Islam: Empire of Faith* has greatly changed the way I saw and thought about Muslims. The Islamic empire had opened roads to scientific and medical advancement. The dark and fearful thoughts that I had before about Muslims and Islam have mainly dissolved through the teaching. The more I learn about the Middle East, the greater the need I feel to partake for a moment in their way of life.[39]

These reflection activities force students to look beyond the content knowledge that they have gained in the course. By addressing the changes in their attitude and perspectives toward Islam and the Middle East, these moments of reflection provide deep self-knowledge beyond the stated learning outcomes of the course.

Areas of Concern for Future Research

The use of guided reflection in these courses was not set up to test its effectiveness as a means for increasing student learning. Rather it was a process into which these courses evolved as a means to increase interaction with students and give them a way to "check in" and express concerns and frustrations. These reflective activities were completely absent from the first online courses that I taught in 2012 and 2013; however, these exercises quickly evolved from being a means to "check in" with students to a moment to provide them with an opportunity to productively reflect on and internalize what they were learning. My own teacher training experience, which heavily emphasized the important role that reflection plays in building community and enhancing learning, influenced the approach and the rationale behind these reflection activities. I did not set out to create a study on the place and effectiveness of guided reflection. Instead, I am offering here my approaches and best practices as developed over four years of teaching nine online courses in a variety of formats and topics.[40] I see this as a starting point for more rigorous study of how guided reflection can enhance student learning in online courses. In particular, those courses focused on non-Western content, which so often encounter unaddressed and unacknowledged biases that students have constructed over years of exposure to mainstream popular and news media. As I continue to teach online courses I will continue to develop these guided reflective practices to build a more substantial body of proof that shows how guided reflection enhances and deepens student learning in online courses about Islam and the Middle East.

Conclusions

The literature shows the important role that reflective practices play in enhancing learning in teaching training scenarios. Barney and Mackinlay expanded on this research, applying reflective journaling practices in a face-to-face course as a mechanism to augment student learning about non-Western subject matter.[41] Their application to a non-Western focused course subject was of particular interest due to the parallels with my own course subject matter. My own experience as a student in an online course environment also influenced my openness to and interest in using these reflective practices. Based on my use of these different levels of guided reflective practice in an online course environment, I find that structured reflection exercises enhance student learning. The reflection activities deepen student learning by providing a safe space in which students can engage in critical self-reflection of their earlier practices and perspectives.

This type of reflective activity has an important place in all learning environments. However, in the online classroom it becomes even more important for keeping students actively engaging in the material, rather than simply completing assignments from a checklist. In particular, guided reflection has an important place in making the study of non-Western cultures and traditions more approachable and relatable. In the instance of my courses, this meant encouraging students to address any biases of Islam, Muslims, and the greater Middle East through their guided reflection assignments. Overall, the results have been very successful. Where these guided reflection activities have required students to understand and contextualize their previous knowledge of this subject matter, often gained from pop culture and news media, within the framework of rigorous academic study of the same subject matter. Such revisions of perspectives uncovered during reflective exercises are more personally meaningful to students and therefore likely to remain with them long after the end of the course. I look forward to seeing additional research and case studies on this subject, which is currently a very new field in the area of collegiate pedagogy.

Notes

1. Katelyn Barney and Elizabeth Mackinlay, "Creating Rainbows from Words and Transforming Understandings: Enhancing Student Learning through Reflective Writing in an Aboriginal Music Course," *Teaching in Higher Education* 15 (2010): 161–173.

2. Muddiest Point Papers are a Classroom Assessment Technique (CAT) that is used to assess where students are having difficulties with the material. Students are asked at the end of a lesson to write down a response to the question "What was the muddiest point?" (the muddiest point being the one that was most unclear or confusing). For more details, see Thomas A. Angelo and K. Patricia Cross, *Classroom Assessment Techniques: A Handbook for College Teachers*, 2nd ed. (San Francisco: Jossey-Bass, 1993).

3. See also Rebecca O'Rourke, "The Learning Journal: From Chaos to Coherence," *Assessment and Evaluation in Higher Education* 23 (1998): 403–413.

4. Corinne Blake, "Incorporating Information Technology into Courses on Islamic Civilizations," in *Teaching Islam*, ed. Brannon Wheeler (New York: Oxford University Press, 2003), 181–190.

5. Joel Blecher, "Pedagogy and the Digital Humanities: Undergraduate Exploration into the Transmitters of Early Islamic Law," in *The Digital Humanities and Islamic & Middle East Studies*, ed. Elias Muhanna (Boston: De Gruyter, 2016), 233–249.

6. Ayla Göl, "Constructing Knowledge: An Effective Use of Educational Technology for Teaching Islamic Studies in the UK," *Education and Information Technologies* 17 (2012): 399–416.

7. Mary Beattie, "Fostering Reflective Practice in Teacher Education: Inquiry as a Framework for the Construction of a Professional Knowledge of Teaching," *Asia-Pacific Journal of Teacher Education* 25 (1997): 111–128; Barbara Larrivee, "Transforming Teaching Practice: Becoming the Critically Reflective Teacher," *Reflective Practice* 1 (2000): 295–307; Dennis Thiessen, "A Skillful Start to a Teaching Career: A Matter of Developing Impactful Behaviours, Reflective Practices, or Professional Knowledge?" *International Journal of Educational Research* 33 (2000): 515–537.

8. Fred Korthagen and Jos Kessels, "Linking Theory and Practice: Changing the Pedagogy of Teacher Education," *Educational Researcher* 28 (1999): 4–17.

9. Some of this literature is also applicable and in fact addresses its methods use in corporate settings and other professional development scenarios. In particular, see Tony Ghayl, *Teaching and Learning through Reflective Practice: A Practical Guide for Positive Action* (New York: Routledge, 2010); and Jennifer Moon, *A Handbook of Reflective and Experiential Learning: Theory and Practice* (London: Routledge, 2004).

10. Minna Körkkö, Outi Kyrö-Ämmälä, and Tuija Turunen, "Professional Development through Reflection in Teacher Education," *Teaching and Teacher Education* 55 (2016): 198–200.

11. Kathleen Cowin, "Enhancing Student Teacher Reflective Practice through Poetry," *The New Educator* 8 (2012): 308–320.

12. For an excellent overview of this literature, see Lisa Jane Choffey, Evelyne de Leeuw, and Gerard Finnegan, "Facilitating Students Reflective Practice in a Medical Course: Literature Review," *Education for Health: Change in Learning and Practice* 25 (2012): 198–203.

13. Sarah Dolphin, "How Nursing Students Can Be Empowered by Reflective Practice," *Mental Health Practice* 16 (2013): 20–23.

14. Ginger Raterink, "Reflective Journaling for Critical Thinking Development in Advanced Practice Registered Nurse Students," *Journal of Nursing Education* 55 (2016): 99–102.

15. Jorge Tricio, Mark Woolford, and Michael Escudier, "Dental Students' Reflective Habits: Is There a Relation with Their Academic Achievement?" *European Journal of Dental Education* 19 (2015): 113–121.

16. Karen Quick, "The Role of Self- and Peer-Assessment in Dental Students' Reflective Practice Using Standardized Patient Encounters," *Journal of Dental Education* 80 (2016): 924–929.

17. Lynn Bye, Shelly Smith, and Helen Monghar Rallis, "Reflection Using an Online Discussion Forum: Impact on Student Learning and Satisfaction," *Social Work Education* 28 (2009): 841–855.

18. Bye, Smith, and Rallis, "Reflection Using an Online Discussion Forum," 847–849.

19. Bye, Smith, and Rallis, "Reflection Using an Online Discussion Forum," 845–846, 851.

20. For a compelling example, see Stephanie Burrell et al., "Getting Started with Portfolios: A Vision for Implementing Reflection to Enhance Student Learning," in *The Learning Portfolio: Reflective Practice for Improving Student Learning*, ed. John Zubizarrata (San Francisco, CA: Jossey-Bass, 2009), 85–97.

21. O'Rourke, "The Learning Journal: From Chaos to Coherence," 404.

22. Gregory F. Barz, "Confronting the Field(note) in and out of the Field: Music, Voices, Text, and Experiences in Dialogue," in *Shadows in the Field: New Perspectives for Fieldwork in Ethnomusicology*, ed. Gregory F. Barz and Timothy J. Cooley (New York: Oxford University Press, 1997), 52.

23. Barney and Mackinlay, "Creating Rainbows," 161–162.

24. Barney and Mackinlay, "Creating Rainbows," 162.

25. Barney and Mackinlay, "Creating Rainbows," 164.

26. For a more in-depth discussion of this, see Megan Boler, "Teaching for Hope: The Ethics of Shattering World Views," in *Teaching, Learning and Loving: Reclaiming Passion in Educational Practice*, ed. Daniel Liston and Jim Garrison (New York: Routledge, 2004), 129.

27. In these cases both Desire2Learn, or D2L, and Moodle were used.

28. This is a model borrowed from my own experience as a student in the Certificate in Collegiate Teaching program offered through the Office of Instruction and Assessment (OIA) at the University of Arizona. I was first exposed to this approach in a course with Dr. Sue Howell on Assessment. I found it to be most effective in creating a virtual community in the online courses that I took as a student and have incorporated it into my own online teaching practices.

29. There is a positive correlation between very personal responses in the initial prompts and increased numbers of comments in the courses that I have taught.

30. *Reel Bad Arabs: How Hollywood Vilifies a People*, directed by Sut Jhally (Northampton, MA: Media Education Foundation, 2006).

31. *Islam: Empire of Faith*, directed by Robert H. Gardner (Arlington, VA: PBS, 2000).

32. Now that you have watched *Reel Bad Arabs*, how do you feel about stereotypes of the Middle East? Do you believe that stereotypes can ever be completely harmless or serve a purpose?

33. Quoted with permission from a public discussion forum post, July 17, 2016.

34. Quoted with permission from the final response paper of a student, August 12, 2016. Importantly, earlier in the response the student classifies herself stating: "My town is extremely small, being predominantly white and Christian, and consisting of one high school."

35. Quoted with permission from the final response paper of a student, January 14, 2014.

36. Quoted with permission from a final response paper of a student, January 14, 2014.

37. There is not a required prompt the final week of classes as students have the final exam and the final reflection paper.

38. Quoted with permission from a student diary entry, March 6, 2016.

39. Quoted with permission from a student diary entry, February 22, 2015.

40. Three courses at Cochise College in Middle Eastern Humanities and Humanities in Contemporary Life, and six courses at the University of Arizona in Middle Eastern Humanities, Introduction to Political Islam, and History of the Modern Middle East, from 1453 to the Present.

41. Barney and Mackinlay, "Creating Rainbows," 162, 167.

LYNDALL HERMAN is a Global Risk Analyst with CARE USA, an affiliated researcher with the Center for Middle Eastern Studies at the University of Arizona, and an instructor at the University of Arizona and Cochise College.

chapter fourteen

TEACHING ISLAM AND GENDER

Shehnaz Haqqani

THIS ESSAY IS NOT SOLELY for teaching about Islam and gender in a course specifically on Islam and gender. It offers resources for incorporating gender into more introductory courses on Islam. In an age when Muslim women and their supposed oppression, as demonstrated by the veil, is a popular topic of discussion—when in a public talk on how *not* to talk about Muslim women, the audience still asks why Islam oppresses women by forcing them to cover their hair—talking about women becomes inevitable. Incorporating women into conversations on Islam is not simply about relevance, however; the subject of women should not be a mere afterthought and instead needs to be recognized as an essential part of the study of Islam and Muslims. The study of Islam, as of other religions and subjects, has historically been largely gendered, although it is on its way to change. The experiences, activities, scholarship, and other contributions of not just women but also of gender and sexual minorities, such as LGBTQ Muslims, to the development of Islam are now a recognized academic area of inquiry. The gendered study of Islam becomes essential particularly in the discourse on authority and Islam, which is currently one of the most studied areas in Islamic studies scholarship. In an age when hashtag activism and Islamic feminism are contributing significantly to the study of Islam, integrating gender into the study of Islam is no longer optional but essential. Ultimately, I hope to contribute to the mainstreaming of gender in courses on Islam, similar to what Beth Baron suggests for the mainstreaming of gender in Middle Eastern studies.[1]

I model my courses after bell hooks's revolutionary pedagogical practices that operate on the belief that learning should be exciting and transformative. Such teaching is an "interplay of anticolonial, critical, and feminist pedagogies," and they make it possible for educators to "imagine and enact pedagogical practices that engage directly both the concern for interrogating biases in curricula that reinscribe systems of domination (such as racism and sexism) while simultaneously providing new ways to teach diverse groups of students."[2] For her, "when education is the practice of freedom, students are not the only ones who are asked to share, to confess. . . . Any classroom that employs a holistic model of learning will also be a place where teachers grow, and are empowered by the process."[3] Particularly in classes focused on historically marginalized individuals and topics, such pedagogy entails embracing inclusiveness in the classroom and the instructor's acknowledgment of students' vulnerabilities—the latter of which may not work in every classroom.

The essay outline is as follows: first, based on my own experiences with Muslim students, I theorize the challenges of teaching Islam classes to Muslims in the American college setting, arguing that their mixed but often confused reactions to a critical study of Islam is directly related to their experiences with Islamophobia. I then offer pedagogical strategies that I have found helpful in teaching about gender issues in Islam to a diverse classroom. I end with resources that I have relied on or recommend for teaching Islam and gender courses; these resources challenge and complicate what might be considered traditional historical Muslim representations of gender in Islam as well as orientalist depictions of Muslim women specifically and gender more broadly.

TEACHING MUSLIM STUDENTS IN THE AMERICAN CLASSROOM

In many academics' experience, teaching students about their own faith can be very challenging. Toni Tidswell, for instance, speaks at length about the issue of "insiders when attempting to engage with their own religious tradition in a critical way," distancing oneself from an exclusivist position to a multiculturalist one.[4] One of my Muslim students once said during introductions on the first day of class, "I'm taking this class because I want to educate everyone about how much Islam honors women." Later, this same student expressed her concern about my teaching about Shiʻi Islam: "I think you shouldn't teach about Shiʻi Islam because what if someone wants to convert to Islam and thinks it's okay to be Shiʻi? . . . You should only teach about Sunni Islam, since it's the majority and therefore right." In a different semester, a Muslim student who was failing had difficulty understanding why he was failing because: "As you know, Professor, I already know all of this stuff."

These are encounters that many educators of Islam experience. Shenila Khoja-Moolji shares her own encounter with a self-identified Sunni Muslim student who contested her decision to allocate an entire class session to Shiʻa Islam because Shiʻa Muslims are a minority and thus by default Sunni Muslims are correct. In response, she recounts, "instead of minimizing his discomfort, I engaged with it by pointing to the ways in which acknowledging multiple histories and interpretations can elicit feelings of uncertainty around one's own identity and history. Yet, it is precisely through such moments of conflicts and discomforts that we can hope to perhaps arrive at a place that creates possibilities for more than one account of history and peoples."[5]

In such cases, it becomes necessary to emphasize the setting and objectives of the course so that students understand what an academic study of Islam entails. I do not propose drawing any clear boundaries between "secular" and "religious" studies of Islam, since these terms carry little weight as such; however, reminding them that the purpose of the course is to historicize and complicate current prevailing attitudes about Islam in both Muslim and non-Muslim imaginations; doing this requires, as Khoja-Moolji suggests, the acknowledgment of multiple histories and interpretations.

One might also consider utilizing Betty Sasaki's proposal for a pedagogy of coalition, which "addresses the ways in which knowledges are dynamically produced in the multiple, intersecting, and often competing narratives of the personal, political, and social. It means reframing the dominant notion of difference as something purely outside oneself to include an interrogation of one's own subjectivity."[6] She adds that the aim of such pedagogy is "not to avoid conflict in the classroom, but rather to expand the ground of oppositions of how we come to know what we know, and how we value or devalue that knowledge. In the process, we forget a critical space in which our students can both recognize and examine the multiplicity of their own subjectivity."[7] Thus, an instructor might consider training Muslim students whose sectarian identities and whose religious beliefs are rarely scrutinized because of their, for instance, Sunni privilege to interrogate their own subjectivity and critically assess how they believe and practice what they do.

When Muslim students exhibit signs of discomfort because of an equal emphasis on the various branches of Islam, the following are some more strategies that demonstrate "neutral enthusiasm" as outlined by John Simmons that "have proven useful in allowing religious studies content to move freely across the supposed boundary between teaching about religion and spiritual guidance in the classroom":[8]

> Power over Truth: concentrate on the impact of religious ideas upon individuals and communities rather than on truth claims of the religion in question.

Behavior before Belief: focus on what adherents do before exploring what they might believe.

Welcome Opposing Viewpoints: be willing to listen to opposing viewpoints or, via videos or guest presentations, balance the *enthusiasm* by inviting detractors into the classroom.

Compare and Contrast Religious Phenomena: . . . [compare and contrast] the unfamiliar with the familiar in terms of beliefs and practices.[9]

ISLAMOPHOBIA, IDENTITY, AND THE MUSLIM STUDENT

Many of the concerns expressed by my Muslim students, including their reactions to some of the "controversial" topics I cover in class (e.g., female-led prayers, sex slavery, and homosexuality) are a result of their struggles as Muslim Americans forced to validate their identity as Americans, on the one hand, and defend their faith against Islamophobes, on the other. Thus, in a class discussion on ISIS and sex slavery, Muslim students insisted that neither ISIS nor sex slavery is or ever was Islamic, and that Islam forbids all forms of ownership of humans as well as violence against others, thereby rendering such conversations ineffective and unnecessary. I want to theorize on this briefly with the objective of inviting other instructors to tread cautiously as they reflect on their experiences with Muslims in the classroom.

The challenges that Muslims face in America influence the ways they negotiate their Muslim identity and inform their reaction to critical, analytical approaches to their religion in classrooms that claim to be educating people about Islam from more balanced perspectives. Most Muslim students in the American college classroom are likely to have self-categorized their identities so that there are often valid gut reactions to the ways Islam is being taught in the classroom. Thus, with Islamophobia causing everyday violence for Muslims, on the one hand, and Muslim-perpetuated terrorism, like ISIS, claiming access to Islam and Muslim identity, on the other, Muslims separate out the different layers of their identity by, in the West, choosing specifically to defend their Muslim identity against both ISIS and Islamophobia.[10] Of course, other possible reasons are due to the fact that most people of faith view their religion as the ultimate truth, thus making it uncomfortable and disconcerting for some Muslim students to witness their religion undergoing the kind of critical analysis that occurs in many college classes.

Muslims' stronger attachment to Islam and Muslimness can also be explained through Henri Tajfel's theory of social identity, which posits that individuals' belonging to or membership in a certain group depends on whether they feel accepted in that group.[11] That is, because of the wide perception in the West that Islam and Muslims are foreign to the American culture, that Muslims are the embodiment of all things non-American, or even un-American, Western Muslims feel a closer connection to their faith than to other layers of their identity. As Nahid Kabir points out, "identity involves emotions and tensions, particularly when the 'self' [Muslims in the West] confronts a crisis, which may polarise identities."[12] Islamophobia, thus, "increases a sense of grievance on behalf of "all Muslims."[13]

Muslims in the West are thus holding on to their identity in a post-9/11 and Islamophobic climate where attempts are made from multiple directions for their identity to be erased and dismissed. The question they are forced to tackle is, who defines Islamic identity? To resist popular Western assumptions that associate Islam with violence and backwardness, to deny any Muslim associations with terrorism, Muslims in the West—indeed, universally—commonly insist that ISIS is not Islamic, that terrorism has no place in Islam, and that anyone who commits violence in the name of Islam is not a Muslim.

PEDAGOGICAL STRATEGIES

Research shows that the key to successful teaching is to "mix things up."[14] Scholars have also learned that "younger students prefer videos, whereas older students favor lectures."[15] Other research also concludes that "pedagogies that promote engagement are most effective."[16] In fact, "the best approach is to use a variety of approaches, 'from teachers teaching students to students teaching and learning from other students,' and students 'constructing' rather than receiving knowledge, with information technology and service experiences added to the mix."[17] As such, I offer here some strategies that have worked well in my classes and that students have enjoyed and found educational.

Debates

My students have found class debates exciting and enriching. I view structured debate as a way to evaluate how well students can argue perspectives that do not reflect their personal views. My classes typically have at least three debates per semester. I allow the students to decide on the topic that they want to debate, and I randomly assign them the position they will be required to support. I provide them with the resources to be able to defend the position they have been assigned and encourage them to rely on other sources as well. Our topics have included: Can non-Muslims speak authoritatively on Islam (the "insider vs. outsider" dilemma)? Can Muslim women pray during menstruation? Was Noor Tagouri's choice to accept an interview with Playboy in 2016 Islamically acceptable? Is homosexuality forbidden in Islam?

Oftentimes, the students are able to see through these debates not only the diversity that is so integral to Islam and the Islamic tradition but also the issues with the statement "What does Islam say about X?" They also learn to be more perceptive and critical consumers of knowledge.

Individual instructors may, of course, structure their class debates differently to suit their class environment, topic, and preferred pedagogical methods. See, for example, Youshaa Patel's blog at the Wabash Center titled "Debates: A Way to Teach Controversial Topics in Islam," where he discusses the ways that class debates have proven for him to be a useful pedagogical strategy.[18]

Dialogues

While debates work for some topics, dialogues and thoughtful discussions are more effective for others. Controversial topics that may necessitate students' sharing of their own personal, religious opinions can be dealt with most productively through dialogues, not debates. Controversial or hot discussion topics enable students to "listen to understand the complexity of the position taken by the other" and give students "the opportunity to reflect thoughtfully on their current opinions and how these opinions compare to others' opinions on these topics."[19] Navita Cummings James, who offers productive class exercises and activities for engaging controversial topics that lie at the intersection of gender and religion in college classrooms, suggests that, among other important reasons, "college-educated students need to be equipped with at least some framework for understanding how to discuss and listen to human sexuality arguments influenced by religion."[20]

Role Plays

Exercises that involve role plays are particularly engaging, fun, and useful. One of my students' favorite class sessions involved an activity where they role-played Muslim legal scholars and the ordinary Muslims seeking their opinions. They had been provided the tools to be able to perform their roles, and their task was to utilize them to demonstrate their understanding of lived Islam. What do Muslims do when they face a question or an issue for which they need religious guidance? Such activities effectively illustrate the realness of Islam and its rules, however "ancient" they might appear to some contemporary observers, including the genuine efforts of many Muslims to adhere to said rules as closely as humanly possible.

Role-playing requires perspective-taking, and "the act of having to articulate the opinions of another promotes empathy, especially when the opinions are those with which we disagree."[21] For specific ideas, particularly in a discussion on women's movements, I recommend Shuler's excellent guide for facilitating the activity.[22]

Guest Speakers

Several times during the semester, my students are exposed to Muslim women, often the scholars whose works we cover in class, to ask questions about their scholarship. This is especially helpful in dealing with a subject that the instructor cannot afford to devote too much attention but that is essential for students' learning. The strategy also exposes students to diverse groups of Muslim women, dispelling myths about Muslims as a monolithic group. Since my class objectives include complicating simplistic views of Islam and Muslims, conversations with Muslim women scholars, activists, and other professionals are a substantial tool to achieve this objective because each guest provides their own understandings of Islam.

I must note, however, that I do not ask our guests to prepare anything in advance for the class, and the entire session is a Q&A on Islam and the scholar's scholarship. Students have expressed deep gratitude for this opportunity, and the guests have enjoyed their time as well, many of whom I've re-invited in other classrooms as well.

CONTEXTUALIZE: PUTTING THINGS IN PERSPECTIVE

I once assigned a reading on women preachers in Saudi Arabia, where the preachers in question promote what many students read as patriarchal values. A discussion ensued about what patriarchy was, whether this was indeed patriarchy or internalized patriarchy, why women themselves might promote such values. What helped them understand was a conversation on whether such women existed in their own lives and communities. The conversation allowed students to reflect on the ways patriarchy is not simply a thing of the past, or foreign, but very much alive and common in their own communities as well. Female and LGBTQ students shared their experiences with sexuality policing, invoking references to recent events in the United States regarding women's clothing, slut-shaming, and gendered double standards promoted by other women.

Useful readings that offer this sort of contextualization include Denize Kandiyoti's article "Islam and Patriarchy" and Leila Ahmed's book *Women and Gender in Islam* to historicize some of the major issues with the ways Muslim patriarchy is imagined and observed today.[23] Ahmed's work, in particular, articulates the role of social, political, economic, and other realities in determining the "status of women in Islam." This point especially helps challenge ideas about religions, including the status of women and sexual minorities in religions, as fixed and bound: just as the political, economic, and social realities of any given community are constantly shifting from one state to another, so, too, is its relationship with religion and religious norms. I have also used Saadia Toor's "How Not to Talk about Muslim Women: Patriarchy, Islam and the Sexual Regulation of Pakistani Women" as a tool through which to examine inconsistent meanings of "Islam" within Muslim contexts and the role of patriarchy and class in determining when "Islam" is applicable or inapplicable.[24]

Inviting students to ask why patriarchy is often associated exclusively with Islam is a useful exercise that they are able to participate in once they have been exposed to scholarship explaining the colonialist legacy of the ways questions about Muslim women are addressed today (e.g., through the scholarship of Laila Ahmed, Denize Kandiyoti, Lila Abu-Lughod, Saadia Toor). Students also learn to acknowledge the role of sensationalist representations of Muslim women that succeed in evoking certain emotions from readers, including leaving the mark on readers that "Muslim women" are victims of a distinct form of oppression called Islamic patriarchy.

PROBLEMATIZE: THE CONSTRUCTION OF "MUSLIM WOMEN"

Contextualizing religion and unfamiliar practices sometimes entails making parallels and comparisons with the familiar. For instance, in a discussion on female-led prayers and the question of whether women could be imams as well as on the husband's authority over his wife, I showed some recent YouTube clips by Christian priests arguing that women could not be pastors and that God has put men in charge of women—and that these were not his (the priest's) words but God's words directly from the Bible. Many Christian students responded with some variation of "This is *not* Christianity! Nobody believes that anymore." The point, however, they learned, was not whether this was Christian or not but that of the religious rhetoric employed by the priest and that of the multiple possible interpretations of Scriptures. Similarly, when a student asked, during our discussion on divorce in Islam, how "Muslim women " in the United States feel about the idea that the husband has unilateral access to divorce, a good place to start was, "If we replace 'Muslim women' with 'Christian women,' does the question make any sense?" Such counter responses illustrate precisely the problem with existing constructions of "Muslim women."

Saba Mahmood critiques this idea of a collective but unreal "Muslim women" in a compelling, critical discussion of the popular tendency in post-orientalist scholarship on gender and Islam:

> With few exceptions, studies produced on gender in Muslim societies tend to focus solely on the lives of women. The problems entailed in the collectivity that the term "Muslim women" indexes immediately become apparent when we compare it to the term "Christian women." Clearly, the latter term, while used to describe activist or devout Christian women, is rarely used to designate women who live in countries as diverse as South Africa, Tanzania, the U.S., Poland, . . . all of which have majority Christian populations. In fact, it is more common to refer to women living in predominantly Christian societies by their nationality, rather than by their relationship to a faith. . . . In other words, the term "Christian women" often refers to women who actively profess the Christian faith and seldom includes those who do not abide by such an allegiance. No parallel distinction, however, seems to hold regarding "Muslim women."[25]

THE "EVERYDAY"

Discussing her pedagogical strategies in her course "Islamic Cultures," Khoja-Moolji writes, "during the course, making the 'everyday' the site of our analysis and plugging in the theories of discourse was productive for interrogating the normative understanding of leadership in early Muslim societies and for highlighting its implications for the discourse on gender."[26] The "everyday," however "mundane and ordinary" it might seem, offers a productive break from "media coverage of aberrations" such as "the kidnapping of approximately three hundred schoolgirls by Boko Haram in Nigeria or the shooting of Malala Yousafzai in Pakistan. Both events have been abstracted from their local contexts and specificities and rearticulated as examples of oppression of Muslim women by Muslim/brown/black men and as illustrations of Islam as an extremist ideology."[27] The problem with a focus on this approach is that it erases other parts of Muslims' lives, such as their social class, race, ethnicity, Khoja-Moolji argues.[28]

Invoking the everyday and lived Islam also helps illustrate the diversity that is inherent not just to Muslims but to all communities of faith. Emphasizing the diversity within Islamic jurisprudence can be a fruitful way both to question the meanings of "Islam" and "Islamic" and to encourage alternative, possibly more egalitarian, modes of engaging Islamic scriptures, as do Muslim feminists and others who are critical of historical interpretations of the Qur'an and hadiths.

Much accessible knowledge available on YouTube presents Islam from the point of view of Muslim men as the educators of Islam, who are often representative of dominant viewpoints and practices—that happen to be patriarchal in many cases. I find it helpful to emphasize the multiplicity of perspectives by providing the more feminist representations of Islam through academic, blog, and internet articles while relying on YouTube lectures for the more dominant perspectives. I begin some class sessions with an introduction to a contemporary Muslim woman (and man, in general Islam courses) who students should know. Through a series called Get to Know a Muslim at the University of Texas at Austin with the College of Liberal Arts Instructional Technology Services (LAITS), initially produced for an online Introduction to Islam class, my co-TA, Bruce Boville, and I took turns writing brief two- to three-minute scripts that I audio-recorded with LAITS resources. These episodes are engaging and offer visuals in a video format and have been received well by students. They are also a way to introduce students to Muslims whom they are unlikely to hear about outside of the classroom and include famous Muslims whom the students did not know were Muslims.

Since "stereotypes about women in Islam in the public domain rarely make allowance for the wide range of Muslim women's experiences and cultural settings," Toni Tidswell suggests, "introducing a wide range of case studies in class can assist in bringing a greater awareness to students who consider they already have a clear understanding of the issues that women face in Islam."[29] This approach "requires the student to balance images of women sentences to stoning in Iran, of being forbidden to drive in Saudi Arabia, of African women enduring clitorectomies not of their choosing, with very different images in Indonesia and India, and others holding high political office in Pakistan, Indonesia, Turkey and Bangladesh."[30] For Tidswell, the learning outcomes she sets for her classes on Women in Islam "include the student's ability to critically approach the subject of women's experience within Islam, and to debate the subject within a student peer group in a constructive, non-confrontational manner," which she acknowledges is a difficult task for "an insider who has grown up in, or has been thoroughly socialized into, a particular religion."[31] She also recommends employing "deep learning approaches" in classes to ensure that students gain a deeper understanding of the subject matter and to "learn to reflect on their own positions in relation to issues under discussion and debate in the classroom."[32] She finds that such moments of struggle for the insider are "quite often a painful and rewarding experience for the entire class as they accompany the individual on the journey."[33]

Islamic Feminism and Islamic Masculinities

Scholarship on gender and Islam has witnessed immense changes in the last few decades.[34] This includes Islamic feminist scholarship, which provides more gender egalitarian interpretations of Islam, including scholarship critiquing Islamic feminism from within.[35] Islamic feminist scholarship encompasses various themes, including unearthing Muslim women's contributions to Islam, particularly through women's biographies;[36] challenging gendered standards of religious, interpretive authority;[37] and reinterpretations of gendered verses of the Qur'an.[38] Scholarship re-evaluating conventional standards and notions of masculinities is also essential to more holistic representations of Islam and gender issues and has recently made major strides.[39]

Anti-/De-colonial Representations of Muslim Women

I rely on Abu-Lughod's "Do Muslim Women Really Need Saving?"[40] and Toor's "How Not to Talk about Muslim Women" to teach students about the impact of how Muslim women and Islam have been imagined by colonists and Westerners, who are often not in touch with the reality of Muslim women. Leila Ahmed's *Women and Gender in Islam* offers an extensive overview of historical Islam and its ahistoricization in colonialist and imperialist depictions of women; her discussion of the hypocrisies of colonialist interventions in the Muslim world offers students the language to articulate the problems with orientalist representations of Muslims. Ahmed's book is also useful in articulating to students the various factors that complicate the trite question "What does Islam say about *X*?" because of Ahmed's critical discussion on the role of politics, economics, culture, time, and setting in determining "women's status in Islam."

Important to note here is that it is imperative to distinguish between the critical scholarship and other production of Muslim feminists and the "native informant" work of public personalities such as Ayaan Hirsi Ali. Saba Mahmood discusses extensively, for instance, the ways in which "the older colonialist discourse on women" is being "reenacted in new genres of feminist literature today, with the explicit aim of justifying the U.S. 'war on terror' in the Muslim world."[41] Surveying some "recently published nonfiction bestsellers written by Muslim women about their personal suffering at the hands of Islam's supposedly incomparable misogynistic practices," Mahmood demonstrates that these autobiographical works are a legacy of colonialist and orientalist representations of Muslim women and argues that these works serve to forge dishonest relationships between these native informant authors and conservative political parties and think tanks in the United States and Europe.

Films

Showing relevance-based films, movies, or documentaries in class, which is my personal preferred method, or outside of class for homework, which might suit other instructors' preferences, is a way to offer students a break from more text-based knowledge. I show approximately three films or documentaries per semester in my classes, often allowing students to vote on a theme when there is some flexibility in the schedule and topics. Some films and documentaries relevant to gender and Islam are as follows:

- *Divorce Iranian Style* is directed by Kim Longinotto and Ziba Mir-Hosseini, the latter of whom is also a scholar of Islam and gender, and depicts the struggles of three couples in Iran as they seek divorce in an Iranian court.
- *Enemy of the Reich* tells the story of Noor Inayat Khan, a Muslim woman fighting the Nazis in the 1940s. The story is compelling particularly because of the commentaries in the film on the role of Sufism in guiding Noor's ethics.
- *Hidden Hearts*, currently in production, chronicles the stories and challenges of British Muslim women married to non-Muslims.
- *Jihad for Love* is a documentary that centers on the struggles of LGBTQ Muslims around the world. A hit with students, this film successfully articulates the challenges that LGBTQ Muslims face in their communities, in Islam, and, perhaps most important, internally as well.
- *The Light in Her Eyes* is the story of Houda al-Habash, a Muslim woman preacher who founded a Qur'an school for girls in Damascus, Syria; the film is framed as the portrayal of a cultural shift in Syria where women reclaim their space within the mosque.
- *The Mosque and Me* is an engaging film on women's place, literally, in mosques, providing a comparison between historical and contemporary positions of women in the mosque.
- *The Scream* highlights the role of women in the one-year Yemeni revolution in 2011, reflecting their hopes and fears about their position in their nation.
- *Shaykha*[42] documents the leadership of three Muslim women—in Turkey, Senegal, and the United States—who practice Sufism.
- *Shugs and Fats* is a web series based on the Brooklyn life of two hijabi girls, Shugufta ("Shugs") and Fatima ("Fats") struggling with different aspects of life as Muslim Americans.
- *Wadjda* features the story of little Wadjda in Saudi Arabia who dreams of owning a green bicycle so she can win a competition with a neighbor kid, Abdullah. When her family refuses to buy the bike for her because riding bicycles is not for girls where she lives, she decides to enter a Qur'an recitation competition that she hopes to win in order to get the money to buy the bike on her own.

Particularly helpful in the case of Muslim feminist engagements with Islam, blogs are an accessible, relatable way to introduce students to alternative forms of knowledge that is not readily given its due credit. Among the questions my students are given from which to select three for their essays throughout the semester is one on the role of blogging, focusing on Muslim feminist and LGBTQ bloggers, in contributing to the development of knowledge on Islam. Exploring these blogs gives students a chance to familiarize themselves with the ways that Muslims today utilize social media to challenge or affirm, or otherwise engage with, established and often mainstream practices of Islam.[43] Students might also consider, however, concentrating on Twitter and hashtags in shaping conversations on Islam. Blogs with active discussions offer students an opportunity to explore what some current potentially contentious topics might be in Muslim communities, and Twitter conversations, often reflecting immediate, urgent concerns that Muslims are facing, allow students to interact with communal issues in real time. In fact, many of my students came to learn about Muslim Women's Day (March 28, launched in 2017) via Twitter when the hashtag went viral. Moody suggests that instructors can "encourage students to follow current events on Twitter," which "allows students to discuss critically how different media outlets cover news and issues."[44]

I also recommend utilizing Muslim feminist projects such as the podcast #GoodMuslimBadMuslim by Zahra Noorbakhsh and Tanzila Ahmed, who cover various topics of relevance to Muslims in the West in humorous, fun, and accessible ways.[45] *Side Entrance*, a Tumblr blog and a project run by Hind Makki, is another useful tool in conversations on women's spaces and inclusion in mosques; it includes "photos from mosques around the world showcasing women's sacred spaces, in relation to men's spaces" and "shows the beautiful, the adequate and the pathetic."[46]

Of course, instructors can determine when and whether social media is a productive tool in their classrooms, which may also be in response to the student's interests and needs. In particular, in a non-social media focused course, some of the pitfalls to avoid when using social media include not overlooking traditional content, not including an excessive amount of YouTube clips, and not teaching in a top-down, hierarchical format that is not collaborative.[47]

Conclusion

In the above discussion, I offer various productive ways to address questions of gender and Islam in an American college classroom. I focus on alternative sources of knowledge—such as nonacademic ones, including blogs, films, the "everyday," conversations with Muslims, and projects that defy heteronormative forms of knowledge and practices of Islam—in an effort to disrupt dominant assumptions of what constitutes legitimate knowledge. These pedagogical tools particularly help in challenging essentialist and naturalized assumptions about Islam and Muslims. Existing power structures operate in ways that shape our perceptions of which sources of knowledge are more legitimate and valuable than others; it is thus not uncommon to marginalize the contributions and knowledge of scholars of color, women, and nonacademic lay individuals in existing curricula. By assigning limited and homogeneous reading lists to our students, we deny them access to the breadth of the sources of knowledge on any given subject, thus effectively reinforcing existing racial and gender hierarchies in the minds of the next generation of thinkers.

NOTES

1. Beth Baron, "A Field Matures: Recent Literature on Women in the Middle East," *Middle Eastern Studies* 32, no. 3 (July 1996): 172–186.

2. bell hooks, *Teaching to Transgress: Education as the Practice of Freedom* (New York: Routledge, 1994), 10.

3. hooks, *Teaching to Transgress*, 21.

4. Toni Tidswell, "Insiders, Outsiders and Critical Engagement: Reflections on Teaching 'Women in Islam' in a Western University," in *The Teaching and Study of Islam in Western Universities*, ed. Paul Morris, William Shepard, Paul Trebilco, and Toni Tidswell (New York: Routledge, 2014), 138.

5. Shenila Khoja-Moolji, "Poststructuralist Approaches to Teaching about Gender, Islam, and Muslim Societies," *Feminist Teacher* 24, no. 3 (2014): 176.

6. Betty Sasaki, "Toward a Pedagogy of Coalition," in *Twenty-First-Century Feminist Classrooms: Pedagogies of Identity and Difference*, ed. Amie A. MacDonald and Susan Sanchez Casal (New York: Palgrave, 2002), 35.

7. Sasaki, "Toward a Pedagogy of Coalition," 36.

8. John Simmons, "Vanishing Boundaries: When Teaching about Religion Becomes Spiritual Guidance in the Classroom," *Teaching Theology & Religion* 9, no. 1 (January 2006): 42.

9. Simmons, "Vanishing Boundaries," 42.

10. Nahid Kabir, *Young British Muslims: Identity, Culture, Politics and the Media* (Edinburgh: Edinburgh University Press, 2012), 9–10.

11. Henri Tajfel, ed., *Human Groups and Social Categories: Studies in Social Psychology* (Cambridge: Cambridge University Press, 1981).

12. Nahid Kabir, *Young American Muslims: Dynamics of Identity* (Edinburgh: Edinburgh University Press, 2014), 29.

13. Kabir, *Young American Muslims*, 29.

14. Richard Felder and Rebecca Brent, "Learning by Doing," *Chemical Engineering Education* 37, no. 4 (2003): 283.

15. Mia Moody, "Teaching Twitter and Beyond: Tips for Incorporating Social Media in Traditional Courses," *Journal of Magazine and New Media Research* 11, no. 2 (2010): 1.

16. Barbara E. Walvoord, *Teaching and Learning in College Introductory Religion Courses* (Malden, MA: Blackwell, 2008), 83.

17. Walvoord, *Teaching and Learning in College Introductory Religion Courses*, 84.

18. Youshaa Patel, "Debates: A Way to Teach Controversial Topics in Islam," Wabash Center Blogs, May 4, 2016, http://wabashcenter.typepad.com/teaching_islam/2016/05/debates-a-way-to-teach-controversial-topics-in-islam.html.

19. Navita Cummings James, "Discussing Gender and Human Sexuality 'Hot Button' Issues: Considering the Role of Religion and Religious Beliefs," in *Activities for Teaching Gender and Sexuality in the University Classroom*, ed. Michael Murphy and Elizabeth Ribarsky (New York: Rowman & Littlefield Education, 2013), 78.

20. James, "Discussing Gender and Human Sexuality," 79.

21. Sherianne Shuler, "Bringing the Gender Movements Alive through Role-Play," in *Activities for Teaching Gender and Sexuality in the University Classroom*, ed. Michael Murphy and Elizabeth Ribarsky (New York: Rowman & Littlefield Education, 2013), 27.

22. Shuler, "Bringing the Gender Movements Alive through Role-Play," 27.

23. Leila Ahmed, *Women and Gender in Islam* (New Haven, CT: Yale University Press, 1992); Deniz Kandiyoti, "Islam and Patriarchy: A Comparative Perspective," in *Women in Middle Eastern History: Shifting Boundaries in Sex and Gender*, ed. Nikki R. Keddie and Beth Baron (New Haven, CT: Yale University Press, 1991).

24. Saadia Toor, "How Not to Talk about Muslim Women: Patriarchy, Islam and the Sexual Regulation of Pakistani Women," in *Introducing the New Sexuality Studies*, 2nd ed., ed. Steven Seidman, Nancy Fischer, and Chet Meeks (New York: Routledge, 2011), 66–174.

25. Saba Mahmood, "Islam and Gender in Muslim Societies: Reflections of an Anthropologist," in *Observing the Observer: The State of Islamic Studies in American Universities*, ed. Zahid Bukhari and Sulayman Nyang (London: IIIT, 2012), 74–75.

26. Khoja-Moolji, "Poststructuralist Approaches," 171.

27. Khoja-Moolji, "Poststructuralist Approaches," 172.

28. Accessible literature that is also helpful in this context includes: Ayesha Mattu, Nura Maznavi, *Love, InshAllah: The Secret Love Lives of American Muslim Women* (Berkeley, CA: Soft Skull Press, 2012); Maria Ebrahimji and Zahra Suratwala, *I Speak for Myself: American Women on Being Muslim* (2011); and Saleemah Abdul-Ghafur, *Living Islam Out Loud: American Muslim Women Speak* (Boston: Beacon Press, 2005).

29. Tidswell, "Insiders, Outsiders and Critical Engagement," 137.

30. Tidswell, "Insiders, Outsiders and Critical Engagement," 137.

31. Tidswell, "Insiders, Outsiders and Critical Engagement," 137.

32. Tidswell, "Insiders, Outsiders and Critical Engagement," 138.

33. Tidswell, "Insiders, Outsiders and Critical Engagement," 141.

34. A longer list of Muslim feminist literature of a broad range of subjects and themes can be found at https://orbala.wordpress.com/books-on-islamic-feminism/.

35. E.g., Raja Rhouni, *Secular and Islamic Feminist Critiques in the Work of Fatima Mernissi* (Leiden: Brill, 2009); Aysha A. Hidayatullah, *Feminist Edges of the Qur'an* (Oxford: Oxford University Press, 2014).

36. E.g., Denise Spellberg, *Politics, Gender, and the Islamic Past* (New York: Columbia University Press, 1994); miriam cooke, *Nazira Zeineddine: A Pioneer of Islamic Feminism* (London: Oneworld, 2010); Yasmin Amin, "Umm Salama and Her Hadith," Master's thesis, American University in Cairo, 2011.

37. E.g., Juliane Hammer, *American Muslim Women, Religious Authority, and Activism More than a Prayer* (Austin: University of Texas Press, 2012); Ayesha Chaudhry, *Domestic Violence and the Islamic Tradition* (2014).

38. E.g., Barbara Stowasser, *Women in the Qur'an, Traditions, and Interpretations* (New York: Oxford University Press, 1994); Sa'diyya Shaikh, "A Tafsir of Praxis: Gender, Marital Violence, and Resistance in a South African Muslim Community," in *Violence against Women in Contemporary World Religions: Roots and Cures*, ed. Daniel C. Maguire and Sa'diyya Shaikh (Cleveland, OH: Pilgrim Press, 2007); Laury Silvers, "'In the Book We Have Left Out Nothing': The Ethical Problem of the Existence of Verse 4:34 in the Qur'an," in *Comparative Islamic Studies* 2, no. 2 (2008): 171–180; Chaudhry, *Domestic Violence and the Islamic Tradition*.

39. Amanullah DeSondy, *The Crisis of Islamic Masculinities* (New York: Bloomsbury, 2013); Lahoucine Ouzgane, ed., *Islamic Masculinities* (London: Zed Books, 2006); Wilson Jacob, *Working Out Egypt: Effendi Masculinity and Subject Formation in Colonial Modernity, 1870–1940* (Durham, NC: Duke University Press, 2011).

40. Lila Abu-Lughod, *Do Muslim Women Need Saving?* (Cambridge, MA: Harvard University Press, 2013).

41. Saba Mahmood, "Religion, Feminism, and Empire: The New Ambassadors of Islamophobia," in *Feminism, Sexuality, and the Return of Religion*, ed. Linda Alcoff and John D. Caputo (Bloomington: Indiana University Press, 2011), 77.

42. Sly Productions, *Shaykha* movie trailer, https://vimeo.com/114093162.

43. A list of Muslim feminist bloggers can be found at https://orbala.wordpress.com/muslim -feminist-blogs/.

44. Moody, "Teaching Twitter and Beyond," 3.

45. Ahmed and Noorbakhsh, #GoodMuslimBadMuslim [Podcast.] http://www .goodmuslimbadmuslim.com/.

46. Makki, *Side Entrance* (blog). http://sideentrance.tumblr.com/.

47. Moody, "Teaching Twitter and Beyond," 8.

SHEHNAZ HAQQANI is an Assistant Professor of Religion at Mercer University. She earned her PhD in Islamic Studies from the University of Texas at Austin.

BIBLIOGRAPHY

Abaza, Mona. "Academic Tourists Sight-Seeing the Arab Spring." *Ahram Online*, September 26, 2011. http://english.ahram.org.eg/News/22373.aspx.

Abou El Fadl, Khaled. *Reasoning with God: Reclaiming Shari'ah in the Modern Age*. Lanham, MD: Rowman & Littlefield, 2014.

Abrahamse, Augusta, Matthew Johnson, Nanette Levinson, Larry Medsker, and Joshua M. Pierce. "A Virtual Educational Exchange: A North-South Virtually Shared Class on Sustainable Development." *Journal of Studies in International Education* 19, no. 2 (2015): 140–159.

Abu-Lughod, Lila. *Do Muslim Women Need Saving?* Cambridge, MA: Harvard University Press, 2013.

Afsaruddin, Asma. *Contemporary Issues in Islam*. Edinburgh: Edinburgh University Press, 2015.

Ahmad, Mumtaz, Zahid Bukhari, and Sulayman Nyang, eds. *Observing the Observer: The State of Islamic Studies in American Universities*. London: IIIT, 2012.

Ahmed, Leila. *Women and Gender in Islam*. New Haven, CT: Yale University Press, 1992.

Ahmed, Shahab. *What Is Islam? The Importance of Being Islamic*. Princeton, NJ: Princeton University Press, 2016.

Aishima, Hatsuki. "Contesting Public Images of 'Abd al-Halim Mahmud (1910–78): Who is an Authentic Scholar?." In *Ethnographies of Islam: Ritual Performances and Everyday Practices*, edited by Baudouin Dupret, Thomas Pierret, Paulo G. Pinto, and Kathryn Spellman-Poots, 170–178. Edinburgh: Edinburgh University Press, 2012.

Ali, Ayaan Hirsi. *Nomad: From Islam to America: A Personal Journey through the Clash of Civilizations*. New York: Free Press, 2010.

Ali, Kecia. Foreword to *Al-Shāfiʿī's Epistle*, xi–xiv. Translated by Joseph Lowry. New York: Library of Arabic Literature/New York University Press, 2015.

———. *Imam Shafiʿi: Scholar and Saint*. Oxford, UK: Oneworld Publications, 2010.

———. *Sexual Ethics and Islam: Feminist Reflections on Qur'an, Hadith, and Jurisprudence*. Revised and expanded ed. London: Oneworld, 2016.

———. "Teaching about Women, Gender, and Islamic Law: Resources and Strategies." Paper presented at the American Academy of Religion Annual Meeting, 2001. http://www.brandeis.edu/projects/fse/muslim/mus-articles/ali-teaching.pdf.

———. "Whose Sharia Is It?" *Huffington Post*, May 29, 2014.

Amelsvoort, Marije, van, Carel van Wijk, and Hanny den Ouden. "Going Dutch or Joining Forces? Some Experiences with Team Teaching in the Netherlands." *Business Communication Quarterly* 73, no. 1 (2010): 96–101.

Anderson, Rebecca S., and Bruce W. Speck. "Oh What a Difference a Team Makes: Why Team Teaching Makes a Difference." *Teaching and Teacher Education* 14, no. 7 (1998): 671–686.

Angelo, Thomas A., and K. Patricia Cross. *Classroom Assessment Techniques: A Handbook for College Teachers.* 2nd ed. San Francisco: Jossey-Bass, 1993.

Anidjar, Gil. "Secularism." *Critical Inquiry* 33, no.1 (Autumn 2006): 52–77. http://www.jstor.org/stable/10.1086/509746.

Appadurai, Arjun. *Fear of Small Numbers: An Essay on the Geography of Anger.* Durham, NC: Duke University Press, 2006.

Asad, Talal. *Genealogies of Religion: Discipline and Reasons of Power in Christianity and Islam.* Baltimore: Johns Hopkins University Press, 1993.

———. *On Suicide Bombing.* New York: Columbia University Press, 2007.

Aslan, Ednan, ed. *Islamische Erziehung in Europa.* Vienna: Böhlau, 2009.

Ayotte, Kevin J., and Mary E. Husain. "Securing Afghan Women: Neocolonialism, Epistemic Violence, and the Rhetoric of the Veil." *NWSA Journal* 17, no. 3 (2005): 112–133.

Badiou, Alain. "September 11, 2001: Philosophy and the 'War against Terrorism.'" In *Polemics,* translated by Steve Corcoran, 15–32. New York: Verso Books, 2006.

Badreya, Sayed. "Saving Egyptian Film Classics." In *This Film Is Dangerous: A Celebration of Nitrate Film,* edited by Roger Smither and Catherine A. Surowiec, 417–420. Brussels: International Federation of Film Archives, 2002.

Bakken, Linda, Frances L. Clark, and Johnnie Thompson. "Collaborative Teaching: Many Joys, Some Surprises, and a Few Worms." *College Teaching* 46, no. 4 (1998): 154–157.

Balakit, Melanie. "State House Passes Anti-Religious Indoctrination Bill." *The Tennessean,* February 29, 2016. http://www.tennessean.com/story/news/2016/02/29/state-house-passes-anti-religious-indoctrination-bill/81107754/.

———. "White County Group Claims Islamic Indoctrination." *The Tennessean,* October 21, 2016, http://www.tennessean.com/story/news/2015/10/20/white-county-group-claims-islamic-indoctrination/74267142/.

Ballard, Lizabeth B., and Ray Anderson. "Two for One: Integrating American History and English III." 1994. ERIC document. https://eric.ed.gov/?id=ED382506.

Ballard, Roger. "Islam and the Construction of Europe." In *Muslims in the Margin: Political Responses to the Presence of Islam in Western Europe,* edited by W. A. R. Shadid and P. S. van Koningsveld, 15–51. Kampen: Kok Pharos, 1996.

Bamman, David, and Noah A. Smith. "Contextualized Sarcasm Detection on Twitter." *Proceedings of the Ninth International AAAI Conference on Web and Social Media,* 2015. http://www.aaai.org/ocs/index.php/ICWSM/ICWSM15/paper/view/10538.

Barlas, Asma. *"Believing Women" in Islam: Unreading Patriarchal Interpretations of the Qur'an.* Austin: University of Texas Press, 2002.

Barney, Katelyn, and Elizabeth Mackinlay. "Creating Rainbows from Words and Transforming Understandings: Enhancing Student Learning through Reflective Writing in an Aboriginal Music Course." *Teaching in Higher Education* 15, no. 2 (2010): 161–173.

Baron, Beth. "A Field Matures: Recent Literature on Women in the Middle East." *Middle Eastern Studies* 32, no. 3 (July 1996): 172–186.

Barz, Gregory F. "Confronting the Field(note) In and Out of the Field: Music, Voices, Text, and Experiences in Dialogue." In *Shadows in the Field: New Perspectives for Fieldwork in Ethnomusicology,* edited by Gregory F. Barz and Timothy J. Cooley, 45–62. New York: Oxford University Press, 1997.

Beattie, Mary. "Fostering Reflective Practice in Teacher Education: Inquiry as a Framework for the Construction of a Professional Knowledge of Teaching." *Asia-Pacific Journal of Teacher Education* 25, no. 2 (1997): 111–128. doi:10.1080/1359866970250202.

Behr, Harry H. *Curriculum Islamunterricht: Analyse von Lehrplanentwürfen für islamischen Religionsunterricht in der Grundschule. Ein Beitrag zur Lehrplantheorie des Islamunterrichts im Kontext der praxeologischen Dimension islamisch-theologischen Denkens*. Bayreuth: Universität Bayreuth Kulturwissenschaftliche Fakultät, 2005. http://www.izir.uni -erlangen.de/docs/IZIR_H.Behr_Dissertation_Curriculum_Islam.pdf.

Bennett, Clinton. "New Directions: The Who, Why, What, How, and Where of Studying Islam." In *The Bloomsbury Companion to Islamic Studies*, edited by Clinton Bennett, 259–282. New York: Bloomsbury, 2013.

Bennis, W. G. "Organizational Development and the Fate of Bureaucracy." In *Readings in Organizational Behavior and Human Performance*, edited by L. L. Cummings, 327–338. Homewood, IL: Irwin, 1973.

Berger, Peter. *The Sacred Canopy*. New York: Anchor Books, 1997.

Berglund, Jenny. *Teaching Islam: Islamic Religious Education in Sweden*. Münster: Waxmann, 2010.

Berkey, Jonathan. *The Formation of Islam: Religion and Society in the Near East, 600–1800*. Cambridge: Cambridge University Press, 2003.

Berkson, Mark. "A Non-Muslim Teaching Islam: Pedagogical and Ethical Challenges." *Teaching Theology and Religion* 8, no. 2 (2005): 86–98.

Black, Cofer. "Joint Investigation into September 11th: Fifth Public Hearing." Joint House/ Senate Intelligence Committee Hearing, September 26, 2002. https://fas.org/irp /congress/2002_hr/092602black.html.

Blake, Corinne. "Incorporating Information Technology into Courses on Islamic Civilizations." In *Teaching Islam*, edited by Brannon Wheeler, 181–190. New York: Oxford University Press, 2003.

Blecher, Joel. "Pedagogy and the Digital Humanities: Undergraduate Exploration into the Transmitters of Early Islamic Law." In *The Digital Humanities and Islamic & Middle East Studies*, edited by Elias Muhanna, 233–249. Berlin: Walter de Gruyter, 2016.

"Bob Jones III Wants to Shed Fundamentalist Label." *Peninsula Clarion*. March 15, 2002.

Bob Jones University. *Student Handbook 16–17*. 2016. http://www.bju.edu/life-faith /student-handbook.pdf.

———. *Undergraduate Catalogue 15–16*. 2015. http://www.bju.edu/academics/resources -support/catalogs/undergrad-catalog-2015.pdf.

Bock, Wolfgang, ed. *Islamischer Religionsunterricht?: Rechtsfragen, Länderberichte, Hintergründe*. Tübingen: Mohr Siebeck, 2006.

Boler, Megan. "Teaching for Hope: The Ethics of Shattering World Views." In *Teaching, Learning and Loving: Reclaiming Passion in Educational Practice*, edited by Daniel Liston and Jim Garrison, 117–131. New York: Routledge, 2004.

Boucher, Dave. "Lawmakers Fear Islamic 'Indoctrination' in TN Classes." *The Tennessean*, September 10, 2015, http://www.tennessean.com/story/news/politics/2015/09/10 /blackburn-alludes--islamic-indoctrination--tn-classes/72015122/.

Bourdieu, Pierre. *The Logic of Practice*. Translated by Richard Nice. Stanford, CA: Stanford University Press, 1990.

———. *The Rules of Art*. Translated by Susan Emanuel. Cambridge, UK: Polity Press, 1996.

———. *Pascalian Meditations*. Translated by Richard Nice. Stanford, CA: Stanford University Press, 1997.

Bowen, Donna Lee, Evelyn A. Early, and Becky Schulthies, eds. *Everyday Life in the Muslim Middle East*. 3rd ed. Bloomington: Indiana University Press, 2014.

Boyer, John W. *The University of Chicago: A History*. Chicago: University of Chicago Press, 2015.

Brewer, Edward C., and Terence L. Holmes. "Communication = Better Teams: A Communication Exercise to Improve Team Performance," *IEEE Transactions on Professional Communication* 59, no. 3 (2016): 288–298.

Brockopp, Jonathan. "The Essential Sharia: Teaching Islamic Law in the Religious Studies Classroom." In *Teaching Islam*, edited by Brannon Wheeler, 77–93. New York: Oxford, 2003

Built, Laura. "Tennessee Mother Fights to Remove Textbook from Schools that Teaches about Islam, Claims Her Child's 'Religious Beliefs Were Violated.'" *New York Daily News*, October 6, 2016, http://www.nydailynews.com/news/national/tenn -mom-fights-remove-school-book-teaches-islam-article-1.2819968.

Bulliet, Richard. *The Case for Islamo-Christian Civilization*. New York: Columbia University Press, 2004.

Burrell, Stephanie, Laurence Miners, Kathryn Nantz, and Roben Torosyan. "Getting Started with Portfolios: A Vision for Implementing Reflection to Enhance Student Learning." In *The Learning Portfolio: Reflective Practice for Improving Student Learning*, edited by John Zubizarrata, 85–97. San Francisco: Jossey-Bass, 2009.

Bush, Stephen S. "Are Meanings the Name of the Game? Religion as Symbolic Meaning and Religion as Power." *Religion Compass* 6 (2012): 525–533. doi:10.1111/j.1749-8171.2012.00361.x.

Bye, Lynn, Shelly Smith, and Helen Monghar Rallis. "Reflection Using an Online Discussion Forum: Impact on Student Learning and Satisfaction." *Social Work Education* 28, no. 8 (2009): 841–855. doi:10.1080/02615470802641322.

Cabezón, José Ignacio. "The Dialectic of Alterity in the Study of Religion." *JAAR* 74, no. 1 (2006): 21–38.

Carapico, Sheila. "No Easy Answers: The Ethics of Field Research in the Arab World." *PS: Political Science and Politics* 39, no. 3 (2006): 429–431. http://www.jstor.org/stable/20451778.

Caufield, Catherine. "The Agency Paradigm: A Pedagogical Tool to Facilitate Nuanced Thinking on Sensitive Issues." *Teaching Theology & Religion* 20, no. 1 (2017): 89–101.

Cheheltan, Amir Hassan. "Writing Is a Dangerous Act: The Situation of Writers in Iran." *Art & Thought on Literature* 103 (2015): 34–37. http://www.goethe.de/ges/phi/prj/ffs /pro/epaper/fikrun_103_en.pdf.

Chih, Rachida. "What Is a Sufi Order?" In *Sufism and the Modern in Islam*, edited by Martin van Bruinessen and Julia Day Howell, 21–38. London: I. B. Tauris, 2007.

Choffey, Lisa Jane, Evelyne de Leeuw, and Gerard Finnegan. "Facilitating Students Reflective Practice in a Medical Course: Literature Review." *Education for Health: Change in Learning and Practice* 25, no. 3 (2012): 198–203. doi:10.4103/1357-6283.109787.

Choudhury, Cyra Akila. "Shariah Law as National Security Threat?" *Akron Law Review* 46 (2012). http://ssrn.com/abstract=2148678.

Cimono, Richard. "'No God in Common': American Evangelical Discourse on Islam after 9/11." *Review of Religious Research* 47, no. 2 (2005): 162–174.

Clark, Janine A. "Field Research Methods in the Middle East." *PS: Political Science and Politics* 39, no. 3 (2006.): 417–423. http://www.jstor.org/stable/20451776.

"Classroom Dialogues." CU Dialogues Program, University of Colorado-Boulder. Accessed September 1, 2016. http://www.colorado.edu/cudialogues/classroom-dialogues.

Cohen, Marica B., and Kate DeLois. "Training in Tandem: Co-Facilitation and Role Modeling in Group Course Work." *Social Work with Groups* 24, no. 1 (2001): 21–36.

Commission on British Muslims and Islamophobia. *Islamophobia: A Challenge for Us All*. London: Runnymede Trust, 1997.

Council on American-Islamic Relations and the Center for Race and Gender at the University of California, Berkeley. "Confronting Fear: Islamophobia and Its Impact in the U.S. 2013–2015." http://www.islamophobia.org/images/ConfrontingFear/Final -Report.pdf.

Cowin, Kathleen. "Enhancing Student Teacher Reflective Practice through Poetry." *The New Educator* 8, no. 4 (2012): 308–320. doi:10.1080/1547688X.2012.726587.

Daniel, Norman. *Islam and the West: The Making of an Image.* 1960. Reprint, Oxford: Oneworld Publishing, 2000.

Davidson, Dan E. "Study Abroad: When, How Long, and with What Results? New Data from the Russian Front." *Foreign Language Annals* 43, no. 1 (2010): 6–26. doi:10.1111/j.1944-9720.2010.01057.x.

Davidson, Lawrence. "Islamophobia, the Israel Lobby and American Paranoia: Letter from America." *Holy Land Studies: A Multidisciplinary Journal* 10, no. 1 (May 2011): 87–95.

Davis, James R. *Interdisciplinary Courses and Team Teaching: New Arrangements for Learning.* Phoenix: American Council on Education and the Oryx Press, 1995.

Deibert, Ron. "Cyberspace under Siege." *Journal of Democracy* 26, no. 3 (2015): 64–78. doi:10.1353/jod.2015.0051.

Delery, Stuart. "Lawfulness of a Lethal Operation Directed against a U.S. Citizen Who Is a Senior Operational Leader of al-Qaʿida or an Associated Force." Department of Justice White Paper, November 8, 2011. http://www.documentcloud.org/documents/602342-draft-white-paper.html.

Derry, Ken. "Believing Is Seeing: Teaching Religion and Violence in Film." In *Teaching Religion and Violence,* edited by Brian Pennington. New York: Oxford University Press, 2012.

Devji, Feisal. *The Terrorist in Search of Humanity.* New York: Columbia University Press, 2008.

Dobkowski, Michael. "A Time for War and a Time for Peace: Teaching Religion and Violence in the Jewish Tradition." In *Teaching Religion and Violence,* edited by Brian Pennington. New York: Oxford University Press, 2012.

Dolphin, Sarah. "How Nursing Students Can Be Empowered by Reflective Practice." *Mental Health Practice* 16, no. 9 (2013): 20–23.

Donner, Fred. "Periodization as a Tool of the Historian with Special Reference to Islamic History." *Der Islam: Journal of the History and Culture of the Middle East* 91, no. 1 (2014): 20–36.

Dressler, Markus, and Arvind Pal S. Mandair, eds. *Secularism and Religion-Making.* New York: Oxford University Press, 2011.

"Dutch Bishop: Call God 'Allah' to Ease Relations." Europe on NBC News.com, August 15, 2017. http://www.nbcnews.com/id/20279326/#.V-_jpYgrLIU.

Eisen, Arri, Anne Hall, Soon Lee Tong, and Jack Zupko. "Teaching Water: Connecting across Disciplines and into Daily Life to Address Complex Societal Issues." *College Teaching* 57, no. 2 (2009): 99–104.

Ernst, Carl W. *Following Muhammad: Rethinking Islam in the Contemporary World.* Chapel Hill: University of North Carolina Press, 2003.

Ernst, Carl W., and Richard C. Martin. "Introduction: Toward a Post-Orientalist Approach to Islamic Religious Studies." In *Rethinking Islamic Studies: From Orientalism to Cosmopolitanism,* edited by Carl W. Ernst and Richard C. Martin, 1–22. Columbia: University of South Carolina Press, 2010.

Esposito, John, and Dahlia Mogahed. *Who Speaks for Islam? What a Billion Muslims Really Think.* New York: Gallup Press, 2007.

Euben, Roxanne. "Premodern, Antimodern or Postmodern?: Islamic and Western Critiques of Modernity: Islamic and Western Critiques of Modernity." *Review of Politics* 59, no. 3 (1997): 429–459.

Felder, Richard, and Rebecca Brent. "Learning by Doing." *Chemical Engineering Education* 37, no. 4 (2003): 283–284. http://www.ncsu.edu/felder-public/Columns/Active.pdf.

Gadamer, Hans Georg. *Truth and Method.* Translated by Joel Weinsheimer and Donald G. Marshall. London: Continuum, 2004.

Gardner, Robert H., director. *Islam: Empire of Faith.* Arlington, VA: PBS, 2000.

Gates, Brian, and Robert Jackson. "Religion and Education in England." In *Religious Education at Schools in Europe: Part 2: Western Europe,* edited by Robert Jackson, Martin Jäggle, and Martin Rothgangel, 65–98. Göttingen: V&R Unipress, 2014.

Gayo-Avello, Daniel. "A Meta-Analysis of State-of-the-Art Electoral Prediction from Twitter Data." *Social Science Computer Review* 31, no. 6 (2013): 649–679. doi:10.1177/0894439313493979.

Gaytan, Jorge. "Instructional Strategies to Accommodate a Team-Teaching Approach." *Business Communication Quarterly* 73, no. 1 (2010): 82–87.

Ghayl, Tony. *Teaching and Learning through Reflective Practice: A Practical Guide for Positive Action.* New York: Routledge, 2010.

Gibson, David. "Bob Jones University Questions 'Fundamentalist' Label." *Huffington Post,* November 11, 2011. http://www.huffingtonpost.com/2011/11/21/bob-jones-university-fundamentalist_n_1106276.html.

Gokhale, Anuradha A. "Collaborative Learning Enhances Critical Thinking." *Journal of Technology Education* 7, no. 1 (1995): 22–30.

Göl, Ayla. "Constructing Knowledge: An Effective Use of Educational Technology for Teaching Islamic Studies in the UK." *Education and Information Technologies* 17, no. 4 (2012): 399–416.

Good, Carter Victor. *Dictionary of Education.* New York: McGraw-Hill Book Company, 1973.

Gorman, Anthony. *Historians, State and Politics in Twentieth Century Egypt: Contesting the Nation.* New York: Routledge, 2003.

Graham, Franklin. Interview on *Now with Bill Moyers,* PBS, January 3, 2003. http://www.pbs.org/now/printable/transcript201_full_print.html.

Green, Emma. "The Fear of Islam in Tennessee Public Schools." *The Atlantic,* December 16, 2015, http://www.theatlantic.com/education/archive/2015/12/fear-islam-tennessee-public-schools/420441/.

Green, Todd. *The Fear of Islam: An Introduction to Islamophobia in the West.* Minneapolis, MN: Fortress Press, 2015.

al-Hakim, Tawfiq. *Return of the Spirit.* Trans. William M. Hutchins. Reissued. Boulder, CO: Lynne Rienner Publishers, 1996. First published 1990 by Three Continents Press.

Hasan, S. S. *Christians versus Muslims in Modern Egypt: The Century-Long Struggle for Coptic Equality.* Oxford: Oxford University Press, 2003.

Hatcher, Tim, and Barbara Hinton. "Graduate Student's Perception of University Team-Teaching." *College Students Journal* 30, no. 3 (1996): 367.

Hayles, N. Katherine. *How We Became Posthuman: Virtual Bodies in Cybernetics, Literature, and Informatics.* Chicago: University of Chicago Press, 1999.

Henderson, Charles, Andrea Beach, and Michael Famiano. "Diffusion of Educational Innovations via Co-teaching." *AIP Conference Proceedings* 883, no. 1 (2007): 117–120.

Hess, Diana E. "Controversies about Controversial Issues in Democratic Education." *PS: Political Science & Politics* 37, no. 2 (2004): 257–261.

Hewer, Chris. "Schools for Muslims." *Oxford Review of Education* 27, no. 4 (2001): 515–527.

Hidayatullah, Aysha A. *Feminist Edges of the Qur'an.* Oxford: Oxford University Press, 2014.

Hirschler, Konrad, and Sarah Bowen Savant. "Introduction: What Is in a Period? Arabic Historiography and Periodization." *Der Islam: Journal of the History and Culture of the Middle East* 91, no. 1 (2014): 6–10.

Hodgson, Marshall G. S. *Rethinking World History: Essays on Europe, Islam and World History*. Studies in Comparative World History. Cambridge: Cambridge University Press, 1993.

Hoffman, Valerie. *Sufism, Mystics, and Saints in Modern Egypt*. Columbia: University of South Carolina Press, 1995.

Hofstadter, Richard. *The Paranoid Style in American Politics*. 1964. Reprint, New York: Vintage Books, 2008.

Høigilit, Jacob, and Frida Nome. "Egyptian Salafism in Revolution." *Journal of Islamic Studies* 25, no. 1 (2014): 33–54.

Holder, Eric. "Speech at the Northwestern School of Law." US Department of Justice, March 5, 2012. https://www.justice.gov/opa/speech/attorney-general-eric-holder-speaks-northwestern-university-school-law.

The Holy Bible. New Revised Standard Version.

hooks, bell. *Teaching to Transgress: Education as the Practice of Freedom*. New York: Routledge, 1994.

Horowitz, Carl. "Immigration and the Culture War." *The Social Contract* 12, no. 2 (Winter 2002): 141–146. http://www.thesocialcontract.com/pdf/twelve-two/xii-2-141.pdf.

Howe, Neil, and William Strauss. *Millennials Rising: The Next Great Generation*. New York: Vintage Books, 2000.

Hughes, Aaron W. *Theorizing Islam: Disciplinary Deconstruction and Reconstruction*. New York: Routledge, 2014.

Huntington, Samuel P. "The Clash of Civilizations?" *Foreign Affairs* 72 (1993): 22–49.

Hussain, Amir. "Confronting Misoislamia: Teaching Religion and Violence in Courses on Islam." In *Teaching Religion and Violence*, edited by Brian Pennington. New York: Oxford University Press, 2012.

———. "Teaching Inside Out: On Teaching Islam." *Method & Theory in the Study of Religion* 17, no. 3 (2005): 248–263.

Hutchins, William M. "Fakhr al-Din al-Razi on Knowledge." PhD diss., University of Chicago, 1971.

———. *Tawfiq al-Hakim: A Reader's Guide*. Boulder, CO: Lynne Rienner, 2003.

Hutchins, William M., ed. and trans. *Egyptian Tales and Short Stories of the 1970s and 1980s*. Cairo: American University in Cairo Press, 1989.

Ivins, Wilson. "Team Teaching in the Southwestern Secondary School." *NASSP Bulletin* 48, no. 290 (1964): 25–30. doi:10.1177/019263656404829004.

al-Jahiz. *Nine Essays of al-Jahiz*. Edited and translated by William M. Hutchins. New York: Peter Lang, 1989.

Jahnke, Keilin, Ann-Perry Witmer, Matthew Tan, and Grace Frances Witmer. "Bringing a Cross-Disciplinary, Contextual Approach to International Service Engineering Learning." Paper presented at ASEEs 123rd Annual Conference & Exposition, New Orleans, LA, June 2016. Paper ID# 14756.

James, Navita Cummings. "Discussing Gender and Human Sexuality 'Hot Button' Issues: Considering the Role of Religion and Religious Beliefs." In *Activities for Teaching Gender and Sexuality in the University Classroom*, edited by Michael Murphy and Elizabeth Ribarsky, 78–86. New York: Rowman & Littlefield Education, 2013.

Jensen, Julia, and Martin Howard. "The Effects of Time in the Development of Complexity and Accuracy during Study Abroad: A Study of French and Chinese Learners of English." *EUROSLA Yearbook* 14, no. 1 (2014): 31–64. doi:10.1075/eurosla.14.02jen.

Jhally, Sut, director, Jeremy Earp, producer, and Jack G. Shaheen, writer. *Reel Bad Arabs: How Hollywood Vilifies a People*. Northampton, MA: Media Education Foundation, 2006.

Jiang, Junyan, and Dali L. Yang. "Lying or Believing? Measuring Preference Falsification from a Political Purge in China." *Comparative Political Studies* 49, no. 5 (2016): 600–634. doi:10.1177/0010414015626450.

Jinkerson, Greg. "Maury Parents Angered over Islam Unit." Spring Hill Home Page, September 3, 2015. http://springhillhomepage.com/maury-parents-angered-over-islam-unit/.

Jones, Robert P., Daniel Cox, Betsy Cooper, and Rachel Lienesch. "Anxiety, Nostalgia, and Mistrust: Findings from the 2015 American Values Survey." Public Religion Research Institute, November 17, 2015.

Kabir, Nahid. *Young American Muslims: Dynamics of Identity.* Edinburgh: Edinburgh University Press, 2014.

———. *Young British Muslims: Identity, Culture, Politics and the Media.* Edinburgh: Edinburgh University Press, 2012.

Kaelble, Hartmut. *Sozialgeschichte Europas: 1945 bis zur Gegenwart.* Munich: C. H. Beck, 2007.

Kamali, Mohammad Hashim. *Shari'ah Law: An Introduction.* Oxford, UK: Oneworld, 2008.

Karatani, Kojin. "Uses of Aesthetics: After Orientalism." *boundary 2* 25, no. 2 (1998): 145–160.

Kassam, Tazim. "Teaching Religion in the Twenty-First Century." In *Teaching Islam,* edited by Brannon Wheeler, 191–216. Oxford: Oxford University Press, 2003.

Kassam, Zayn. "Engendering and Experience: Teaching a Course on Women in Islam." In *Teaching Islam,* edited by Brannon Wheeler, 124–143. Oxford: Oxford University Press, 2003.

Khalfaoui, Mouez. "Islamunterricht im europäischen Kontext: Gibt es einen 'Euro-Islam' in der Schule?." In *Kindheit und Jugend in muslimischen Lebenswelten: Aufwachen und Bildung in deutscher und internationaler Perspektive,* edited by Sabine Andresen and Christine Hunner-Kreisel, 235–253. Wiesbaden: SV Verlag, 2010.

———. "Medrese: Religiöse Wissensvermittlung in der islamisch geprägten Welt und darüber hinaus." *Schweizerische Zeitschrift für Religions- und Kulturgeschichte* 108 (2014): 449–464.

Khoja-Moolji, Shenila. "Poststructuralist Approaches to Teaching about Gender, Islam, and Muslim Societies." *Feminist Teacher* 24, no. 3 (2014): 169–183.

Khorchide, Mouhanad. "Der islamische Religionsunterricht in Österreich." In *Österreichischer Integrationsfond 5* (2009). http://www.integrationsfonds.at/fileadmin/content/AT/Downloads/Publikationen/n5_Dossier_Islamischer_Religionsunterricht.pdf.

Kidd, Thomas. *American Christians and Islam: Evangelical Culture and Muslims from the Colonial Period to the Age of Terrorism.* Princeton, NJ: Princeton University Press, 2009.

Kiefer, Michael, and Irka-Christin Mohr, eds., *Islamunterricht, Islamischer Religionsunterricht, Islamkunde: Viele Titel—Ein Fach?* Bielefeld: Transcript, 2009.

Kincheloe, Joe L., Shirley R. Steinberg, and Christopher Darius Stonebanks, eds. *Teaching against Islamophobia.* New York: Peter Lang, 2010.

Klein, Julie Thompson. "Interdisciplinarity." In *Encyclopedia of Science, Technology, and Ethics,* edited by Carl Mitcham, 1034–1037. Detroit: Macmillan Reference USA, 2005.

———. *Interdisciplinarity: History, Theory, and Practice.* Detroit: Wayne State University, 1990.

Klein, Julie Thompson, and William H. Newell. "Internationalizing the Curriculum." In *Handbook of the Undergraduate Curriculum: A Comprehensive Guide To Purposes, Structures, Practices, and Change,* edited by Jerry G. Gaff and James L. Ratcliff, 393–415. San Francisco: Jossey-Bass, 1997.

Körkkö, Minna, Outi Kyrö-Ämmälä, and Tuija Turunen. "Professional Development through Reflection in Teacher Education." *Teaching and Teacher Education* 55 (2016): 198–200. doi:10.1016/j.tate.2016.01.014.

Korthagen, Fred, and Jos Kessels. "Linking Theory and Practice: Changing the Pedagogy of Teacher Education." *Educational Researcher* 28, no. 4 (1999): 4–17. doi:10.2307/1176444.

Kozinets, Robert. "Netnography." In *The Sage Dictionary of Social Research Methods*, edited by Victor Jupp, 135. London: Sage Publications, 2006.

Kumar, Deepa. "Framing Islam: The Resurgence of Orientalism during the Bush II Era." *Journal of Communication Inquiry* 34, no. 3 (2010): 254–277. doi:10.1177/0196859910363174.

Kurzman, Charles, and Carl W. Ernst. "Islamic Studies in U.S. Universities." *Review of Middle East Studies* 46, no. 1 (2012): 24–46.

bin Ladin, Usama. "To the Americans." In *Messages to the World: The Statements of Osama bin Laden*, edited by Bruce Lawrence and translated by James Howarth, 160–172. London: Verso Books, 2005.

Lamptey, Jerusha T. "Boko Haram: Not My Sharia." *Time*, May 8, 2014.

———. *Never Wholly Other: A Muslima Theology of Religious Pluralism.* Oxford: Oxford University Press, 2014.

Larrivee, Barbara. "Transforming Teaching Practice: Becoming the Critically Reflective Teacher." *Reflective Practice* 1, no. 3 (2000): 295–307. doi:10.1080/713693162

Lavey, Nate. "Commentary—The Poetry of Jihad." *The New Yorker* Videos, 2015. Accessed September 3, 2016. http://video.newyorker.com/watch/commentary -the-poetry-of-jihad.

Lean, Nathan. *The Islamophobia Industry: How the Right Manufactures Fear of Muslims.* New York: Pluto Press, 2012.

Letterman, Margaret R., and Kimberly B. Dugan. "Team Teaching a Cross-Disciplinary Honors Course: Preparation and Development." *College Teaching* 52, no. 2 (2004): 76–79.

Levy, Pierre. *Becoming Virtual: Reality in the Digital Age.* New York: Plenum, 1998.

Lewis, Bernard. "The Roots of Muslim Rage." *The Atlantic Monthly*, September 1990, 47–60.

Lewis, Phillip. "Imams, Ulema and Sufis: "Providers of Bridging Social Capital for British Pakistanis?" *Contemporary Asia* 15, no. 3 (2006): 273–287.

Lewis, Tyson E. "Teaching with Pensive Images: Rethinking Curiosity in Paulo Freire's *Pedagogy of the Oppressed*." *Journal of Aesthetic Education* 46, no. 1 (Spring 2012): 27–45.

Lincoln, Bruce. *Holy Terrors.* Chicago: University of Chicago Press, 2003.

Lipka, Michael. "Muslims and Islam: Key Findings in the U.S. and around the World." Pew Research Center, 2017. Accessed May 4, 2017. http://www.pewresearch.org /fact-tank/2017/02/27/muslims-and-islam-key-findings-in-the-u-s-and-around -the-world/.

Luther, Martin. *On War against the Turk.* In *Luther's Works*, edited by Robert C. Schultz, 46:155–205. Philadelphia: Fortress Press, 1967.

Mahfouz, Naguib. *Cairo Modern.* Translated by William M. Hutchins. Cairo: American University in Cairo Press, 2008; New York: Anchor Books, 2009.

———. *Palace of Desire.* Translated by William M. Hutchins. New York: Doubleday & Cairo: American University in Cairo Press, 1991; New York: Anchor Books, 1992.

———. *Palace Walk.* Translated by William M. Hutchins. New York: Doubleday & Cairo: American University in Cairo Press, 1990; New York: Anchor Books, 1991.

————. *Sugar Street*. Translated by William M. Hutchins. New York: Doubleday & Cairo: American University in Cairo Press, 1992; New York: Anchor Books, 1993.

Mahmood, Saba. "Islam and Gender in Muslim Societies: Reflections of an Anthropologist." In *Observing the Observer: The State of Islamic Studies in American Universities*, edited by Zahid Bukhari and Sulayman Nyang, 70–81. London: IIIT, 2012.

————. "Religion, Feminism, and Empire: The New Ambassadors of Islamophobia." In *Feminism, Sexuality, and the Return of Religion*, edited by Linda Alcoff and John D. Caputo, 77–102. Bloomington: Indiana University Press, 2011.

Maier, Carol, and Françoise Massardier-Kenney. *Literature in Translation: Teaching Issues and Reading Practices*. Kent, OH: Kent State University Press, 2010.

Malik, Maszlee. "Islamische Bildung in Großbritannien: Ein Überblick." In *Religionen in der Schule und die Bedeutung des islamischen Religionsunterrichts*, edited by Ucar Bülent, Martina Blasberg-Kuhnke, and Arnulf Scheliha, 291–304. Osnabrück: Universitätsverlag Osnabrück, 2010.

Mariuma, Yarden. "Taqiyya as Polemic, Law and Knowledge: Following an Islamic Legal Term through the Worlds of Islamic Scholars, Ethnographers, Polemicist and Military Men." *Muslim World* 104, no. 1-2 (2014): 89–108.

Martin, Florence, and Michele A. Parker. "Use of Synchronous Classrooms: Why, Who, and How?" *MERLOT Journal of Online Learning and Teaching* 10, no. 2 (2014): 192–210.

Marzano, Robert J. "Fostering Thinking across the Curriculum through Knowledge Restructuring." *Journal of Reading* 34, no. 7 (1991): 518–525.

Masud, Muhammad Khalid, Brinkley Messick, and David S. Powers, eds. *Islamic Legal Interpretation: Muftis and Their Fatwas*. Cambridge, MA: Harvard University Press, 1996.

Mathison, Sandra, and Melissa Freeman. "The Logic of Interdisciplinary Studies." *National Research Center on English Learning and Achievement*. Report Series 2, no. 33 (1998). ERIC document.

Mattson, Ingrid. "How to Read the Qur'an." In *The Study Quran: A New Translation and Commentary*. Edited and translated by Seyyed Hossein Nasr, Caner K. Dagli, Maria Marissa Dakake, Joseph B. Lumbard, and Mohammed Rustom, 1587-1600. New York: HarperOne, 2015.

McDonald, Kevin, director. *Life in a Day*. DVD. National Geographic, 2011.

Meijer, Wilna A. J. *Tradition and Future of Islamic Education*. Münster: Waxmann, 2009.

Menocal, María Rosa. *The Ornament of the World: How Muslims, Jews, and Christians Created a Culture of Tolerance in Medieval Spain*. New York: Back Bay Books, 2003.

Modood, Tariq, Anna Triandafyllidou, and Barrero Zapata. *Multiculturalism, Muslims and Citizenship: A European Approach*. London: Routledge, 2006.

Mogahed, Dalia, and Fouad Pervez. "American Muslim Poll: Participation, Priorities, and Facing Prejudice in the 2016 Elections." *Institute for Social Policy and Understanding*. March 2016.

Mohr, Irka-Christin. *Islamischer Religionsunterricht in Europa: Lehrtexte als Instrumente muslimischer Selbstverortung im Vergleich*. Bielefeld: Transcript, 2006.

Moody, Mia. "Teaching Twitter and Beyond: Tips for Incorporating Social Media in Traditional Courses." *Journal of Magazine and New Media Research* 11, no. 2 (2010): 1–9.

Moon, Jennifer. *A Handbook of Reflective and Experiential Learning: Theory and Practice*. London: Routledge, 2004.

Moosa, Ebrahim. *Ghazālī and the Poetics of Imagination*. Chapel Hill: University of North Carolina Press, 2005.

Morris, Pamela K. "Team Teaching of Creative Advertising and Public Relations Courses." *Journal of Advertising Education* 20, no. 1/2 (2016): 44–53.

Morro, William." Violence and Religion in the Christian Tradition." In *Teaching Religion and Violence,* edited by Brian Pennington. New York: Oxford University Press, 2012.

Morrow, Lance. "The Case for Rage and Retribution," *Time,* September 12, 2001. http://content.time.com/time/nation/article/0,8599,174641,00.html.

Moskin, Julia. "During Ramadan, Dates Are a Unifying Staple." *New York Times,* June 16, 2015.

Müller, Rabeya, Lamya Kaddor, and Harry H. Behr, eds. *Saphir 5/6: Religionsbuch für junge Musliminnen und Muslime.* Munich: Kösel, 2008.

Murawski, Wendy W., and Lisa Dieker. "50 Ways to Keep Your Co-Teacher." *Teaching Exceptional Children* 40, no. 4 (March 2008): 40–48.

Murphy, Robin M. *How Social Trauma Affects How We Write: Post 9/11 Rhetorical Theory and Composition Pedagogy.* Lewiston, NY: Edwin Mellen Press, 2010.

al-Musawi, Mushin J. ed. *Arabic Literature for the Classroom: Teaching Methods, Theories, Themes and Texts.* New York: Routledge, 2017.

Newell, William H. "A Theory of Interdisciplinary Studies." *Issues in Integrative Studies* 19 (2001): 1–25.

Olsen, Jonathan, Annette Zimmer, and Markus Behr. "Real Success with a Virtual Exchange: The German and American Politics Electronic Classroom." *PS: Political Science and Politics* 39, no. 2 (2006): 351–355.

Omar, Hussein. "The State of the Archive: Manipulating Memory in Modern Egypt and the Writing of Egyptological Histories." In *Histories of Egyptology: Interdisciplinary Measures,* edited by William Carruthers, 174–184. New York: Routledge, 2015.

O'Rourke, Rebecca. "The Learning Journal: From Chaos to Coherence." *Assessment and Evaluation in Higher Education* 23, no. 4 (1998): 403–413. doi:10.1080/0260293980230407.

Osterhammel, Jürgen. *Colonialism: A Theoretical Overview.* Princeton, NJ: Marcus Wiener, 1997.

Palmer, Jeremy. "Arabic Diglossia: Teaching Only the Standard Variety Is a Disservice to Students." *Arizona Working Papers in SLA and Teaching* 14 (2007): 111–122.

Parker-Jenkins, Marie. *Children of Islam: A Teacher's Guide to Meeting the Needs of Muslim Pupils.* London: Trentham Books, 1995.

Pasto, James. "Islam's 'Strange Secret Sharer': Orientalism, Judaism, and the Jewish Question." *Comparative Studies in Society and History* 40, no. 3 (July 1998): 437–474. http://www.jstor.org/stable/179271.

Patel, Youshaa. "Debates: A Way to Teach Controversial Topics in Islam." Wabash Center Blogs, May 4, 2016. http://wabashcenter.typepad.com/teaching_islam/2016/05/debates-a-way-to-teach-controversial-topics-in-islam.html.

Pennington, Brian K., ed. *Teaching Religion and Violence.* New York: Oxford University Press, 2012.

Pfiffner, James P. "US Blunders in Iraq: De-Baathification and Disbanding the Army." *Intelligence and National Security* 25, no. 1 (February 2010): 76–85.

Pinto, Paulo G. "Creativity and Stability in the Making of Sufi Tradition: The Tariqa Qadiriyya in Aleppo, Syria." In *Sufism Today: Heritage and Tradition in the Global Community,* edited by Catharina Raudvere and Leif Stenberg, 117–135. New York: I. B. Tauris, 2009.

Plank, Kathryn M. "Team Teaching." *IDEA Paper* 55 (2013). ERIC document.

Quick, Karin. "The Role of Self- and Peer-Assessment in Dental Students' Reflective Practice Using Standardized Patient Encounters." *Journal of Dental Education* 80, no. 8 (2016): 924–929.

Radsch, Courtney. "From Cell Phones to Coffee: Issues of Access in Egypt and Lebanon." In *Surviving Field Research: Working in Violent and Difficult Situations*, edited by Chandra Lekha Sriram, John C. King, Julie A. Mertus, Olga Martin-Ortega, and Johanna Herman, 91–107. New York: Routledge, 2009.

Rall, Harris Franklin. *The Life of Jesus*. New York: Abington Press, 1917.

Raterink, Ginger. "Reflective Journaling for Critical Thinking Development in Advanced Practice Registered Nurse Students." *Journal of Nursing Education* 55, no. 2 (2016): 99–102. doi:10.3928/01484834-20160114-08.

Reinhart, A. Kevin. "On the 'Introduction to Islam.'" In *Teaching Islam*, edited by Brannon Wheeler, 22–45. New York: Oxford University Press, 2003.

Repko, Allen F. *Interdisciplinary Research: Process and Theory*. Los Angeles: SAGE, 2008.

Richardson, Joel. *The Islamic Antichrist*. Los Angeles: WND Press, 2015.

Roberts, Sam. "Gamal al-Ghitani, Egyptian Novelist with a Political Bent, Dies at 70." *New York Times*, October 21, 2015.

Rohan, Brian, and Maram Mazen. "In Egypt, Clamp on Academic Freedoms Sparks Scholar Backlash." Associated Press, February 18, 2016. http://bigstory.ap.org /article/c47aef5e5eb24f988779bd8e410a4d84/egypt-clamp-academic-freedoms -sparks-scholar-backlash.

Ruprecht, Louis. "Caught between Enlightenment and Romanticism: On the Complex Relation of Religious, Ethnic and Civic Identity in a Modern 'Museum Culture.'" In *Rethinking Islamic Studies: From Orientalism to Cosmopolitanism*, edited by Carl W. Ernst and Richard Martin, 203–223. Columbia: University of South Carolina Press, 2010.

al-Sabouni, Marwa. *The Battle for Homs: The Vision of a Young Architect in Syria*. New York: Thames & Hudson, 2016.

Said, Edward W. *Covering Islam: How the Media and the Experts Determine How We See the Rest of the World*. New York: Vintage Books, 1997.

———. *Orientalism*. New York: Random House, 1979.

Sasaki, Betty. "Toward a Pedagogy of Coalition." In *Twenty-First-Century Feminist Class-rooms: Pedagogies of Identity and Difference*, edited by Amie A. MacDonald and Susan Sanchez Casal, 31–57. New York: Palgrave, 2002.

Schweber, Simone. "Fundamentally 9/11: The Fashioning of Collective Memory in a Christian School." *American Journal of Education* 112, no. 3 (2006): 392–417. http://www .jstor.org/stable/10.1086/500714.

Shaefer, Richard. "Let's Talk about Religion." *Perspectives on History*, May 2010. Accessed April 29, 2017. https://www.historians.org/publications-and-directories/perspectives -on-history/may-2010/controversy-in-the-classroom/lets-talk-about-religion.

Shaffer, Robert. "Open Your Eyes: Followers of Islam Are Real Threat." *Wyoming Tribune Eagle*, March 30, 2016.

Shafik, Viola. *Popular Egyptian Cinema: Gender, Class, and Nation*. Cairo: American University in Cairo Press, 2007.

El Shakry, Omnia. "'History without Documents': The Vexed Archives of Decolonization in the Middle East." *American Historical Review* 120, no. 3 (2015): 920–934. doi:10.1093 /ahr/120.3.920.

Shohat, Ella. "Gender in Hollywood's Orient." *Middle East Report* 162 (1990): 40-42.

Sholkamy, Hania. "Why Is Anthropology So Hard in Egypt?." In *Between Field and Text: Emerging Voices in Egyptian Social Science*, edited by Seteney Shami and Linda Her-rera, 119–136. Cairo Papers in Social Science, vol. 22, no. 2. Cairo: American University in Cairo Press, 1999.

Shuler, Sherianne. "Bringing the Gender Movements Alive through Role-Play." In *Activities for Teaching Gender and Sexuality in the University Classroom*, edited by Michael Murphy and Elizabeth Ribarsky, 26–34. New York: Rowman & Littlefield Education, 2013.

Siddiqui, Sohaira. "Beyond Authenticity: ISIS and the Islamic Legal Tradition." Jadaliyya .com, February 24, 2015. http://www.jadaliyya.com/pages/index/20944/beyond -authenticity_isis-and-the-islamic-legal-tra.

Silverstein, Brian. "Sufism and Modernity in Turkey: From the Authenticity of Experience to the Practice of Discipline." In *Sufism and the Modern in Islam*, edited by Martin van Bruinessen and Julia Day Howell, 39–60. London: I. B. Tauris, 2007.

Simmons, John. "Vanishing Boundaries: When Teaching about Religion Becomes Spiritual Guidance in the Classroom." *Teaching Theology & Religion* 9, no. 1 (January 2006): 37–43.

Smart, Ninian. *Dimensions of the Sacred: An Anatomy of the World's Beliefs*. Berkeley: University of California Press, 1996.

Smith, Aaron, Lee Rainie, and Kathryn Zickuhr. "College Students and Technology." Pew Research Center, July 19, 2011. Accessed October 10, 2016. http://www.pewinternet .org/2011/07/19/college-students-and-technology/.

Smith, Barbara Leigh. "Taking Structure Seriously: The Learning Community Model." *Liberal Education* 77, no. 2 (1991): 42–48.

Smith, David Charles. "Protestant Anti-Judaism in the German Emancipation Era." *Jewish Social Studies* 36, no. 3–4 (1974): 203–219.

Smith, J. Z. "Basic Problems in the Study of Religion." In *On Teaching Religion*, edited by Christopher I. Lehrich, 20–27. New York: Oxford University Press, 2013.

———. *Imagining Religion: From Babylon to Jonestown*. Chicago: University of Chicago Press, 1982.

———. "The Introductory Course: Less Is Better." In *On Teaching Religion*, edited by Christopher I. Lehrich, 11–19. New York: Oxford University Press, 2013.

———. *On Teaching Religion*. Edited by Christopher I. Lehrich. Oxford: Oxford University Press, 2013.

Squires, Geoffrey. "Interdisciplinary in Higher Education in the United Kingdom." *European Journal of Education* 27, no. 3 (September 1992): 201–210.

Starnes, Todd. "'There Is No God but Allah'? School Accused of Islamic Indoctrination." Foxnews.com, September 10, 2015, http://www.foxnews.com/opinion/2015/09/10 /there-is-no-god-but-allah-school-accused-islamic-indoctrination.html.

Stille, Alexander. "Who Murdered Giulio Regeni?" *The Guardian*, October 4, 2016. https:// www.theguardian.com/world/2016/oct/04/egypt-murder-giulio-regeni.

Stommel, Jesse. "Critical Digital Pedagogy: A Definition." *Digital Pedagogy Lab*. November 18, 2014. http://www.digitalpedagogylab.com/hybridped/critical -digital-pedagogy-definition/.

The Study Quran: A New Translation and Commentary. Edited and translated by Seyyed Hossein Nasr, Caner K. Dagli, Maria Marissa Dakake, Joseph B. Lumbard, and Mohammed Rustom. New York: HarperOne, 2015.

Taylor, Leah, and Jim Parsons. "Improving Student Engagement." *Current Issues in Education* 14, no. 1 (2011): 1–33.

Telhami, Shelbi. "American Attitudes toward the Middle East." *The Brookings Institution*. July 11, 2016.

Tenenbaum, Gershon, Som Naidu, Olugbemiro Jegede, and Jon Austin. "Constructivist Pedagogy in Conventional On-Campus and Distance Learning Practice: An Exploratory Investigation." *Learning and Instruction* 11, no. 2 (2011): 88–111.

Thatamanil, John. "Comparative Religion after 'Religion.'" In *Planetary Loves: Spivak, Post-coloniality and Theology*, edited by Stephen D. Moore and Mayra Rivera, 238–257. New York: Fordham University Press, 2011.

Thiessen, Dennis. "A Skillful Start to a Teaching Career: A Matter of Developing Impactful Behaviours, Reflective Practices, or Professional Knowledge?" *International Journal of Educational Research* 33, no. 5 (2000): 515–537. doi:10.1016/S0883-0355(00)00032-X.

Tidswell, Toni. "Insiders, Outsiders and Critical Engagement: Reflections on Teaching 'Women in Islam' in a Western University." In *The Teaching and Study of Islam in Western Universities*, edited by Paul Morris, William Shepard, Paul Trebilco, and Toni Tidswell, 136–142. New York: Routledge, 2014.

Trentman, Emma. "Arabic and English during Study Abroad in Cairo, Egypt: Issues of Access and Use." *Modern Language Journal* 97, no. 2 (2013): 457–473. doi:10.1111/j.1540-4781.2013.12013.x.

Tricio, Jorge, Mark Woolford, and Michael Escudier. "Dental Students' Reflective Habits: Is There a Relation with Their Academic Achievement?" *European Journal of Dental Education* 19, no. 2 (2015): 113–121. doi:10.1111/eje.12111.

Ucar, Bülent. "Der Islamische Religionsunterricht in Deutschland: Aktuelle Debatten, Projekte und Reaktionen." In *Islamische Erziehung in Europa*, edited by Ednan Aslan, 87–108. Vienna: Böhlau, 2009.

United Nations. Charter of the United Nations. June 26, 1945. http://www.un.org/en /charter-united-nations/.

Vande Berg, Michael, Jeffrey Connor-Linton, and R. Michael Paige. "The Georgetown Consortium Project: Interventions for Student Learning Abroad." *Frontiers: The Interdisciplinary Journal of Study Abroad* 18 (2009): 1–75.

van de Ven, Andrew H., and Paul E. Johnson. "Knowledge for Theory and Practice." *Academy of Management Review* 31, no. 4 (2006): 802–821.

"Wabash Center for Teaching and Learning in Theology and Religion." Accessed April 15, 2017. http://www.wabashcenter.wabash.edu/.

Wadud, Amina. *Inside the Gender Jihad: Women's Reform in Islam*. Oxford, UK: Oneworld, 2006.

Wagner, Rick. "Islam Removed from Draft Tenn. 7th Grade Social Studies Standards." *Kingsport Times News*, September 25, 2016, http://www.timesnews.net/Education /2016/09/25/Islam-removed-from-draft-Tenn-7th-grade-social-studies-standards.

Walsh, Kenneth T. "George W. Bush's 'Bullhorn' Moment." *U.S. News*, April 25, 2013. http://www.usnews.com/news/blogs/ken-walshs-washington/2013/04/25 /george-w-bushs-bullhorn-moment.

Walvoord, Barbara E. "Students' Spirituality and 'Big Questions' in Introductory Religion Courses." *Teaching Theology and Religion* 11, no. 1 (2008): 3–13.

———. *Teaching and Learning in College Introductory Religion Courses*. Malden, MA: Blackwell, 2008.

Waterson, Robert A. "The Examination of Pedagogical Approaches to Teaching Controversial Public Issues: Explicitly Teaching the Holocaust and Comparative Genocide." *Social Science Research & Practice* 4, no. 2 (2009): 1–24.

Watson, Foster. *The Encyclopedia and Dictionary of Education; a Comprehensive, Practical and Authoritative Guide on all Matters Connected with Education, Including Educational Principles and Practice, Various Types of Teaching Institutions, and Educational Systems throughout the World*. London: Sir I. Pitman & Sons, 1921–22.

Weissberg, Jay. "Fires, Heat Trouble Egyptian Film Preservation." *Variety*, July 31, 2010. http://variety.com/2010/biz/news/fires-heat-trouble-egyptian-film-preservation -1118022406/.

Wheeler, Brannon, ed. *Teaching Islam*. New York: Oxford University Press, 2003.

———. "What Can't Be Left Out: The Essentials of Teaching Islam as a Religion." In *Teaching Islam*, edited by Brannon Wheeler, 3–21. Oxford: Oxford University Press, 2003.

Willaime, Jean Paul. "Religious Education at Schools in Europe." In *Religious Education at Schools in Europe: Part 2: Western Europe*, edited by Robert Jackson, Martin Jäggle, Martin Rothgangel, 99–119. Göttingen: V&R Unipress, 2014.

Williams, Raymond. *Keywords: A Vocabulary of Culture and Society*. Oxford: Oxford University Press, 1976.

Wilmsen, David. "What Is Communicative Arabic?." In *Handbook for Arabic Language Teaching Professionals in the 21st Century*, edited by Kassem M. Wahba, Zainab A. Taha, and Liz England, 125–138. New York: Routledge, 2013.

Wood, Graeme. "What ISIS Really Wants." *The Atlantic Monthly*, March 2015. http://www.theatlantic.com/features/archive/2015/02/what-isis-really-wants/384980/.

Woods, Charlotte. "Researching and Developing Interdisciplinary Teaching: Towards a Conceptual Framework for Classroom Communication." *Higher Education* 54, no. 6 (2007): 853–866. doi:10.1007/s10734-006-9027-3.

Younes, Munther. *The Integrated Approach to Arabic Instruction*. New York: Routledge, 2015.

al-Zawahiri, Ayman. *Shifaʾ sudur al-muʾminin*, Ilmway.com. http://www.ilmway.com/site/maqdis/MS_13066.html.

al-Zawahiri, Ayman. "Jihad, Martyrdom, and the Killing of Innocents." In *The Al Qaeda Reader*, edited by Raymond Ibrahim, 141–171. New York: Broadway Books, 2001.

INDEX

media, 1, 17, 19, 44, 51–53, 74–75, 96, 136–139, 162, 174, 176, 178–79, 210; critical media studies, 137; media discourse, 174–85
millennials, 148, 150–51
misogyny, 31, 173, 176–77. *See also* gender, patriarchy
Mohr, Irka-Christin, 58
Moosa, Ebrahim, 22
Morrow, Lance, 109–111, 114, 119–20
Muslim-majority states, 55, 133, 181
Muslim-minority states, 55, 58, 65–66, 128, 139
Muslim student associations, x, xi, 11
Muslim students, x, 26–28, 53, 57, 58, 63, 89, 162, 203–5

Newell, William H., 98
new media pedagogy, 9, 12–13, 16
9/11, 3, 28, 50, 68–70, 81–82, 90, 96, 109–11, 119, 125, 130, 132–33, 138, 147, 149, 176, 179, 206

Obama, Barack, 68, 111, 114
Olsen, Jonathan, 13
online courses, 188–99
orientalism, 23, 29–32, 68, 75–76, 82–85, 131, 132, 137, 203, 212
Orientalism, 29, 37, 132
O'Rourke, Rebecca, 191
Oyarzun, Beth Allred, 12

Parker, Michele A., 12–13
Patel, Youshaa, 207
patriarchy, 169–70, 173, 177–78, 181–83, 208–9, 211. *See also* gender, women
pedagogy of coalition, 204
Pedagogy of the Oppressed, 30
Pfiffner, James, 184
philosophy, 36, 39, 64
podcasts, 214
politics, 113, 136, 175, 177–78, 180–82, 185
popular culture, 81, 97, 162. *See also* films, media, social media
postcolonial theory, 71, 131–32
post-orientalism, 210
Protestantism, 69–73, 75–76, 165, 174–75. *See also* Christianity
public schools, 24–25, 28, 30, 59–65

al-Qāʻida, 3, 109, 113–14, 119
Qurʼan, xii, 24, 27, 38, 73–74, 77, 130, 134, 146, 168, 179–80

racism, 23, 31, 68, 130, 136, 191
Razi, Fakhr al-Din al-, 83
reflective learning, 4, 9, 188–99, 211
Reinhart, A. Kevin, 126, 177
religious minorities, 61, 175
role plays (pedagogical technique), 207–8
romanticism, 29–30
Runnymede Report, 129
Rushdie, Salman, 111, 129, 133

Sabouni, Marwa al-, 89–90
Said, Edward, 29–30, 37, 78, 131–32
Sasaki, Betty, 204
scholastic fallacy, 35–37
secularism, 26, 28, 29, 30, 50–51, 58, 64–65, 70–72, 78–79
September 11, 2001. *See* 9/11
Shafʻi, Imam, 166–67
Shaham, Ron, 170
shariʼa, 52, 68–69, 75–76, 117, 135, 154, 161, 165, 167, 180–82
shaykh, 39–41
Shia, 60, 64, 68
Sholkamy, Hania, 42
Silverstein, Brian, 38–39
Simmons, John, 204
Skype, 9, 10, 14, 16–17
Smart, Ninian, 71–74, 77
Smith, J. Z., 110, 119, 174
social media, x, 13, 14–15, 17–18, 20, 45, 53, 126, 214. *See also* Facebook, Twitter
sola fide fallacy, 70–71, 73
stereotypes, 13, 19–20, 70, 71, 74–75, 125, 126, 127, 129, 133, 136, 137, 139, 192, 194–95
study abroad, 13, 19, 42, 45–46, 150
Sufism, 38–41

Tajfel, Henri, 205
taqiyya, 68
taste, 22, 28–29, 31–32
teacher training, 60, 188–90
Teaching Islam, 2, 71, 147, 163, 189
team teaching, 97–106
terrorism, 24, 50, 113, 133, 138, 149, 161, 173, 176, 178, 183–84, 206. *See also* violence
textbooks, 18–19, 24, 28, 56–60, 165
textual production, 157
Thatamanil, John, 71, 78
Tidswell, Toni, 203, 211